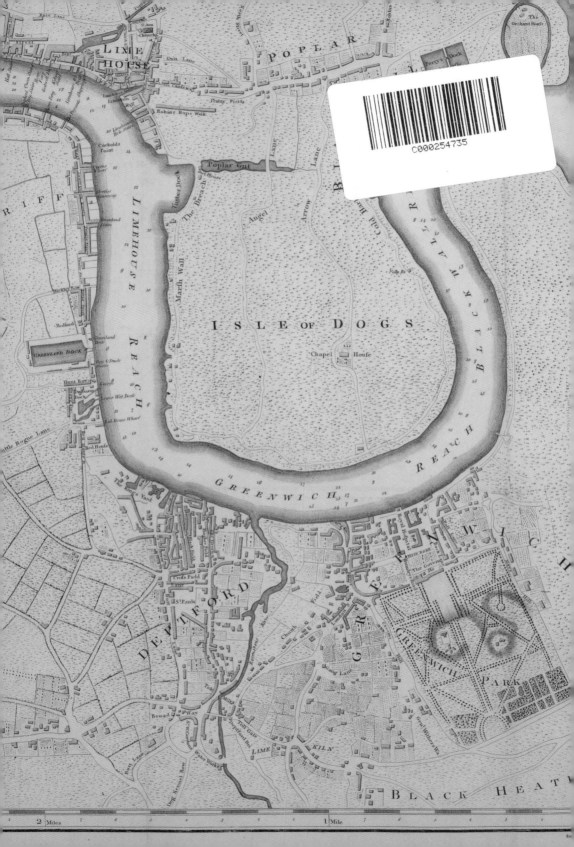

TRADING IN WAR

TRADING IN WAR

LONDON'S MARITIME WORLD IN THE AGE OF COOK AND NELSON

MARGARETTE LINCOLN

YALE UNIVERSITY PRESS
NEW HAVEN AND LONDON

Published with assistance from the Annie Burr Lewis Fund.

For information about this and other Yale University Press publications, please contact:
US Office: sales.press@yale.edu   yalebooks.com
Europe Office: sales@yaleup.co.uk   yalebooks.co.uk

Set in Adobe Garamond Pro by IDSUK (DataConnection) Ltd
Printed in Great Britain by Gomer Press Ltd, Llandysul, Ceredigion, Wales

Library of Congress Control Number: 2017952551

ISBN 978-0-300-22748-2

A catalogue record for this book is available from the British Library.

10 9 8 7 6 5 4 3 2 1

CONTENTS

PLATES

ACKNOWLEDGEMENTS

One of my aims in writing this book was to recover people lost to history. It is only fair, then, to begin by thanking all those people, many of them volunteers, who have helped to make digitized newspapers and other texts available online. Without them, I would still be looking for a lot of the material I needed for the book.

I am extremely grateful to Maggie Hanbury and to all the staff at the Hanbury Agency. I am lucky to have found such a good literary agent. At Yale University Press, my thanks go to Robert Baldock for his support and encouragement, and to Rachael Lonsdale, Samantha Cross and Daniel Coyne for further guidance. I am indebted to Charlotte Chapman for copy-editing. I should also like to thank the anonymous readers of the proposal and the complete draft for their valuable suggestions.

Authors of books like this always owe a great debt to people who have helped along the way. Anne Currie, formerly of the National Maritime Museum, helped me to track down useful material, Peter Henley and his family have given extremely generous access to their family archives, and Thomas Antoniw kindly showed me around Trinity Green Almshouses, Whitechapel. Librarians and archivists have given expert assistance. I'm grateful to staff at the following institutions: the National Maritime Museum's Caird Library, the National Archives, the Museum of London's Archaeological Archive, the London Metropolitan Archives, the British Library, the Institute of Historical Research, the Greenwich Heritage Centre, Lewisham's Local History and Archives Centre, and Tower Hamlets Local History Library and Archives. Particular thanks go to John Boneham, reference specialist at the British Library; to Richard Meunier, Deputy Archivist/Curator, and to his colleagues at the Royal London Hospital Archives and Museum; to Vicky Holmes, Archivist, Port and River Collections at the Museum of London Docklands, and to Colin Gale, Archivist at Bethlem Museum of the Mind. I would also like to thank Steve Clarke in the National Maritime Museum's IT Department for helping me to safeguard my research files.

Many scholars have given generous help. Matthew Davies commented on early ideas, Brian Lavery shared new information about Deptford dockyard, Alex Werner and Derek Morris advised on sources for the history of the West India Company. I gained much from contributing to the 2016 symposium of the Docklands History Group, organized by Chris Ellmers, and from the 2016 conference of the London and Middlesex Archaeological Society. My thanks also go to Vivienne Richmond and to the History Department at Goldsmiths College, London, for providing such a stimulating intellectual environment for research. Most of all, I owe a great debt to Roger Knight. I have been fortunate, throughout this project, to have benefitted from his suggestions, help and encouragement. He early advised on how best to shape the proposal and he has commented in detail on draft chapters, saving me from many errors. I'm very grateful for his time and for his generosity in sharing his knowledge.

Finally, I thank my family for their support, most especially my husband, Andrew, who has read every word, suggested improvements with unfailing tact, and cheerfully accompanied me on long walks in search of Thames wharves and slipways. Without him, maritime London would not be nearly as much fun. This book is for him.

NOTE ON CONVENTIONS

In quotations, original spelling, punctuation and capitalization have been retained throughout.

£ s. d. denotes the pre-decimal currency in Britain of pounds, shillings, and pence. Under this system there were four farthings in a penny, twelve pennies in a shilling and twenty shillings in a pound.

The Bank of England calculates that goods and services costing £1 in 1760 would cost £1 17s. 6d. in 1800, and £138.80 in 2016: https://www.measuringworth.com/ukcompare.

Before decimalization, Britain used imperial units of weight. There were 16 ounces (ozs) to the pound (lb), 14 pounds to a stone, 2 stones to a quarter, and 4 quarters to a hundredweight.

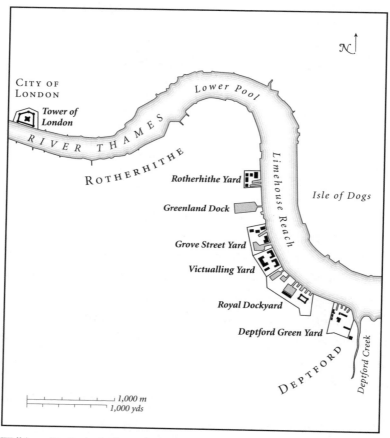

Wells's yard in Rotherhithe and, in Deptford, Barnard's two shipyards and the royal naval and victualling yards.

INTRODUCTION
Forgotten Histories

L ondon's alluring maritime districts snaked downriver from London Bridge on either side of the Thames. On the northern bank, east of the Tower of London, stretched Wapping, Shadwell, Ratcliff and Limehouse. To the south lay the wharves of Southwark and Bermondsey, then Rotherhithe, Deptford and Greenwich. London Bridge marked the farthest, western point of the Thames navigable by tall-masted sailing vessels. The stretch of river from there to below Limehouse was the Pool of London, always noisily crowded with thousands of vessels bringing goods from overseas or other parts of Britain. Ships were anchored alongside each other, two or three abreast, leaving a channel of river in the middle for others to pass. The congestion was increased by hundreds of lighters or barges carrying goods from ships in the lower reaches of the Thames to wharves and warehouses in the heart of London. To add to the confusion, there were also hundreds of watermen ferrying passengers across or up and down the river. Ceremonial barges, belonging to the nobility or official organizations, could be travelling at speed. In the mid-eighteenth century, London was still small enough to be crossed quite easily on foot, and it had a well-regulated hackney coach service. But officials and courtiers often preferred water to dusty road transport.

1

Their launches, rowed by up to eight men, could make an impressive nine knots with the tide, about 10 miles an hour, if only in short bursts.

The tide itself was a dramatic feature of riverside life. The difference between high and low water was conservatively reckoned to average about 10 feet (3 metres) before the Victorian Embankment narrowed the river.[1] London travellers were as conscious of the tides then as we are of major roadworks today. When wind and tide were favourable, ships would hoist sail and crowd upriver all at once to unload. Typically, there would be over 1,800 vessels trying to cram into a space that held only 500. London was the largest city in the world and the Thames was one of the world's busiest waterways, yet in spite of this activity, the river gave Londoners a sense of open space and freedom from crowded streets, much as it does now. It also offered an ever-changing spectacle and a source of news, the comings and goings of myriad vessels acting as barometers of trade, national defence and diplomacy.

There was never just one 'maritime London'. The City had a major role as a financial and commercial centre, a hub for invisible trade and maritime services, including insurance and shipping intelligence. The City's governing body, the Corporation of London, had historic powers over the port and the river. But it was the tapestry of different businesses, cultures and peoples along the Thames that made the most immediate impression on tourists and residents alike. Specialized maritime institutions such as Lloyd's, and powerful merchant houses that later became merchant banks, have left documentary archives allowing their corporate histories to be known. In this book the focus is on London's riverside communities whose texture of life is harder to reconstruct. Yet it is the lives of ordinary people, as well as tales of the rich and famous, which allow us to connect with history. An account of a local riot prompts us to think about how people lived in the busy maritime districts. These parishes were becoming more industrialized by the decade and were crucial to Britain's colonial ambitions, its overseas trade and its war efforts. One sign of their importance is that most benefited from the 1711 Act to build new churches in the capital. The fact that Greenwich and Deptford gained from the Act, while not strictly part of the city, shows how the metropolis was spreading. Together these districts made up the maritime London that famous seamen, such as the explorer Captain James Cook and Admiral Nelson, would have known.

This book is set in the turbulent decades when Britain struggled first to retain its colonies in North America and then fought against Revolutionary France. It covers the period from the radical 1760s, blighted by the St George's Fields Massacre when troops fired into a crowd of unarmed civilians, to the short-lived Peace of Amiens in 1802, an interlude in the long wars against Napoleon, and beyond. That year, 1802, also saw the opening of London's West India Docks. For city merchants, the most important thing about this momentous and costly development was that the enclosed waterfront reduced pilfering. For ordinary people, the new docks changed work patterns and a way of life for ever.

This is the story of how people in maritime parishes along the Thames coped with the American Revolutionary War, and then dug deep to ensure Britain's overseas trade continued to grow during the war with France, a crucial factor in Napoleon's defeat. The riverside districts had a total permanent workforce of several thousand and expanding populations. In the eighteenth century, the inhabitants of Limehouse doubled to nearly 9,000 and in Rotherhithe they tripled to over 10,000. Deptford, a densely populated town, had over 18,000 inhabitants by the end of the century and was far greater than any other London 'suburb' yet to be engulfed by the capital. These maritime districts were also subject to the influx of shifting peoples as seamen came and went, and they were notoriously unruly, affected by increasing industrialization and growing social unrest. London's riverside seethed with activity, becoming one of the wonders of the age. Nothing in the world could match the Port of London: the volume of its trade doubled between 1770 and 1795 alone. Yet it came under increasing strain from congestion, crime and labour disputes. This is also the story of how London's port was reformed to counter the pressures of growing trade and prolonged warfare.

Uniquely, at Deptford, royal naval and victualling yards lay next to private shipyards, which built and repaired vessels for the navy as well as for commerce. It was a period when the demand for ships was unprecedented due to recurrent warfare and long-distance trading. Skilled, enterprising shipbuilders with a little capital could do very well. In the 1770s, William Barnard, who already part-owned one shipyard in Deptford, leased a second. He found, as Britain went to war with its American colonies, that there was enough business to keep both yards working at full stretch. Naval vessels were provisioned at Deptford's victualling yard. From October to April, the air would have been full of the noise of hogs and oxen being slaughtered. In these cooler months, the meat was cut, salted, then packed tightly in barrels for the navy. Such was the demand for seamen's biscuit that in 1775 new ovens were built and extra men hired to keep up production. Teams of bakers at the yard's twelve ovens could produce 14,400 lbs (6,500 kg) of biscuit a day and worked at capacity for months on end.[2]

Even so, these maritime districts retained rural elements. The acres of asparagus grounds in Deptford, like those at Battersea and Gravesend, were famously productive. By the mid-1790s, the annual crop weighed 2,000–4,000 lbs (900–1,800 kg). And when, in 1794, the Board of Agriculture made a survey of the cows supplying the metropolis with milk, it recorded that cow-keepers in Kent (including Rotherhithe, Deptford, Greenland Dock, New Cross and Bermondsey) kept nearly 700 animals, while those in Limehouse, Poplar and Ratcliff maintained upwards of 400. These grazing cows would have lent a pastoral aspect; open fields and acres of market gardens were still only a short step from industrial sites. Yet the strain of London's expansion was already taking its toll on the water quality of the Thames. At low tide in summer, the banks between Westminster Bridge and Deptford stank. One wag, taking a boat downriver between the 'back-sides' of Wapping and the Isle of Dogs on the left and the 'back-sides' of Rotherhithe, Deptford and Greenwich on the right, grumbled that it was as if their combined populations had taken a dose of laxatives.[3] The City of London was urged to supply the mud as manure to farmers, but baulked at the expense.

In these crowded maritime communities, local politics had an uneasy relationship with City affairs and the government of the nation as a whole.

The question of who, exactly, took local decisions was a tangled business. The City's Corporation, led by the Lord Mayor and powerful aldermen, appointed people to lucrative jobs in the port and on the river. It was jealous of its privileges. But maritime London stretched across several counties, each with its own Members of Parliament. East of the Tower, beyond the boundaries of the City, maritime parishes north of the Thames were in Middlesex. (Today, these districts are known as 'Tower Hamlets'. The term was current in the eighteenth century to describe settlements between the Tower and the eastern boundary of Middlesex at the River Lea. But it was mostly associated with the militia: inhabitants had to provide two regiments of militia, under the command of the Constable of the Tower or Lieutenant of Tower Hamlets, to guard that fortress in times of emergency.) South of the Thames, Southwark and Rotherhithe lay in Surrey, whereas Deptford and Greenwich were in Kent. Naturally, local politics coloured life in the different parishes.

Another power to be reckoned with was Trinity House, which licensed river pilots and was responsible for pilotage on the Thames. It was independent of the City and run by a court of elder brethren under a master. To complicate matters, the watermen and lightermen on the river were mostly licensed by their own organization, the Company of Watermen and Lightermen, though its licensing officials were appointed by the Mayor. Watermen were famously belligerent, and the Company's concern to control their working practices distinguished it from City livery companies who served their members' economic interests.

London's riverside districts, with their transient populations of young seamen, were volatile and easily stirred by rousing talk. The late 1760s and early 1770s were the heyday of popular demonstrations in favour of the radical politician John Wilkes. When pro-Wilkite crowds gathered in St George's Fields in May 1768, publicans in Rotherhithe and Wapping at once boarded up their houses to avoid damage by the rioting mob. Social conflict in Britain was aggravated by the revolutionary wars against the American colonies from 1775 and then France in 1793, which split public opinion. The country seemed to be taking up arms against those claiming to fight only for liberty. Among London's riverside populations, the forces of law and order struggled to contain the brutal and criminal elements that threatened Britain's commercial and imperial success. Violence was never far from the surface. Clashes between armed smugglers and custom-house men were commonplace. Radical ideas threatened to disturb the peace of these communities at the very time when the nation was battling to defend its imperial interests overseas. Loyalists in these districts had to work hard to counteract disruptive forces, although in the case of war with France, once the revolutionaries had executed their king most Britons were united against them. Surprisingly, there was no regular Thames police force until 1798, although pilfering from cargo ships reached scandalous proportions. Still, the Marine Police, with its office in Wapping, pre-dated the Metropolitan Police by some thirty years – an indication of the importance attached to trade, especially in wartime.

Within the maritime parishes, respected families provided a measure of stability. In Wapping, the hard-working Henley family prospered from the coal trade and government contracts, and the wives of explorers James Cook and William Bligh lived in cautious gentility while their husbands were away. Their knowledge, gleaned from their husbands' letters, provided neighbours with a link to distant imperial ventures, as did much everyday conversation with the sea captains based locally. South of the river, in Deptford, the Barnard family won government contracts to build warships in their private shipyards, while the canny Slade dynasty squeezed as much profit as they could from their connections with the naval dockyard. The ups and downs of all these lives mirrored the fortunes of war and trade.

The contribution made by ordinary maritime Londoners to Britain's wars, which in this period extended across oceans and continents, is hardly known. Yet their lives offer new perspectives on epoch-making events. Mobilization put pressure on all families connected with the sea but the impact of war was not always negative. Some shipowners welcomed the chance to make money from privateering. There were more employment opportunities. Local tradesmen could even benefit from troop reviews at home by selling refreshments to onlookers at inflated prices. Also, in wartime, the naval yards at Woolwich and Deptford were treated as sites of national importance, bolstering local pride. The Admiralty's regular, well-publicized inspections added drama to the daily round. George III himself, when out riding, sometimes dropped by to survey dockyard activity.

In this period, too, riverside communities had a special connection to government-sponsored voyages of exploration, which set off from the banks of the Thames. Earlier in the eighteenth century, a voyage to the Pacific would have daunted even the stoutest sailor, but increasingly it was no more to be dreaded than a common passage to the East Indies. When in 1768 Captain Cook set out for Tahiti, taking Joseph Banks and other experts to study plants and wildlife, one reporter saw the expedition as 'Gentlemen of Fortune' embarking on a 'tour of pleasure'.[4] In a difficult period when seamen were demanding higher wages and Wilkes was agitating for parliamentary reform, no wonder some thought that the voyage was an elite sideshow. In contrast, dockside populations warmed to shipments of exotic animals – stunning Arab horses, tame Indian elephants and big cats from the jungles of Southeast Asia – and jostled for a glimpse of them. The openness of the riverside districts to novelty is reflected in the industries alongside the Thames that were sites of technological experimentation. Machines were invented to improve conditions for seamen and new methods of ship construction were trialled. All these developments helped to make the riverside a hotbed of rumour and speculation. They fuelled industrial rivalry and encouraged entrepreneurship.

Warfare meanwhile brought growing unease about the role of women in society, particularly as radical ideas gained hold. In London's maritime parishes, women anyway carried more domestic responsibility than was usual for the time, being left to cope when seafaring menfolk were absent from home. Even in peacetime, local men might be forced to work abroad; lack of employment opportunities in the early 1770s drove many to serve as soldiers in the East India Company or to work in the Dutch trade. These turbulent decades had a notable impact on women. At one end of the economic spectrum we find instances of mothers accused of murdering unwanted babies by drowning them in the river or bog-house. At the other end, we find capable widows carrying on their dead husbands' businesses in wartime. William Barnard's widow, Frances, is one example of the latter. She ran the shipyard which built ships for the navy until her sons were old enough to take over.

There was a more light-hearted side to life. The American Revolutionary War, for instance, and the post-war boom years in the 1780s, presented riverside communities with many opportunities for social events and entertainment. Regular ship launches attracted thousands of onlookers from all classes, although not everyone in the crowd supported the war. Military reviews, charity balls, regattas, church ceremonies and victory celebrations were lively distractions. Charitable giving, annual events such as the water processions of Trinity House, and civic occasions attended by royalty all offered platforms for outward displays of gentility and respectability. These rituals marked the social calendar, and while they attracted pickpockets, they played a part in controlling social behaviour. The same can be said for charitable institutions such as almshouses, charity schools and the Marine Society, which sent poor boys to sea.

When war with Revolutionary France came in 1793, Britain seemed better prepared than in 1775. The logistics involved were impressive but rarely reported. Only when upwards of 7,000 tons of hay were shipped from London for the British cavalry in Flanders did newspapers think it worth mentioning. Later the prodigious quantity of salted provisions, peas, biscuit, flour and other stuffs being stockpiled for the navy also drew comment. The yards along the Thames were busy constructing warships and frigates to allegedly new designs – signalling that vessels for the fleet would be at the forefront of technology. The relentless pace of work produced its own tensions among the workforce. From 1796, two regiments of the City of London militia guarded Deptford and Woolwich dockyards. Each regiment had 600 men, serving for six months in rotation. The rigorous steps government took to deter radicalism in these areas were costly but vital: the presence of troops secured the yards and helped to preserve order.

The river at work, in all its guises, was one of the sights of London. This book reveals the importance of London's quaysides during a crucial period when inhabitants were caught up in wars of global proportions. What did it feel like to live in one of the riverside parishes? Each contained pivotal buildings where people of all classes, preoccupations and political persuasions came together, their paths entwined by wartime events. Equally, each had dimly lit, 'no-go' areas where even burly seamen were subject to attack. The story begins with an exploration of the main thoroughfares and buildings in these expanding districts. It uncovers the activities that went on within them: shipbuilding and industrial experiments, the build-up to war, crime and prostitution, moneymaking and leisure. It considers what people understood by 'liberty' during these revolutionary years and it gives insights into anxious, often violent lives. It describes varied, personal experiences, interleaved with dramatic national events, and recalls communities effectively lost to history. The story bristles with personal anecdotes that bring the past alive. In sum, it reveals a maritime London, on both banks of the Thames, that pre-dates the capital's east–west divide.

1

LONDON'S RIVERSIDE

A seaman in the 1760s, returning after a long voyage and heading upriver on the evening tide, might well come ashore at St Catherine's Stairs, just below the Tower. If he headed east for Wapping, he would soon be on familiar territory. In the fading light, he might wish to avoid the area of Execution Dock, on a bend of the river towards the middle of the Wapping foreshore. Tarred gallows stood there, below high-water mark. As late as 1760, Captain John Tune had been hanged at Execution Dock for piracy on the high seas, although his crime had taken place a mere 3 leagues out from Folkestone. He had boarded a neutral ship in wartime, assaulted the master and stolen cloth worth £148. His exploit was hardly in the same league as the crimes of Blackbeard and other notorious pirates of the 'Golden Age' of piracy some half a century earlier, but the punishment was just as horrific. After death, Tune's body was left swinging from the gallows until the tide had washed over the corpse three times, symbolically cleansing him of his sins. Then it was cut down and hung in chains near Blackwall, on the eastern side of the Isle of Dogs, as a warning to others. Two years later, another captain, James Lowry, was hanged at Execution Dock for murdering one of his crew. Almost all seamen were deeply superstitious; it was a place to shun.

So, rather than heading for Wapping Dock (a narrow road banked above marshland, curving with the foreshore and edged by dank alleyways crammed with timber tenements), a returning seaman might instead strike north for Ratcliff Highway. This ran east–west along gravel upland and marked Wapping's northernmost boundary. Also a narrow road in spite of its name, and badly paved, it boasted no fewer than thirty-six pubs and taverns along its half-mile extent. Many were the jealously guarded haunts of the Portuguese, Dutch or Genoese. Brawls and stabbings among the different nationalities might flare up in a moment.[1] It was a world apart, and one of the sights of London for anyone who dared walk its length. There were seamen here from every discovered continent, of every physical description, clustered in small groups arguing and joking in different languages which, given their habit of also using nautical jargon, made the general babble utterly incomprehensible to those not used to the sea. The Highway was irregularly lit by oil lamps, but in the gathering dusk it was already a place of danger as snatches of song and drunken conversation spilled out from alehouse doors into the street.

London's poor were still wedded to cheap gin, most likely distilled illegally and ruinous to health. A large glass, mixed two to one with water, could be bought from a gin shop for a penny but it was often ordered by the half pint for three pence. Even regular beer drinkers might call for a pint of purl, or beer – often warmed – with a slug of gin. Alcohol kept out the cold, blunted cares and offered the desperate a welcome oblivion. A seaman newly landed with money in his pocket might intend to seek out some woman he trusted, perhaps one he had stayed with before, but in each pool of lamplight there would be women of the town coaxing him for something to drink. Not infrequently, sailors fresh from the sea woke up the next day with no money at all, and perhaps no watch or shoe buckles either.

The public houses along Ratcliff Highway were at the centre of communal life. Seamen might seek lodgings in one of them and stay carousing all day. The taverns offered backgammon, shuffleboard, singing and perhaps dancing. Many also offered skittles, and although it was illegal to bet on the game, many did, prompting violent disputes. Local constables would casually frequent public houses to learn the latest gossip and track down criminals. Constables even used the more reputable establishments, such as the Virginia Planter, as places to lock up suspects before interrogation. By day, the various drinking houses along the Highway were absorbed into the colourful attractions of the street as a whole. There were shops to cater for a sailor's every need: ship chandlers, providing tools and ships' equipment; slop shops, offering cheap, ready-made clothing; brandy and tobacco stores, signalled by the wooden figure of a black Indian, with a crown and a kilt of tobacco leaves; pawnshops, where clothes outnumbered pledged goods of every description; and brothels. Workers in all these premises were anxious to accost and reel in the unsuspecting seaman to take his money. Just as they accommodated him, so his custom was essential to them. If smaller businesses prospered, it was down to sailors' money. And some shops, specializing in curios and novelties, would be on the lookout for any exotic goods that seamen might care to sell.

The Highway, a major thoroughfare, was a hubbub of noise, which began even before dawn had properly broken. Grumbling drivers of heavy carts made their way to join queue points near the river, where they stood, braving the cold, aiming to get work carting unloaded cargoes away from the quayside. In Lower Thames Street carts were banned before 4 a.m. in summer and 7 a.m. in winter, but outside the City there were fewer rules. Washerwomen, on their way to help with households' regular washing days, were also out and about while it was still dark, hurrying to light kitchen fires early in order to boil water. Soon there would be street sellers, peddling fresh milk, fish or greens from market, calling out their wares in shrill tones calculated to get attention. Other hawkers would be carrying trays of clay pipes, ribbons or pies. Ballad sellers would pitch up on street corners to gather a crowd, sing the latest ballad and hope to sell the words, printed on single sheets, for a few pennies. And wherever there was a crowd there would be pickpockets, equally fixed on making a living.

Ratcliff Highway has often received a bad press. In the Elizabethan age, John Stow described it as 'a continual street, or rather a filthy straight passage, with Lanes and Allyes, of small Tenements inhabited by Saylors and Victuallers'; in Victorian times it was denounced as 'the head-quarters of unbridled vice and drunken violence – of all that is dirty, disorderly, and debased'.[2] But between these two periods, before a rapid increase in population brought squalor in the nineteenth century, residents included families who were comfortably off, as well as the poor. One indication of the varied employment along its route is that workshops made it particularly susceptible to fire. Newspapers regularly reported premises being gutted and rebuilt. So by day, people visited perfectly respectable shops – cheesemongers, shoe shops and silversmiths – and it was at night that pedestrians needed to take particular care and prosperous taverns had to guard against burglary.

Follow Ratcliff Highway eastwards and you come to Shadwell. By the middle of the eighteenth century the demand for unskilled labour, especially for coal heaving, had brought a rough, uncouth population to Shadwell that neighbouring parishes looked down on, even in this part of the world. The newcomers – often Irish – were housed by creating yards, courts and alleys within existing streets. The names of these makeshift developments – Vine Court, White Lyon Yard, Bear Court – indicate that they covered the back yards of inns, or occupied sites which had once been the garden grounds of older houses. As London's trade grew and the demand for manual labour increased, these tenements became overcrowded and seedy. River work was subject to weather – if a severe frost or unfavourable winds made the Thames unnavigable for any length of time, labourers were laid off. Conditions for their families soon became desperate and Lower Shadwell rapidly developed a reputation for being poverty-stricken. But Shadwell's family-owned shipbuilding yards on the riverside were largely profitable. Owners expanded their businesses, invested in shipping and even engaged in international trade.[3]

Ratcliff, a hamlet to the east of Shadwell, via Broad Street, was also full of inns and alehouses. A favourite haunt of captains and seamen for centuries, its population increased markedly from the 1780s. Ratcliff housed many small businesses: watchmakers, shoemakers, ropemakers, coopers, pickled salmon sellers, druggists and linen drapers. Some of its taverns were substantial, such as the City Arms at Ratcliff Cross, which also sold herbal eye-water. Ratcliff Cross, the alley running to the river between Broad Street and its continuation, Narrow Street, was an established meeting point for seamen. It was also a well-known staging point for passenger coaches and goods wagons. Here watermen waited to ferry passengers across the river, wary of the ebb tide which ran very strong between 'The Cross' and Horse Ferry, 300 metres or so eastwards. Narrow Street, which continued all the way to Limehouse, was crowded with timber buildings but had rows of fine houses too, some occupied by mariners' widows who rented spare rooms to supplement their income.

Many of the substantial, two- or three-storey, brick-fronted buildings on Narrow Street had shops at pavement level and industrial premises to the back. An early Georgian terrace survives on the south side, giving an impression of the street's former appearance. The larger premises incorporated arched passageways so that horse-drawn wagons could reach yards to the rear. Some buildings combined living quarters and a warehouse in one development. In the 1780s, Charles Argil, a ship chandler dealing in cordage, had his warehouse on this street with the doors fronting the river. Such arrangements made it easier to transport rope. After all, some local roperies manufactured rope that was up to 23 inches (58 cm) thick, and if width was not a consideration then length could make rope a heavy load. Large sailing vessels used an incredible amount. Nelson's *Victory*, for example, needed over 26 miles (42 km).

Easy access to the river doubtless encouraged smuggling and the receipt of stolen goods by water. But the land tax was always higher for properties on the waterfront and owners may have regarded opportunities for illegal trade as fair compensation.[4] On Narrow Street, too, stood the Bunch of Grapes (now just called The Grapes). Built around 1720, it was a landmark, although not much more than 15 feet (4.5 m) wide. A pub had stood on the site from Tudor times. Owing to its riverside location it was rumoured to be much used by press gangs. Seamen would be plied with drink, only to wake up the following morning on a ship already making its way down the Thames to the sea.

Still heading east, Narrow Street was the route to Limehouse and the lime kilns that gave the area its name. In what was once a desolate spot, limestone was heated to produce lime for mortar and agriculture. But by mid-century the area also had sawmills, timber yards and brickworks. Farther east still lay Limehouse Causeway where, in the 1780s, a small group of Cantonese seamen set up home – the beginnings of London's first Chinatown. Inland, the heath was carefully laid out as market gardens, which supplied London's voracious food markets. Along the Limehouse riverfront were solidly built houses with ladders descending to the foreshore, and shipyards where barges and ships were fitted out and repaired. Here, as in Ratcliff, some pubs backed onto the river. Proprietors found it easier to keep a boat and travel by water than trust roads, which, on the outskirts of town, were notorious for footpads.

In time, the riverside buildings became increasingly patched, higgledy-piggledy and shored up against the tide, but the 1760s were years of steady expansion. Limehouse was soon absorbed into an extensive industrial area. In 1770 Limehouse Cut was opened to provide a shortcut for grain and malt barges to join the River Lea at Bromley by Bow, sparing them the circuitous route around the Isle of Dogs. The navigation of the River Lea had itself just been redeveloped into a canal to reduce transport times and to bring gunpowder to London from the royal gunpowder mills at Waltham Abbey. All these developments increased the importance of Limehouse. And across the windswept marshland, on the eastern side of the Isle of Dogs, was Blackwall, a shipbuilding centre since the Middle Ages. The various smells of local industries drifted on the wind: smoke, tar, sugar refining, sawdust, leadworks and, above all, the musty smell of waterlogged wood.

Churches

London's maritime parishes housed transient, seafaring populations but they were also home to close-knit communities for whom a focal point was their local place of worship. The Anglican churches in Ratcliff, Limehouse, Shadwell and Wapping brought residents together and, by association, helped to reinforce the areas' maritime identity. The oldest church, St Dunstan and All Saints, at the north end of Ratcliff, dates from medieval times. It was given the dramatic title of 'Church of the High Seas' because of its historic links with merchants and shipbuilders. From its tower, it still flies the Red Ensign, the same flag that English and British merchant ships have flown since at least the time of Charles II. To the southeast, St Anne's church in Limehouse provided a useful landmark for navigation. One of fifty new Anglican churches approved by Act of Parliament in 1711 to cater for London's expanding population and to counter the worrying numbers of Dissenters in outlying parishes, it was completed in 1724, although not consecrated until 1730. Above its 200-foot (61-m) high tower, by permission of the Crown, it flies the navy's White Ensign. Visible for miles around, it became a Trinity House sea mark and featured on navigation charts for this part of the river. To returning seamen, its flag must have represented welcome proof that they would soon reach port. Allegedly, any babies born during a voyage would be taken promptly to St Anne's to be registered and baptized.

St Paul's Shadwell, rebuilt in 1669, was known as 'the Church of Sea Captains' because they accounted for most of its congregation. Several have monuments on the church's walls and many more are buried in the church-yard. It was Captain Cook's parish church: he worshipped here when he lived in Shadwell with his wife, early in their marriage, and in 1763 his eldest son was baptized here. St Paul's rose above a centre of maritime activity. The trades clustered around it included roperies, timber yards, sail-makers, coopers, breweries and a flourishing market. A path, raised in places on stilts above marshland, led from the church to the Thames. It terminated at the Prospect of Whitby public house. Formerly known as 'The Devil Tavern', perhaps reflecting the quality of its clientele, it was rebuilt after a fire in 1777 when it was renamed after a Whitby collier that brought coal from the Northeast to London and overwintered nearby.

St George-in-the-East, Wapping, was only a short walk away and another of the churches to result from the 1711 Act. Consecrated in 1729, it was set behind houses just above Ratcliff Highway and also frequented by seafarers. Of the fifty churches approved by Parliament in 1711, only twelve were actually built. Each was over budget and the money ran out. So it is significant that a quarter of the churches prioritized for completion were built in London's maritime parishes where dissent was rife: in Limehouse, Wapping and, as we shall see, Deptford and Greenwich. With the exception of St Paul's in Deptford, which was designed by Thomas Archer, the architect of these wonderful new churches was Nicholas Hawksmoor. He intended them to 'work' on the viewer and create an intense spiritual effect.[5] The striking 'pepper-pot' towers of St George-in-the-East and its wide principal tower are deliberately uplifting. While Protestant Dissenters had been at liberty to worship as they pleased since the Toleration Act of 1689, they were still barred from public office and political life. The Anglican churches, towering over the homes of parishioners, were constant reminders of the power of the established, national religion. Their clocks chimed the hours that regulated the working day. The churches also became marks of social segregation: the rich attended in their carriages, the less well-off on foot.

The churches appealed to the well-to-do and are certainly imposing, even unsettling. St Anne's was still surrounded by open fields in the mid-eighteenth century, but soon prompted a row of fine houses along Church Lane, now Newell Street, boasting gardens that opened directly onto church ground. St Dunstan's in Ratcliff likewise attracted the comparatively affluent; from mid-century the area around it was home to a group of wealthy widows.[6] This may have been a factor in the church deciding to employ women in roles seemingly aligned with their housekeeping duties. At that time, the bunch of keys that many women carried at their waist was a visible sign of their responsibility for domestic management, and in the 1790s, St Dunstan's had a sextoness and female officials who unlocked the pews. Of course, whenever congregations were particularly large, as when Communion was celebrated (on Easter Day, Whit Sunday, Christmas Day and Good Friday), thieves were drawn to the crowd. Those who attended evening lectures in church were similarly at risk of being jostled and robbed on the way home.

Another indication of the social mix in Wapping is found in a contemporary anecdote from 1802. A minister had been engaged to give a charity sermon at the old church of St John's near Wapping Old Stairs, rebuilt in 1760 despite retaining just a tiny parish. The minister, Mr Hill, had a reputation for peppering his sermons with jokes, which usually went down well. On this occasion, observing that he had a large congregation of mostly seafaring folk, not renowned for being religious, he began by exclaiming that he had 'come to preach to great sinners, notorious sinners, profane sinners', in short (warming to his theme and punning on the sound of the word), 'Wapping Sinners'. The joke backfired horribly: 'this climax operated like an electric shock through all the congregation, and highly offended the inhabitants of that *polite* part of the town'.[7] The Wapping congregation was prepared to be called a bunch of sinners but not to have its neighbourhood slighted as a place likely to house them.

The presence of other significant churches in Wapping served as a reminder of the way in which the sea united different peoples in the same endeavour. By Well Close Square lay the Danish Church, built in 1696 at the expense of the King of Denmark. In Princes Square there was a church for the Swedes, built about 1729. Portuguese sailors worshipped in a chapel at the upper end of Virginia Street, close to Ratcliff Highway. Stepney as a whole was a centre for Dissenting communities and in Wapping there remained numerous places of worship for them. The Independent Stepney Meeting was on Bull Lane, just a hundred metres or so west of St Dunstan's. At the bottom of Old Gravel Lane there was the meeting house of the Independents. There was another, for Presbyterians, in Broad Street. The Quakers had a meeting house in Gracechurch Street and another, with a small school attached, in Ratcliff. It was not unheard of for some residents on Sundays to worship at both church and meeting house.

In contrast, penal laws prohibiting Catholic worship remained in force until the last quarter of the eighteenth century. In the 1760s, Wapping's parish officials suppressed a Roman Catholic mass-house at the back of trade premises near Saltpetre Bank (now Dock Street). The priest and about twenty 'mean-dressed people' made their escape through a back door.[8] Irish immigrants in the maritime districts worshipped secretly in people's houses. There was another private mass-house in Virginia Street. Yet the number of Catholics in Wapping seems to have been comparatively low, if still a concern to the authorities.

The physical environment of Wapping seemed to reinforce the moral choices open to its inhabitants. St George-in-the-East pointed to the path of virtue; Execution Dock stood as a reminder of the fate awaiting transgressors. Ratcliff Highway offered temptations, while the wharves and industries along Wapping Dock displayed the wealth that could be gained through hard work. Tellingly, local churches often had law enforcement apparatus nearby. The old church of St John's was the site of the 'cage' where constables imprisoned offenders overnight until they could find a magistrate. There was a watch-house at St Dunstan's used as a base by the local watchmen, and again a place where offenders or just the drunk and disorderly might be restrained. But even small watch-houses kept a fire and could provide a warm refuge for those in trouble. Perhaps, after all, there was some synergy between watch-houses and the charitable work of the church.

Civic buildings

Other landmarks included local charity schools, also featured on contemporary maps. Well-endowed schools acted as powerful reminders not only of the need for Christian kindness but also of the money to be made in maritime-related industries. Raine's Hospital in Fowden Fields, Wapping, was exceptionally well known. This charity school for girls had been built in 1737 by the brewer, Henry Raine, who owned a brewhouse nearby at New Crane Wharf. When it came to endowing the school, Raine displayed the same application and attention to detail that had helped him to make a fortune in the first place. He stipulated that forty girls were to be taught to read, write and do housework so that after three years of education they could be put out to service. No Dissenters were to be admitted. He made provision for one girl each year to receive a dowry, and lots were drawn for this. The girl with the winning ticket received the dowry only if school governors approved of her husband-to-be (who had to be an Anglican). For a poor girl, the dowry was truly life changing. It added to the reputation of Raine's Hospital and the annual drawing of lots became an event.

Such was the demand for places at the school that it sometimes housed as many as forty-eight girls. They were selected from the more promising pupils at a school Raine had set up earlier in Old Gravel Lane. This admitted fifty girls and fifty boys. Unusually, the boys were instructed in arithmetic as well as reading and writing, which would fit them for navigation and specialist trades. Raine also set aside funds to allow them to be apprenticed at the end of their schooling. His endowments were specific and well regulated. They were clearly intended for the long-term benefit of the maritime parishes north of the river, contributing to residents' sense of cohesion and self-worth. Raine's Hospital attracted notable supporters, including Francis Holman, the marine painter, a trustee from 1780 to 1785.

Another significant landmark was the London Hospital, at the northernmost point of these maritime districts. It had been set up as a charity in 1740 to provide free medical care to those in the east of the city. Specifically, it aimed to help manufacturers, merchant seamen and their wives and children. It rapidly outgrew its first rented accommodation and governors decided to raise funds for purpose-built premises. The only site they could acquire was on the Whitechapel Road, surrounded by fields and on the edge of Mile End Old Town. They had misgivings, thinking that a hospital ought to be more centrally located, but construction proceeded as fast as they could raise funds. The new building opened in 1757, although it was not completed for another two years. The wings that were planned could not be afforded for another ten. The long struggle to raise money for the hospital helped to endear it to local people, who welcomed the efforts made on their behalf.

Care in the hospital was at first rudimentary but had some success, not least because people with contagious diseases and pregnant women were not admitted (it was a time when many died in childbirth). The hospital was well publicized from the outset. Newspapers carried notices of governors' meetings, of its annual sermon and feast, and reports of major donations. From 1785 it trained medical students, advertising its lectures on anatomy, midwifery and other branches of medicine. Its anatomy college was the first in the country to be based in a hospital. One of its founders, the surgeon William Blizard, introduced the practice of walking the wards, now an essential part of medical education, although he is also believed to have been the last surgeon to give consultations in coffee houses. The college raised the hospital's profile and made the community proud to possess an institution of importance. By 1800 the hospital had become part of London's expanding eastern parishes, although it still backed onto fields.

Wapping, Shadwell, Ratcliff and Limehouse had been quick to establish workhouses for the poor in the early decades of the eighteenth century. Their crowded sites had little to recommend them. In contrast, local almshouses ranged from underfunded, shabby places of real poverty, catering for small numbers, to proud institutions that really did offer residents a comfortable old age. Trinity House of London, incorporated by Henry VIII, had almshouses (which can still be seen) on the north side of Mile End Road 'for 28 decayed masters and commanders of ships, mates and pilots, and their wives and widows'.[9] Trinity House ran two more almshouses in Deptford, which have long since disappeared. These were powerful symbols of the Corporation's status and also of private munificence, since seafaring men left legacies to these institutions. The almshouses in Mile End, for example, had been built in 1695 on land provided by Captain Henry Mudd of Ratcliff. They were well designed and built around a chapel. Replicas of 42-gun warships still feature on each gable, and Mudd and his widow, who also donated, are commemorated on a wall plaque. Such almshouses signalled the importance of seafaring and the responsibility of care that wealthy citizens accepted for those who had given their lives to working in Britain's interest.

Freemasonry, another community activity, was a strong social force in the maritime districts from the 1760s. Masons, who excluded women, met fortnightly in public houses when they voted funds to help widows, the sick or those in debt. There were six lodges in Wapping alone. The oldest, established about 1733, was the Dundee Arms Lodge, No. 9. In 1763 its members purchased the freehold of a warehouse in Red Lion Street, which ran north–south to the river just west of Wapping New Stairs, and held their meetings in two rooms on the first floor. They installed two oil lamps to light the entrance, making the building more of a landmark. It became known as the Wapping Assembly Rooms because on days when there was no meeting, masons let out the larger room, 44 feet by 25 feet (13.5m by 7.6m) for public dances.

The prevalence of freemasonry in maritime districts is another indication of the affluence and level of education of many inhabitants. Masons were invariably literate and could afford fees. Freemasonry's emphasis on mutual support and charity was useful in an environment where men risked personal capital in business ventures and could lose all if they became bankrupt. The masonic emphasis on morality and personal liberty also chimed well with the spirit of the times. Masons supported civil obedience and respect for law. The Dundee Arms Lodge notably spent £30 on a double-handed 'sword of state' in 1761 to mark the coronation of George III, and displayed it at their meetings. But they were also active in contemporary debates about the nature of liberty. Their view of liberty was essentially that of the philosopher John Locke, as set out in his *Two Treatises of Government* in 1690. Like most Britons, they upheld the constitutional monarchy; they believed that allegiance to a ruling power secured their safety and property. Yet they also believed that within this form of government, based on trust and consent, they retained their liberty – understood to include social responsibilities as well as customary freedoms. One indication of the kind of debate about liberty that Wapping masons might have enjoyed is that John Wilkes, the radical politician, attended one of their meetings in June 1770, at the height of his notoriety.[10]

Wapping residents

Wapping's mixed population resulted in pockets of poor-quality and slum housing but also large fine houses owned by the 'middling sort'. This group is usually defined as having annual incomes of between £61 and £200.[11] Wapping was a major centre for supplying food and equipment to the thousands of ships that used the Thames each year. Wapping Wall, a mile-long road hugging the northern bank of the Thames, had over fifty ship chandlers and dozens of other maritime businesses, from suppliers of anchors, sails and ropes to brewers and bakers of ship's biscuit.[12] Many of these industries were essential to London's economic success. Some local merchants were also large-scale contractors to the navy. The most powerful might also have investments in the coastal coal trade, or contracts to service the ships of the East India Company and the Hudson's Bay Company, with interests extending to the farthest reaches of empire. Much of Wapping High Street had been rebuilt in brick after a fire in 1673. These were the properties inhabited by merchants and businessmen who needed to live by the river. The area of Wapping above Ratcliff Highway was more prosperous, and beyond the fields in Mile End Old Town about half the taxpayers were of the 'middling sort'.[13] As Wapping merchants made money, so they were tempted to move to Mile End Old Town or farther afield. Their business premises, though, remained by the river.

Labourers and sailors lived in the squalid alleys off Wapping High Street or in equally poor housing farther north of the Thames. The houses were jerry-built of timber, often just one or two storeys high with one room to a floor. They were overcrowded, with different families or lodgers occupying different floors, and offered little privacy. Elizabeth Waite, a witness at an Old Bailey trial in 1762, explained that she could vouch for what had taken place in her next-door neighbour's house because the houses had only a thin wainscot partition between them: 'We can very well hear common conversation in her house as we sit in our own.'[14]

Wapping had its crime hot spots. One of the most notorious was Saltpetre Bank, a badly lit, narrow hill leading north from Ratcliff Highway with a reputation for bawdy houses, pawnshops and dubious lodging houses. It took its name from nearby glassworks. (Glass-making tended to be near the river because it needed heavy sand, coal and potash, which were easier to bring by water.) There were some small tradesmen in Saltpetre Bank, carpenters and the like, but it was a dangerous area. The narrow lane was frequented at all hours of the night by criminals, prostitutes and seamen. It had at least four public houses, the Black Boy alehouse being the most disreputable, where stolen goods were often fenced.[15] As trade increased on the river, the number of thefts from barges and ships increased too, and the waterfront became the haunt of river pirates.

Crossing the river

Thanks to the Thames, London's maritime districts were well connected. In the mid-eighteenth century, to cross the Thames anywhere between Vauxhall and Limehouse cost four pence when the boat was rowed with more than one man, each pulling on an oar, and two pence if it had just one oarsman sculling more slowly. A simple crossing was not without its dangers. Boats might be overloaded in spite of regulations. There were collisions, and sometimes passengers drowned. Even hardened seamen avoided a night crossing, when the ebb tide could be dangerously strong. But by and large, numerous watermen offered easy communication between the maritime districts on each side of the Thames.

While Wapping's businessmen and merchants thought nothing of walking to the City, to the Royal Exchange or to catch the latest maritime news in specialist coffee houses, many people in the maritime districts east of the Tower rarely saw the need to venture into central London. They were more likely to take a boat to other maritime parishes south of the Thames. Thriving shipwrights and tradesmen had business interests on both sides of the river, which contributed to a varied picture of industry. An advertisement for a Rotherhithe 'smith's and anchor-smith's shop' in 1796 gives an insight into this activity. It had a riverside frontage of 42 feet (12.8m) with a crane, different types of forges, a shop and two-storey warehouse, counting house, coal cellars, smith and braziers' shops, stowage and a yard. The stock to be sold included ship stoves and hearths, ship bells, thirty-five iron and wood anchors, iron from Sweden and Russia, rolled plate and twenty cauldrons of coals.[16] Windmills were another sign of industry. From Wapping and extending downstream along the Isle of Dogs, windmills lined the northern bank of the Thames. Still more could be seen south of the river. They were first used to grind corn but by the end of the century were more likely to be crushing oilseed.

As in the northern parishes, the churches to the south served to orientate those on the river. Opposite Wapping and slightly to the east lay the Rotherhithe peninsula, marked by the spire of St Mary the Virgin. Next to the church was a charity school, originating in a free school for just eight sons of seafaring men in the 1600s; much expanded, it occupied the site for fifty years from 1742. Nearby, Rotherhithe's great wet dock had been home to London's whaling industry in the early part of the century; it was renamed Greenland Dock because of the many ships that sailed to the Arctic in search of whales. The stench of whale blubber being rendered in cauldrons on the quayside had once filled the air, but the trade declined. In contrast, the expansion of shipbuilding at Rotherhithe can be gauged by the fact that mid-century it had just three docks while by 1792 it had eleven. Its timber merchants imported vast quantities of wood from northern Europe and had strong links with Scandinavia. Their success signalled that although trade had its ups and downs, the Rotherhithe community possessed resilience and the skills to seize opportunities and remain economically buoyant.

If Rotherhithe was fast becoming an industrial powerhouse, it still retained acres of market gardens. In 1770 an entrepreneur opened the St Helena Gardens and Tavern in pastureland to the south. It was a rather genteel attraction for a while, offering fresh rolls, coffee and tea by day, and music and dancing in the evening. But as industrial activity expanded on Rotherhithe's foreshore, the gardens, with their walkways, ponds and Chinese pavilions, were increasingly patronized by artisans, dockyard workers and their families. The grounds must have offered a welcome relief from the noise and smells of the shipbuilding yards. But even here there was no escaping the maritime identity of the district: alongside the southern reaches of the gardens lay a rope-walk for the stretching and twisting of fibre into ship's rope.

Deptford dockyard

To the east of Rotherhithe lay Deptford. Henry VIII famously set up a royal dockyard here in 1513 although royal ships had been built on this stretch of the river since the early fifteenth century. The royal dockyards were the largest industrial complexes of the age, using some of the most advanced machinery in the world. They took in a variety of heavy, raw materials and turned them into intricate vessels. The work was impressive:

massive felled trees came on site and were stripped, sawn into ribs and planks, then used for construction. While Britain's other naval dockyards outstripped it in size, Deptford always had a special importance because, closest to the Admiralty and Navy Board in London, new methods of working and new materials were routinely trialled there.

Just upstream of the royal dockyard was the victualling yard, or naval supply depot, officially founded in 1742. It was known as 'the Red House' after the original storehouse of red brick, and was itself a landmark for seamen. It held tons of naval stores, clothing, food, tobacco and rum. Already by mid-century it occupied some 11 acres; it suffered repeated fires and, whenever rebuilt, was always enlarged. From October to April, when the yard's butchers slaughtered livestock for the navy, the roads leading up to it were periodically dangerous and congested. As many as 800 oxen a week could be driven from Smithfield meat market across London or Blackfriars Bridge and down the Old Kent Road, bellowing and jostling, to the yard's gates. The whole complex was surrounded by a high brick wall to deter theft and sabotage, with the main entrance guarded by a porter's lodge.

By the second half of the eighteenth century, the naval dockyard gave Deptford a particular character and pride. A plan of 1774, made for King George III, shows that it was almost a village in itself, now covering at least 30 acres. Within its walls were houses and gardens for the yard officers who needed to live onsite to supervise the work, which might be determined by the tide rather than the clock. They included the master attendant, the storekeeper, the 'clerk of the cheque' (who approved all expenditure) and the dockyard's own surgeon. The master shipbuilder's house still exists. There were stables for horses, and a coach house. Official buildings included a tap-house and a pay-office. As for shipbuilding facilities, it had a large basin for ships; two wet docks (a double, covering 2 acres, and a single of 1.5 acres); six building slips (three on the river and three on one side of the basin, all surrounded by timber berths); two mast ponds with a series of locks to maintain water levels, and drainage to the river; nine saw pits; a mould loft where shipwrights drew out full-sized cross-sections of ships; a sail room for cutting and sewing sails, with storage for them; a large smith's shop with several forges for making anchors; storehouses for oakum (unravelled rope) with a store for pitch nearby so that caulkers could stir the two together and use the mixture to plug the seams of ships; a building for steaming wood into curved shapes; workshops for block-making, wheel-making and painting; and a rigging house. The yard also had huge store-houses, great timber berths, anchor wharves with long racks for their storage, kilns, a pump house and a line of cranes.[17] It provided moments of high drama for those watching from the other side of the river. Artists were inspired to produce views of great masts being swung into warships and ship launches that drew thousands.

Deptford was in Kent, therefore not strictly part of London. It was more of an industrial satellite, although already joined to Rotherhithe in the west and to Greenwich in the east, making a continuous ribbon of development. The town was large and populous by the standards of the day, with about 10,000 residents in 1700, growing to an estimated 18,282 by 1801, according to the census that year, which did not take into account transient populations such as seamen. Historically, it was divided into Upper and Lower Deptford. Upper Deptford had grown from a settlement around an important bridge at Deptford Broadway, where the London-to-Dover road crosses Deptford Creek. The Ravensbourne tributary flows into the Thames through this creek, which, being tidal, was used to power early industries. Farther north, Lower Deptford had grown from a fishing village on the bank of the Thames, and was chiefly occupied by shipbuilding and associated trades. Alongside the naval dockyard, it had impressive private ship-yards with large workforces although there were still local fishermen in the area. The two parts of the town were linked by Butt Lane, now Deptford High Street, only sparsely populated until the mid-eighteenth century.

Shipbuilding dominated Deptford, rather like a car manufacturing plant might dominate a town today. The town was overwhelmingly popu-lated by artisans, labourers and mariners. It was highly dependent on wage labour and far larger and more built up than any of London's other 'suburbs'. Local businesses relied on the income that came from the dockyard, either directly through government contracts, or indirectly from the wages of dockyard employees. Its total workforce mid-century was about 1,000 men; the annual salary bill more than £20,000. So the dockyard was responsible for considerable spending power in the town, even allowing for late payment of wages. If ever work was short in the naval yards, shipwrights and carpenters might join private yards, or help with the harvest, or build timber houses locally.

In the 1770s, Deptford dockyard employed 400 or more shipwrights alone. They built and repaired vessels, but also dismantled old vessels, salvaging timber. As with most skilled crafts of the time, there was a seven-year apprenticeship before a novice qualified as a shipwright. Wages were not very high but the work was constant so apprenticeships were highly sought after and carefully limited. Once out of apprenticeship, shipwrights were skilled workers and not easily replaced. They were not just literate – their skills extended to complex draughtsmanship. Shipwrights could band together to demand wage increases, especially in wartime. Difficult labour relations were endemic in the dockyards. And as the men could communicate effectively to other naval dockyards in Chatham, Portsmouth or even Plymouth, there was combined strike action on many occasions.

Shipwrights knew that they were of national importance and had collective bargaining power. Their status helped to give Deptford a distinctive culture and self-confidence. They owned their own tools and worked in gangs with elected 'team leaders', or quartermen. It was a job for life, while one's health lasted. And although there was no consistent pension scheme, naval dockyards kept older men in employment, on the understanding that the younger took on some of their work. Younger men seem to have done this willingly, knowing that when their time came they would need the same help. The system worked well because most workers were from close-knit communities with extended families.

By the 1770s it was obvious that Deptford dockyard would decline: Chatham and Portsmouth were attracting more government investment. The problem was that large warships found it hard to get up to Deptford due to silting in the Thames, and ships were getting larger. The navy already built its largest vessels at Woolwich and Portsmouth where the water was deeper. Those launched at Deptford already had to be taken down to Woolwich to have their heavy guns installed, as this made them sit deeper in the water. But, for the time being, there was plenty of work for Deptford. Even in peacetime there were smaller ships and transports to build, and others to repair or break up.

Living in Deptford

Most of the houses in Deptford were timber framed. This technique endured – in a district of expert carpenters – long after other builders had turned to brick. Dockyard workers were entitled to take offcuts of wood, or 'chips', as one of the perks of the job, so long as the timber was less than 6 feet (1.8 m) in length. Allegedly this entitlement was open to abuse, with workers carefully sawing wood to just under this length, then taking it home. Whatever the truth, much local housing was augmented with dockyard timber. It was common for London artisans to live comfortably with their families in narrow, two- or three-room houses on several floors. A skilled dockyard worker could afford to rent a three-room house and there was nothing mean about such accommodation, given the standards of the day.[18] Inventories show that people who lived in these houses did so in respectability and comfort. They owned books, prints, tea sets, fine fabrics and birdcages. The truly poor lived in sheds and shacks that have not survived to be documented.[19] As late as 1800 newspapers carried adverts for new-built, three- and four-room houses in Deptford, specifically intended for shipwrights and other workers in the dockyard, only five minutes' walk away. These houses had 'closets, fire places, wash-houses', and open yards or gardens behind. The annual rent was affordable at a little over £6 for each house.[20]

All Deptford residents, and travellers just passing by, would have known the Centurion public house. It stood at the Deptford Broadway end of Butt Lane and had long been a staging post between London and Dover. In the 1750s and 1760s, its landlord was Tom Storey, a former gunner who had sailed around the world with Commodore George Anson. At the outset of war with Spain in 1739, Anson had been given command of a squadron of six ships and ordered to attack Spanish possessions in the Americas. He met with disaster from the outset. Sailing in 1740, later than planned, two of his ships failed to make it round Cape Horn and returned to England. Another was wrecked off Chile. Scurvy, caused by a lack of vitamin C, made short work of the remaining crews. By 1742, Anson had to take all survivors onto his flagship, *Centurion*. They suffered unspeakable hardship crossing the Pacific. Then, within sight of the Philippines, Anson had the enormous good luck to fall in with a Spanish treasure ship carrying more than a million pieces of eight. After a brisk fight, the Spanish galleon surrendered. Anson was a rich man for life and the lowliest sailor on board had wealth beyond his dreams. When they finally returned to Portsmouth, after a voyage of three years and nine months, the treasure was conveyed to London in thirty-two wagons and paraded in triumph through the city.

Thomas Storey probably set up as a publican on the strength of his prize money. Anyone who survived that terrible voyage deserved credit, and Storey clearly capitalized on his achievement, naming his pub after Anson's ship. He died in January 1762, having established a successful business.[21] The pub's location secured a trade in ready money rather than the usual credit. Coaches to and from Blackheath, Greenwich, Deptford and London stopped here and, as an established concern, it became a centre for a range of activities. Auctioneers sent pre-sale catalogues there for public view. Auctions themselves might take place there, as in June 1788 when building land on Butt Lane was sold (a sign of Deptford's increasing expansion).[22] In 1797, the Centurion was rebuilt to include six bedchambers, a club-room, two parlours, a tap-room, bar, large kitchen, roomy cellars, yard and stabling, when the annual rent on an eighteen-year lease was £20 18s.[23]

To Greenwich

In the early summer of 1768, Captain Cook was often in Deptford dock-yard, carefully overseeing the fitting out of his ship, *Endeavour*, for his first voyage to the Pacific. He had taken command of it on 27 May and it was being modified to carry what we would now call a team of scientists. From Deptford dockyard he had a clear view of the twin domes of Greenwich Hospital farther east. This baroque masterpiece, designed by Sir Christopher Wren and Nicholas Hawksmoor for retired and disabled naval seamen, showed the value Britain placed on its navy and on control of the seas. It was home to nearly 2,000 men who led a monotonous existence, although a fairly comfortable one by eighteenth-century standards. From 1741, to make communal life more bearable, they had been allowed two shirts a week, rather than just one.

Although busy, Cook had opportunities to renew his acquaintance with both Deptford and Greenwich. Before sailing, it would have been natural for him to visit the Royal Observatory in Greenwich, where astronomers were recording observations to help seafarers who still mostly navigated by the stars. Cook's voyage had been prompted by the Royal Society to satisfy a thirst for greater knowledge about the planet, and he was due to record the Transit of Venus from Tahiti. Accurate observations of this phenomenon would allow astronomers to calculate the distance of the Sun from the Earth. That said, the expedition had won Admiralty support because it offered a pretext to search for the undiscovered continent widely supposed to be in the southern hemisphere. Cook would certainly have wanted to meet Nevil Maskelyne, the new Astronomer Royal at Greenwich. Maskelyne was just publishing lunar tables that allowed mariners to calculate their longitude in order to determine their position at sea. The first edition of his *Nautical Almanac*, containing tables with instructions for their use, was published in 1767, supported by the Royal Society. Cook was to take with him copies of the *Nautical Almanac* for the years 1768 and 1769, together with the latest scientific instruments, so that he could calculate his longitude as accurately as possible. Charles Green, an assistant astronomer at the Observatory, was to accompany him on the voyage. Green would also observe the Transit of Venus and help to chart the exact position of newly discovered land.

In Deptford, many walked to their work in the dockyard. If Cook fell in with local ways and set off early on foot to Greenwich, he would soon have regretted, as many did, the absence of a quick direct route. The first landmark was St Nicholas's church, which had served Lower Deptford since the twelfth century, although it had been heavily rebuilt in the seventeenth. St Nicholas is the patron saint of sailors and the church had strong links with both Trinity House and the East India Company, which had once built its vessels nearby. Many seamen and explorers before Cook, including Sir Francis Drake, had been blessed at St Nicholas's before setting out to sea. Deptford had a second church, St Paul's, given to Upper Deptford by the Act of 1711 for building new churches, and made a separate parish. With more room for expansion, it became the larger parish of the two.

As Cook passed St Nicholas's, taking the ancient road aptly named 'Stowage', the rising sun would catch the eastern side of the church tower and the rooftops of old Trinity House, the Corporation's earliest headquarters. These Trinity almshouses included a hall and twenty-one two-storey houses in Cook's time. The Corporation's second Deptford almshouses, built with thirty-one units, stood on Church Street opposite the burial ground of St Paul's. These almshouses reflected on the standing of Trinity House and the corporation strived to maintain them well, which was more than could be said of the local workhouses. The workhouse in the parish of St Nicholas was tucked behind the dockyard, near the local cockfighting pit, and occupied the decaying mansion house on the estate of Sir John Evelyn, grandson of the famous diarist. Sir John still had many tenants in Deptford but no longer lived there. The other Deptford workhouse, in the parish of St Paul, was located on the main shopping street, Church Street.

Stowage led Cook to Deptford Creek where it widened to meet the Thames. There was no bridge here yet, so those unwilling to make a detour to Deptford Bridge and the Centurion had to take a ferry. The banks of the Creek were marshy, piled with domestic waste from the almshouses, and the water itself was polluted by adjacent industries. In the low-lying fields just upstream were noxious copperas works. This valuable product, hydrated ferrous sulphate, was essential to many industrial processes, especially textiles; it was used as a dye fixative and a dye-darkening agent. It was also used to blacken leather and to make ink. Lumps of the mineral iron pyrite were brought up the Thames from the Sussex coast. Near Copperas Lane, the rocks were covered in water in a great pit, over 100 feet (30.5 m) long and 15 feet (4.5 m) broad at the top, subdivided to reduce loss from leaks. After oxidation, the rocks produced a dilute solution of hydrated ferrous sulphate and sulphuric acid, a valuable by-product. The chemical process took four years so the industry was heavily capitalized but yielded good profits. The liquid flowed into a cistern, was drained off into a boiler 8 feet (2.5 m) square and then simmered to concentrate the products. This took twenty days and much coal, after which materials were left to cool. Cook may have taken an interest in the chemical process since he was curious about all means to preserve health at sea, and the navy had used 'elixir of vitriol' (sulphuric acid) to treat scurvy, ineffectively of course.

Nearby, too, there were potteries producing 'Deptford Ware'. These potteries could not compete with the makers of fine china. They specialized in stoneware jugs for domestic use and in industrial products such as chimney pots, sugar moulds, flowerpots and crucibles. The potteries saw increased local demand due to the expansion of Deptford and Greenwich, and Deptford Ware long retained a niche in the London market. A large pottery at the mouth of the Creek included kilns, wharves, stabling, millhouses and warehouses. And of course, along the creek, there were mills for grinding corn.

Once on the other side, in Greenwich, Cook would have taken a marshy path to Church Street where St Alphege's had been rebuilt, another beneficiary of the 1711 Act to make new churches in the capital. There were many naval families living in Greenwich. Before its roads were widened and improved in the early decades of the nineteenth century, the town retained a rural character and much of its medieval layout. To the west of Greenwich Hospital, with its infirmary and brewhouse, there was still an open-air market twice a week, selling meat, fish and vegetables. Some said that naval officers liked to install their wives at Greenwich while away at sea, because it had few attractions that might tempt them into debt. But its cleaner air and views of the Thames and Blackheath had long drawn gentlemen retired from military service. The painted ceiling in the refectory of Greenwich Hospital, completed by the artist James Thornhill in 1725, invited admirers who paid a small fee for entry. (The room became known as the Painted Hall, and inmates were dismissed to dining rooms below.) But the town was not the attraction it later became. Nelson's lying-in-state in the Painted Hall before his funeral in 1806 did much to raise the profile of Greenwich. Like other maritime districts, the population was mixed. There were well-built brick houses for genteel families in streets leading away from the centre, along Maze Hill and Croom's Hill, but taverns and alleys near the river had a bad reputation. Oyster women and fish sellers congregated at the stairs leading to the Thames, particularly around the Ship Tavern in Fisher's Alley.

The Greenwich pensioners (as they were known), were liable to cause trouble in the town. Some inmates of the hospital had their wives and families nearby, who might take in washing or work as servants. Other inmates were more disruptive. Many were still quite young, if maimed. Pensioners did not work and, once admitted, could not marry. They got drunk, brawled and consorted with prostitutes in local bawdy houses. The Greenwich workhouse committee found much to occupy its time. Originally next to St Alphege's, the workhouse had outgrown the building by 1765 and its governors began to rent land off Maidenstone Hill, close to an area where the grandest houses in the parish were being built on the edge of Blackheath. Its male paupers worked in gangs, repairing the roads, and would have been highly visible.[24] Some indication of the quality of life in the town centre is glimpsed from the committee's work. It repeatedly prosecuted townspeople for allowing their hogs to run about the parish, or their servants to tip ash, household rubbish or the contents of cesspits into the public road.

As Cook walked away from the river and towards Greenwich Park, he would have found more reputable establishments: the Spread Eagle, which had stabling for twenty horses, coach houses and a blacksmith's shop, and the Greyhound Inn and coffee house, both in Stockwell Street. Stagecoaches set out for London twice daily from here, and the 'middling sort' of traders and artisans lived in this area. The association of Anti-Gallicans for Kent had met for their annual feast in the Greyhound in 1767 and Alderman Wilkes had joined them.[25] This is another indication of the vibrancy and intellectual interests of the maritime parishes. The society of Anti-Gallicans was a dining club for gentlemen announced at the end of the War of the Austrian Succession in 1748. Its first regular meeting place was the Ship Tavern at Ratcliff Cross. As its name implies, members combined anti-French sentiment with conviviality, but their club also raised funds for charity, including sending poor boys to sea, and in the 1750s and1760s it also offered prizes to encourage British commerce. It thrived in areas where military interests and rivalry in trade encouraged anti-French prejudice. Branches soon spread to other parts of the capital, including, by the 1770s, to Greenwich and the assembly rooms in Mile End.

As Cook strode by Greenwich Park, up the steep hill to the Observatory, he would have enjoyed the unique prospect of the winding river, with London in the distance. Greenwich apart, the maritime districts north and south of the river were busy industrial places, as was the river itself, crowded with vessels of all descriptions. Perhaps Cook, conversant with Trinity almshouses at Mile End and Deptford, and within sight of hundreds of pensioners idling around Greenwich Hospital, may have had his ambitions spurred by the impression of so many seafaring people dragging out the end of their lives in inaction and boredom.

River and identity

From at least the time of Daniel Defoe's description in the 1720s, London's riverscape had been a source of incomparable wonder and fascination:

> The whole river, in a word, from London-Bridge to Blackwall, is one great arsenal, nothing in the world can be like it.[26]

Later essayists and commentators, writing for the enjoyment of middling readers, habitually poked fun at the 'low life' there, helping to neutralize the disquiet it caused. In terms of opulence, the banks of Rotherhithe and Wapping could hardly match the buildings on either side of the river in London's centre. Even so, contemporaries grew proud of London's bustling maritime districts. This is evident in John Barrow's account of his travels in China in 1793. Barrow was Private Secretary to the Earl of Macartney, who led an embassy to China in an (unsuccessful) attempt to open up trade. On reaching Tianjin, then a coastal trading centre and gateway to the capital, Beijing, Barrow expected to see a scene comparable to that on the Thames. He was disappointed:

> We entered the suburbs of the large city of Tien-sing, stretching, like London on the Thames, for several miles along each bank of the river Pei-ho. But neither the buildings nor the river would bear any comparison, even with those parts about Redriffe and Wapping. Every thing, in fact, that we had hitherto seen, wore an air of poverty and meanness.[27]

Maritime London was understood to be a powerhouse essential to national prosperity. Varied industries along the riverbanks were acknowledged indicators of Britain's imperial reach and huge trading capacity. Increasingly, the authorities took steps to ensure that London's maritime areas were as well controlled as resources permitted. There would be consequences, both good and bad, for the people who lived there.

2

OPPORTUNITIES AND PRESSURES OF
A WORLD CITY

When, in 1784, Michael Henley sat in his counting house in Wapping and paid the first school bill for his younger daughter's harpsichord and dancing lessons, he could be forgiven a moment's self-congratulation. Born in Rotherhithe, most probably, Henley received scant education himself and was apprenticed in 1757 to a waterman and lighterman. This meant gruelling work on the river in all weathers.[1] When opportunities came, Henley seized them. In time, he set up as a coal merchant. All London's coal came from the Northeast, and was transported ashore in lighters or barges from colliers anchored in the Thames. The Company of Watermen and Lightermen played a part in the retailing of coal, which explains how Henley came to the trade. His granddaughter claimed that he also spent time in the navy, which would account for his understanding of ships and the sea. Certainly, skilled watermen were likely to be pressed or recruited into the navy. By the 1770s, Henley owned barges and had even saved enough to invest in his own ships. He started to transport coal to London from the coalfields in Northumberland and Durham on his own account. It was a steadily expanding trade, he had good contacts, and he built up a reputation for being reliable and trustworthy. He also drove a hard bargain.

37

The money Henley made, he reinvested in the business, accumulating more ships. It was usual in those days to have shares in a number of ships in order to spread risk. Henley was a pioneer of sorts in that he tended to own his vessels outright, though in a few cases he shared ownership with a trusted captain. Henley's premises were in the Hermitage, Wapping, a narrow street just north of the foreshore. He had married prudently and set up home in the back streets of Shadwell before moving to progressively better houses in Wapping High Street. In 1773 he was able to buy a wharf and warehouse for the equipment needed to run his ships: spare sails, ropes, anchors, rations and clothing. He got these items cheaply at auction, whenever prize ships were sold, or there were sales of government surplus stock, or businesses went bankrupt and sold up. Later he ran his own sail loft, making and repairing sails for his fleet. Henley tended to buy older vessels, mostly built on the Northeast's coast, where shipbuilders were known to turn out strongly constructed ships. These he maintained well. They might be overhauled and repaired in the Thames but he also took advantage of voyages to the Northeast to have them refitted in northern yards where he trusted shipwrights to do a good job. He looked to buy medium-sized vessels that could carry a range of bulk cargoes and which, if over 200 tons, could even serve as naval transports.

When the American Revolutionary War broke out in 1775, Henley was well placed to contract his ships to the government, carrying troops and supplies to conflict zones. This tactic was immediately profitable and he began to shift the emphasis of his business away from the coal trade, continuing to diversify his cargoes even after the war ended. By 1790 he owned nine vessels. He used them in the Northeast coal trade but also sent them to the Baltic and to the West Indies for timber. When war with France loomed, Henley deftly focused on shipowning so that he could take advantage of the anticipated boom in the shipping industry. During the French Wars from 1793, his ships operated as transports to the West Indies, the Mediterranean and later the Baltic. He supplied coal to overseas bases, fleets and troops. He also won government contracts to supply coal to the naval dockyards at home. Officials told him when a dockyard was running low and he would send supplies until the limit of his contract had been reached. There were opportunities for fraud. As a matter of routine, the masters of his ships treated dockyard officers to food and drink when making deliveries; the practice greased the wheels when Henley applied for future contracts. Possibly it also encouraged officials to wink at dubious practices. His labourers could, for example, unload coal into dockyard bins so that, from the facing side, coal seemed to be piled high. Further back, the mound fell away steeply so deliveries could be less than the amount ordered and paid for.

Apart from the occasional setback, as in 1803 when Plymouth dock-yard accused Henley's firm of delivering short weight, the company prospered.[2] In the thirty years from 1775 to 1805, over seventy ships passed through Henley's hands, although some he only part-owned, and some he bought for immediate resale or breaking up. By 1805 he had a steady fleet of fifteen vessels, not counting his river boats needed for loading and unloading cargo. He became one of the most important shipowners on the Thames. The range of his business, the skills and contacts needed to build it up and his own personal drive meant that his shipping operation was both a source of pride and enormous excitement to him. The coal and transport trade was not simply a matter of carrying bulk goods from one port to another. Masters had to be vetted and hired for the voyage. They, in turn, had to engage crews. These men had to be supplied with food. Wages had to be paid out to their families in their absence. Ships had to be overhauled and equipped. There were contracts to negotiate, cargoes to find, customs duties to pay, records to keep and issues with authorities to smooth over. As many vessels as possible had to be kept at sea at the same time – it was like keeping plates spinning in the air. And all the time there was the sense of becoming a man of substance, in the capital city of the foremost industrial nation of the world.

Henley had a firm grasp on accounts but he was not wonderfully literate: in retirement, when he no longer had access to clerks, his second wife, Ann, well educated and of independent means, wrote letters for him. Yet he early attained positions of community responsibility. In 1781 he was one of the trustees responsible for overseeing poor relief in Wapping.[3] At the same time, he cannily profited from the work of paupers in the workhouse. He contracted with several workhouses for oakum picking – unravelling old rope to produce material that, mixed with tar, made ships watertight. In wartime, when hard-pushed to find crews for his ships, he even scoured workhouses to look for men. But Henley had the reputation of being a good employer: hard but fair.

In the Hermitage, there were other men like Henley, all driving their businesses forward and adding to the bustle on the Wapping foreshore. Henley knew who to go to for reliable supplies, who would rent him out more storage space on a temporary basis, who would give legal advice, who would tip him off that a new government contract was about to be advertised. From the outset, he set about establishing a business that would generate wealth for his family. He had two sons, Michael and Joseph, and he paid a series of tutors in Wapping to educate them in the ways of commerce. They learned reading, a good hand and, most importantly, merchants' accounts. Their future was mapped out for them: they would enter the business and master the detail from the bottom up. Joseph, the oldest, took to this regime from the first. He joined the firm in the 1780s, showing the same conscientious zeal as his father, the same reluctance to waste hard-earned money on needless expense, the same ruthless ability to get the best terms available. This mindset was simply held to be good business sense; like his father he took pride in being both competent and highly respected.

Michael Henley also had two daughters. Their education was somewhat different. While they inherited a sense of pride in their station and a respect for the ways of business, they were sent to a genteel school in Wandsworth where they learnt music, dancing and other accomplishments as well as reading and writing. Clearly, Henley thought the local offer unsuitable for his daughters' education. And yet his household patronized a range of Wapping establishments, from linen drapers to furniture makers, circulating the wealth Henley had amassed and contributing to the buoyancy of the local economy. While he might have chosen to get his own coat 'scoured' or cleaned rather than invest in a new one, the family bills even for new shoes and repairing old ones were substantial. Henley bought his wigs locally – it was cheaper to wear wigs than to have a hairdresser visit your house regularly to dress your hair. And he purchased a lot of china, which suggests that he did much entertaining. He also arranged for celebratory dinners at local taverns; the itemized bills show that he treated guests handsomely. He kept all such receipts with the same attention to detail as he kept his business records.[4] This type of behaviour, collectively, formed the base for Britain's growing commercial wealth, based on sea power. Michael and Joseph Henley steered the company with sense and skill for sixty years or so, at the centre of economic activity on the river. In time they passed on a considerable fortune, and their heirs became landed gentry.

Civil disturbance

Meanwhile, London's expansion and industrialization brought worker unrest. Civil disorder was particularly high in 1768. That year, bread prices doubled. Unemployment and hardship sparked demonstrations, marches, petitions and strikes. Much of this unrest took place in the spring, coinciding with parliamentary elections. There were riots involving numerous trades. The most violent centred on two groups: the silk weavers in Spitalfields, who rose up when their masters threatened to cut wages, and the coal heavers in Shadwell and Wapping, who also rebelled against conditions of employment. Coal heaving was dirty, dangerous and badly paid. It was controlled by local publicans, known as 'undertakers'. They marshalled the gangs of workers (mostly Irish immigrants), insisted that the men buy their drink from them, and sometimes even paid them in base coinage. Now coal heavers went on strike, demanding higher wages and a fairer employment system.

On the night of 20–21 April 1768, coal heavers in Shadwell besieged the tavern belonging to John Green. He had been organizing scab labour to break the strike. Swearing that they might as well hang as starve, they threatened to 'have his heart and liver, and cut him in pieces and hang him on his sign'.[5] Green had weapons to protect his premises. He fired on the mob from his windows and killed at least two men, holding the crowd off that night. Though prosecuted, he was never punished for these deaths. The authorities had little sympathy for coal heavers, who were mostly Catholics and viewed with suspicion. On 26 July, seven convicted 'ring-leaders' were hanged in Sun Tavern Fields, off Ratcliff Highway. The place of execution – in Stepney rather than the more usual Tyburn – was clearly intended to intimidate local labourers. Allegedly a crowd of 50,000 Londoners turned out to watch, but law officers had planned for trouble. From 6 a.m. that day, more than 300 soldiers and bands of constables summoned from other districts patrolled the streets. Michael Henley would probably have been among the spectators, as anxious as anyone that the coal heavers' strike was broken. In 1768 he was living in Shadwell and still working as a waterman, but with ambitions to set up as a lighterman, moving freight from ship to shore.

After the executions, around a hundred of the king's guards were ordered to set up a base in an empty cooperage near St James's Stairs, Wapping, to keep the peace. Some argued that to use soldiers in this way was against the constitution, but tradespeople in Wapping and Shadwell were grateful that the mob was kept in check. The situation remained volatile and soldiers confronted desperate men daily. At the end of July two guards were killed. Coal heavers watched them go into a house, then followed, seizing a kitchen poker and shovel on entering. Caught unawares, the soldiers were bludgeoned to death.[6]

That year, too, the radical thinker John Wilkes returned from exile in Europe and was elected MP for Middlesex. He had been outlawed for seditious libel after appearing to criticize King George III in No. 45 of *The North Briton*, a weekly satirical paper. Now Wilkes, a libertine, friend of freedom and shameless self-promoter, became the hero of the underprivileged. He capitalized on the wave of industrial disputes and widespread economic distress that prevailed after a particularly hard winter. The frost in January had been so sharp that a small fishing boat was found trapped in some islands of ice on the Thames. Its crew were all frozen to death, one youth still sitting eerily erect, as if alive. Only desperate poverty drove people to work in such conditions.

In spring, the coal heavers who marched in protest down Ratcliff Highway chanted, 'Wilkes and Liberty, and coal heavers for ever!' They had no vote. Before Parliament was reformed in 1832, there were two types of constituencies: counties and boroughs. In England, each type sent two representatives to Parliament (though the City of London sent four). Political representation had become scandalously unequal across the country because, over the centuries, borough towns had grown at different rates or even declined. Some were nothing but villages with very few voters; others were swelling conurbations. Worse still, the new industrial cities in the north had no representation at all. Only adult males with freehold property could vote, but individual boroughs might limit the franchise slightly differently.

Patronage and the local aristocracy had a huge influence on the way people voted. Although bribery was rarely used to change minds and buy votes, many still expected to be 'treated' for voting as patronage or their inclination dictated. Some candidates wished to become MPs just to gain power. John Durand, for example, made money as a captain in the East India Company, then set up as a London merchant, and simply bought his Aylesbury seat in 1768. He voted in favour of Wilkes's election that year but soon sided with the government against Wilkes. He had shipping interests in Rotherhithe and focused on getting lucrative government contracts for the supply of troops overseas. He was fifteen years in Parliament and never once spoke in the House.

Wilkes's election in Middlesex was a surprise in 1768, though there had long been calls for political reform. During the first half of the century, Middlesex had routinely elected country gentlemen, usually one Whig and the other Tory. Whigs favoured a strong parliament and tended to draw support from industrialists and merchants. Tories backed a strong monarchy, although one they hoped would be under their influence, and tended to represent the interests of landowners. Wilkes probably succeeded because Middlesex was by now the most urbanized of counties and too many gentlemen lived there for any one elite family to wield influence. The development of its inner parishes, both residential and industrial, helped to foster radical views, for which Wilkes provided a timely focus. He was not responsible for the civil unrest that year but certainly exploited it.

Nearly 3,000 voters took part in the 1768 Middlesex election. Most were in business. Crucially, its voters included not only wealthy merchants and manufacturers but also lesser tradesmen – grocers, carpenters, booksellers and weavers. While the commercial class in general backed Wilkes, the bulk of his Middlesex supporters were shopkeepers and petty tradesmen (though Michael Henley was not yet prosperous enough to vote). Enthusiasm for Wilkes was strongest in the troubled eastern areas of London: in the riverside parishes of Shadwell and Wapping he received 74 per cent of all votes cast. Perhaps small traders were hit when labourers had little money and credit was stretched to the limit. Or perhaps resentment against the aristocracy was a factor. Whatever the case, Wilkes, a brilliant politician, convinced tradesmen voters that he stood for reform and liberty.

By the end of April, in a shocking reversal, Wilkes was locked up in the King's Bench Prison. Regardless of popular support, he was still an outlaw charged with writing libel and had yet to prove that he was being detained illegally. Social disturbance reached the maritime parishes. On 5 May, several hundred sailors boarded merchant ships, took down the sails and swore they would not sail until masters raised their wages. On 9 May, watermen protested noisily outside Mansion House. The next day about 5,000 seamen from vessels anchored in the Pool of London massed in Westminster. Not all supported Wilkes but, emboldened by his protest, they marched to complain about pay and conditions of work. That same day, nervous troops opened fire on an unarmed Wilkite crowd that had gathered outside the King's Bench Prison. A number were killed or wounded and it was soon termed the 'St George's Fields Massacre'.[7] That day, too, about 500 sawyers destroyed Charles Dingley's mechanical sawmill in Limehouse by the Thames. It was not so much a political protest as an early case of workers damaging machines that would rob them of employment, but the authorities were thoroughly rattled. The wind-powered mill was repaired at public expense and an Act of Parliament passed against machine breaking, although the Act was also prompted by the wrecking of cotton-spinning machines in the north of England. Radical thought was so much in the forefront of people's minds that some even quipped that the owner of the Boot and Crown public house in London's Bridge Street should be arrested for libel since his pub sign placed the boot triumphant over the crown.[8]

The government was worried about the security of the naval dockyard in Deptford. Merchants, losing money while shipping was trapped in the river, called for stern measures to quell the rioting. To keep the peace, the militia was stationed on vital approach roads to Deptford and Greenwich. As was usual, these were men serving far from home, who could be tasked with restraining local populations unconnected to them. All the same, two soldiers were sentenced to be flogged in the Tower for getting drunk, joining the mob in Southwark and roaring out, 'Wilkes and Liberty for ever!' They would regret supporting Wilkes's views in No. 45 of *The North Briton*. They each received forty-five lashes, three times, over five days. Afterwards they were ordered to be drilled on the parade ground for forty-five days and fed short rations, so that their bellies as well as their backs would be pained by that celebrated number.[9]

Wilkes, being a convicted prisoner, could not take up his seat in the House. He was formally expelled from it the following February for publishing libel. This only increased his power to inflame popular protest. Middlesex voters returned him unopposed at a by-election that February. Again the House expelled him. A month later, he was re-elected and once more expelled, but this time Parliament declared him incapable of being re-elected. Now it was no longer a question of whether a person, convicted of libel and blasphemy, expelled from the House of Commons and outlawed, was fit to enter Parliament. Rather, it was a question of whether voters had the right to elect their own representative. As Wilkes put it, 'whether the people have an inherent right to be represented in Parliament by the man of their free choice'.[10] Some pundits even argued that Parliament, in declaring Wilkes incapable of re-election, had exercised arbitrary powers and usurped the rule of law. The contest now centred on fundamental civil liberties.

Some of Wilkes's followers formed the Society of Gentlemen Supporters of the Bill of Rights. They raised funds to clear Wilkes's debts, knowing that when released from prison he would otherwise be rearrested for the money he owed. They also made unprecedented use of the press to publicize Wilkes's cause. So, the (pro-Wilkes) *Middlesex Journal* enthusiastically reported a Society meeting on 30 March 1770 in the Mile End Assembly Rooms. As described, the entire road from Whitechapel to the assembly rooms seethed with people. The procession was led by a band, followed by leaders in their coaches, then supporters, all wearing blue cockades and shouting, 'Wilkes and Liberty!' Londoners, angered by social inequality, had at last found an effective means to voice their discontent.

Wilkes himself was astute enough to behave with restraint. He encouraged supporters to raise peaceful petitions across England in his cause. These petitions strongly condemned Parliament's treatment of Wilkes but were presented respectfully to the King. The Society for the Bill of Rights, alongside Whig politicians, actively encouraged them. Middlesex submitted two; the City of London and Surrey followed. In Kent, Canterbury sent its own petition. Many of Kent's local gentry opposed the movement but others cooperated with City radicals to raise a county petition, calling upon the King to disband Parliament. William Pitt, first Earl of Chatham and the Whig leader credited with obtaining victory for Britain in the Seven Years War (1756–63), sent his steward to Deptford and Greenwich in December 1769 to drum up support for the Kent petition. Three hundred freeholders promptly signed it. By the end of 1769, thirty-one petitions had been submitted.

Wilkes was released from prison in 1770 and rose to power in the City on a wave of support. In 1774 he was chosen to be Lord Mayor. In October that year he was again elected MP for Middlesex and was finally allowed to take his seat in the House. The Bill of Rights Society continued to be a force for radicalism until the following year when the crisis with the American colonies deteriorated into war. An early supporter of the colonists, the Society was then out of tune with the times, losing popularity as people rallied behind Britain's armed forces.

Wilkes slowly moderated his radical views. The Gordon Riots in the summer of 1780 proved a turning point. Londoners rioted because Lord George Gordon, leader of the Protestant Association, pandered to religious prejudice by spreading rumours that government planned a return to popery and absolute monarchical rule. Parliament had passed the Catholic Relief Act in 1778, removing some of the official discrimination against Catholics. Just as there had been a petitioning movement pleading Wilkes's cause, so now groups lobbied for the Act's repeal. Petitions were left in Wapping alehouses to be signed – often just lists of names, so people supposed they were protesting about grievances. When government seemed to ignore the petitions, violence erupted. London and Southwark were in flames, the mob broke prisoners out of jails, and loyalty to Protestantism became an excuse to settle old scores, chiefly with Catholics. The maritime parishes to the east escaped more lightly than the City, but the Mass-house in Wapping's Virginia Street was destroyed and Catholic homes were set on fire. Whitechapel was one of the areas that had provided many signatures for the anti-Catholic petition, and violence was considerable there. Tellingly, most of those who had signed the petition were lesser tradesmen, not the labouring poor.[11]

London's authorities were slow to react. There was no professional police force and Justices feared they would become targets themselves if they read the Riot Act. Hesitation allowed the situation to become terrifying. Rioters wreaked havoc until army regiments, the militia and the garrison of the Tower were summoned. Soldiers had orders to fire on groups of more than four who refused to disperse. The Surrey Militia turned back the mob at Blackfriars Bridge, though not before rioters had released prisoners from Surrey jails. The Northampton Militia stood ready to guard Greenwich, Deptford and Blackheath. Two warships sailed from Deptford to Woolwich with orders to guard the ordnance there and convict labour along the riverside was suspended. Greenwich Pensioners were issued 300 muskets, pikes and poles when a mob threatened Greenwich

Hospital with fire and destruction. After a week of rampage, order was slowly restored but authorities claimed at least 210 had been shot dead and another 75 had died of their wounds. The actual figure may have been higher still.[12] Wilkes himself led troops against rioters who attacked the Bank of England. He believed in reform but saw at once that insurrection on this scale would have destructive consequences. Many adherents to the radical cause thought Wilkes a traitor and deserted him.

Wealthy Catholics had been targeted during the rioting, but the unrest was not just caused by religious hatred or poor people wanting to hit back at the rich. The Protestant Association's petitions were clearly associated in people's minds with earlier petitions for reforming Parliament. Gordon presented his petition to the House on the very day that unequal representation was being debated. Petitioning was held to be a fundamental right of the British people. Supporters of both petitioning movements had expressed fears that Britain's prized constitution was being corrupted. One reason why the Gordon protests got out of hand was that George III had appeared to ignore demands rather than give them the attention they deserved.

There were growing racial tensions, too. By the end of the American Revolutionary War in 1783, there were between 5,000 and 10,000 black men and women in London. Many had served on merchant ships or in the military. Some arrived as servants. There were also groups of South Asian sailors, or 'lascars'. Lascars helped crew East India Company ships to London; afterwards, the Company boarded them in Blackwall and elsewhere until they could sail home. In maritime districts, they joined a host of other nationalities: Scandinavian, Dutch, Portuguese and Spanish sailors, and still others from destinations along major trading routes. Each group had its own support network and, depending on length of stay, its own social circle. These might not be exclusive: in the 1780s white Londoners as well as black paid to dance to black music at so-called 'black hops'.[13] Asian, Black and Chinese seamen seem to have been treated fairly in law, receiving good representation if their cases came to trial, but within maritime communities there was cultural conflict. Different races may well have served side by side at sea, but sexual jealousy came into play on land. White men resented the preference that some women showed for black sailors.[14] Lascars allegedly cut and ill-treated women in 1780.[15] Contemporaries assumed the lascars were avenging themselves on women who had passed on sexually transmitted diseases but they may have been responding to cultural differences.

The charity of some black sailors was equally well publicized, perhaps in support of the growing movement to abolish slavery which further divided opinion. Londoners saw huge social inequalities. The powerful West Indian merchants who upheld the slave trade seemed an implacable force but sailors must have felt the incongruity of some of their number working alongside free black men at sea while others helped to transport Africans into slavery.

Rivalries to the south

South of the river, labour unrest was also a grave concern, adding to the pressure of long-standing commercial rivalries. The brothers John and William Wells, whose family boasted a range of local ship-related interests, took over Thomas Stanton's Rotherhithe yard in the mid-1760s. It stood just above Greenland Dock on the site of today's Surrey Docks Farm and often changed hands. Among notable vessels, it built the *Carcass*, in which Nelson sailed to the Arctic as a midshipman in 1773. The brothers expanded the yard to construct ever-larger ships for the East India Company. Towards the end of the century, the Barnard family acquired this Rotherhithe yard. It had a mast house and a mast slip, which allowed the Barnards to extend their interests into the fitting as well as building of ships.

Meanwhile, William's two sons, also John and William, took half a share in Perry's extensive yard in Blackwall on the eastern shore of the Isle of Dogs. The East India Company had established the shipyard in the early seventeenth century. By 1779 it was owned by John Perry, whose family had worked their way up in the yard over decades. Perry ran it for nearly ten years, creating the Brunswick Dock on marshland to the east in 1789–90.

He took his son-in-law, George Green, into the family business, then sold half of it to the Wells brothers in 1798. The new partnership expanded operations until Blackwall was considered the largest private yard in the world. When its owners were faced with proposals for an enclosed West India Docks at the end of the century, they petitioned Parliament for compensation, pointing out that their own wet dock had not only cost a fortune but involved surmounting engineering problems that at times threatened catastrophe. Problems had been overcome only 'by unremitting and expensive Perseverance and Exertions'.[16] The phrase could well have been applied to the work of many shipyard owners along the river. The fates of different yards were often intertwined. Private shipbuilders constantly competed for business, though they might sometimes lease vacant slipways to rivals; many were subject to takeovers or driven to ambitious expansion projects. Individuals had to be ready to seize opportunities but careful not to overextend capacity.

If the Thames foreshore from Wapping to Limehouse was a mass of wharves and maritime-related trades, its southern bank was also busy. From the parish of Southwark St Olave and Bermondsey, stretching eastwards to Greenwich, the river frontage was crammed with more wharves, then shipbuilding yards, timber merchants, ship-breakers, ropeyards, tar houses, iron foundries and anchorsmiths. Residents to the south also depended heavily on the business of Deptford's naval dockyard.

One shipyard owner, William Barnard, came from an established shipbuilding family based in Ipswich and Harwich. Despite being outside London, his father, John, had managed to win naval contracts during the War of Jenkins' Ear (1739–48). The Navy Board's practice in such cases was to assign an overseer to make sure the private yard was built to the navy's specification. By chance, the work was overseen by Thomas Slade, a shipwright in the royal dockyards and destined to become the most skilful naval architect of the century. He encouraged John Barnard to take on more naval work. Soon the shipbuilder had such a standing locally that he was chosen to welcome Princess Charlotte, future wife of George III, when she landed at Harwich in 1761, presenting her with a basket of grapes from his greenhouse.

For his services, he was offered a knighthood but brushed the offer aside and said he would rather just have another naval contract. Here was another man proud of his status with no wish for honours. Given Barnard's contact with Thomas Slade, it is no surprise that he apprenticed his son, William, as a shipwright in Deptford dockyard. Afterwards, William returned to Ipswich where he built his first ship under the watchful, and sometimes interfering, eye of his father. But William had decided that London was the place to make a shipbuilding career. He had already married Frances Clarke, a local girl from Rotherhithe in 1760. He realized, too, that while he might build up his business by winning naval contracts, he would need another source of income whenever warship building was at a low ebb. This was where the East India Company came in.

Founded in 1600, at first the Company built its own ships for the long voyage to the East: at Deptford, then Blackwall. From about 1627, it saw that it was easier to hire ships. Soon a cartel of shipowners was building East Indiamen to tight specifications and leasing them to the Company for a fixed price. Vessels generally made four voyages to India or China before being judged too worn for the arduous voyage, although from 1788, once ships began to be copper-bottomed, they might make six voyages. Interim repairs were usually carried out in the yard where ships had been constructed. Better still for that yard, when a ship was decommissioned and broken up, its owner had a preferential right to build another 'on the ship's bottom'. Each ship was run by a managing owner known as the 'ship's husband'. These were sometimes shipbuilders too. If not, the manager worked with a preferred builder who regularly got the contract to build the replacement ship. Once these business links were forged, there was a guaranteed source of long-term income. The strength of this cosy relationship was reflected in the specialized language all shared.

Even so, during the second half of the eighteenth century, shipbuilding for the Company became less certain. Owners still had a preferential right to replace a worn ship but there was no guarantee that the Company would give them permission to build. This was because owners themselves had set up an elaborate system designed to limit overcapacity in the Company's fleet and ensure that their vessels were fully and continuously employed. In the 1780s, too, the Company began to assert more control over hiring arrangements. In busy periods, it did agree to hire extra ships but it would not always guarantee that these could be replaced after the standard number of voyages. And sometimes the Company insisted that once a ship had been tendered it had to be built in twelve months or the right of replacement would lapse. Worse still, despite protests from the Wells brothers and others, it experimented with building ships in India. So, the relationship between the Company, ship's husband and shipbuilder could be stressful and needed management, but it offered some security for the Thameside yards, which had a virtual monopoly on the work.

In 1763, William Barnard fulfilled his ambition to return to London. He went into partnership with William Dudman and Henry Adams, jointly managing a 9-acre shipyard strategically located at Grove Street, Deptford, between Greenland Dock and the Navy Victualling Office. The location was extremely convenient for someone who wanted to build ships for the navy. Adams was always a 'silent partner'. He had his own yard in Hampshire and aimed to profit from this venture without the bother of active management. The partners leased the Grove Street yard from Sir John Evelyn for £315 a year and had to sign a bond to the value of £10,000 to guarantee that they would meet the terms of the lease, which shows the level of risk involved.[17] The yard had a large wet dock, two dry docks and three building slips, as well as a house where Dudman lived. It was one of the larger premises on the Thames and, in busy periods, could provide work for over 300 men. The young Barnard profited from Dudman's experience (who was fifteen years his senior), and began to work hard to establish himself in his profession. A surviving miniature shows a handsome, slight man, in a fashionable high-necked coat, wearing his own hair, powdered. He looks good-humoured, intelligent and slightly strained. It is the face of a man under pressure.

From the first, Barnard set about making the contacts that would help him succeed in his ambition to be one of the foremost shipbuilders on the Thames. He presented himself as a man skilled in traditional shipbuilding skills but also as a forward thinker, open to new ideas. He was attracted to problem solving and gained a reputation for clear thought. In 1779, when the East Indiaman *York* ran aground off Margate in a violent gale, he was called to give advice. The ship belonged to Sir Richard Hotham, a self-made man who had done well out of his hat-selling business and who owned several East Indiamen. Barnard managed to get the ship to dry dock in Deptford by building a watertight box to cover the irreparable hole in its hull. Keen to make a name for himself, he wrote a paper explaining how to salvage vessels that had been driven ashore and damaged in this way. The Astronomer Royal, Nevil Maskelyne, presented it to the Royal Society and it was later published, demonstrating that Barnard was an ingenious mathematician. In 1785 he was elected to the Society for the Encouragement of Arts, Manufactures and Commerce (now the Royal Society of Arts). John Perry had already been made a member in 1782. Top shipbuilders could claim to be highly skilled innovators; they contributed to the practical, scientific thinking that helped to advance Britain's industrial revolution.

Shipbuilders at the level of Barnard or Perry relished chances to enlarge their skills. Their task in building East Indiamen was to balance conflicting demands of speed, security and the commercial requirement for maximum cargo space. The Company had long favoured ships of 500 tons or 800 tons. (The smaller size was often registered at 499 tons to avoid the expense of carrying a chaplain or surgeon on board, which ships above 500 tons were obliged to do.) In the 1770s, the Company suddenly turned against using the larger ships, probably because whenever one was wrecked, the financial loss was huge. Shipbuilder William Wells commented revealingly, 'I looked upon it as fettering the hands of genius; the East-Indiamen are the only ships a builder has an opportunity of shewing himself in.'[18] But from 1785, it began to encourage ships of 1,200 tons, particularly for the China trade. Although the measurement of tonnage had been tightened up since the mid-1770s, these large East Indiamen still had more capacity than their measurements implied and were designed to evade the heavy tax on tonnage. In this key area, the skill of the shipbuilder came into play. Builders also warranted ships fit to make the long voyage east.

The safety of thousands of pounds' worth of cargo depended on their expertise, as well as on the skill of the ships' crews.[19]

In 1772, Barnard's partner William Dudman died and Barnard took over sole management of the Grove Street yard, though at some point he took Dudman's son into partnership and allocated a one-fifth share to him. If anything, Barnard now pushed himself even harder. In 1779, for example, he offered to build a 64-gun ship for the navy in just forty-two months. That year, too, he was able to afford to lease the Deptford yard near the Stowage earlier used by the East India Company. It included two houses, warehouses, storehouses, counting houses, stables, a dry dock, a piece of meadow land, gardens, timber yards and three building slips. He extended its dry dock and built a plank yard and an oval garden. He also installed his family in the larger of the two houses, an impressive three-storey brick building on Deptford Green. In ten years, from 1780 to 1790, the two Barnard yards completed an astonishing forty-one vessels: twenty-eight for brokers of the East India Company and thirteen for the navy.[20]

Barnard was a Dissenter and worshipped at a Deptford meeting house, but that did not prevent him being elected churchwarden in St Nicholas's parish, an office which brought status and power. Church officeholders served in rotation, which guarded against corruption but also limited the burden of service on any one individual. In St Nicholas's one of the two churchwardens rotated yearly but as a rule each served two years, providing continuity. Elected officials in this parish typically included naval dock-yard officials and private shipbuilders as well as other property owners. Barnard, although busy, unusually served three years from 1791 to 1793. He had been a member of the vestry committee in the 1770s and party to local workhouse accounts from at least 1782. The social prestige of being a churchwarden is indicated by the fact that even Dissenters worshipping elsewhere, as Barnard did, consented to serve. The office had its trials. When the parish of St Paul was set up, a disproportionate amount of land was taken from the parish of St Nicholas. As a result, the cost to residents of maintaining the poor in St Nicholas's was over twice as much as in

St Paul's.[21] (Poor relief was administered by the parish: wealthier residents paid a property tax, 'the Poor Rate', to fund it.)

From 1793, when the lease expired on the Grove Street yard, Barnard was involved in a legal dispute with his partners. He wanted to focus on his Deptford Yard. They wanted to continue with the partnership and, worse still, Adams claimed that the yard in Deptford Green was part of the business owned by the partnership. Eventually, the matter was settled out of court in 1794, but it took its toll. Worn out by legal wrangling and overwork, Barnard died in 1795, leaving two sons and three daughters. He willed everything to his capable wife, Frances, who was fifty-eight at the time of his death.

Politics in Surrey and Kent

Politics south of the river differed from politics in the north. Southwark, a hub for noxious processing trades, had seen rapid growth and radicalism had taken hold there from the 1760s. Here, Joseph Mawbey, a wealthy vinegar distiller, had been elected to Parliament as a Whig in 1761. He became a supporter of Wilkes and a leader in the petitioning movement of 1769–70, which sought to get Wilkes established in the House of Commons. Mawbey instigated the petition for Surrey and helped to organize others further afield. In the 1774 election, he offered himself as a candidate for Surrey but the gentry of the county were determined to keep him out. Even so, 88 per cent of voters in Rotherhithe backed him, showing that Surrey's eastern parishes had been affected by radical ideas. Eighty per cent of the voters in Deptford and Greenwich who were qualified to vote in Surrey also chose Mawbey.[22] (One flaw of the electoral system was that some voters were entitled to vote in several constituencies.) The following year, Mawbey succeeded at a by-election – the first openly radical MP to be returned for Surrey. Again, the county's eastern parishes gave him the highest number of votes. Mawbey easily defeated the other Opposition candidate, Sir Francis Vincent junior. Vincent was the son of the previous MP and voters were becoming exasperated by parliamentary seats being passed from father to son within one landed family.

Surrey's gentry, even those who supported the Opposition, bitterly resented the growing influence of businessmen like Mawbey. There were similar tensions in Parliament itself. Mawbey was an active member and often spoke with blunt good sense, claiming to be above party. But although he held his seat until 1790, his election did not guarantee him a voice. Aristocratic members sneered at his lowly origins, mocked him for keeping pigs (which he fed on the husks of barley used in distilling), and often drowned out his speeches with their taunts.

Any radical opinion springing from Deptford and Greenwich was even less likely to be expressed in Parliament. Both towns were included in the area represented by the two MPs for Kent. So, before 1832, these large and growing conurbations with important dockyards were almost as unrepresented as the great new industrial cities in northern England. Already a prosperous and bustling town, Deptford's population rose by a third in the eighteenth century. Greenwich, too, saw a marked increase in well-to-do residents. In the second half of the century, the numbers of wills from Greenwich proved by the prerogative court of Canterbury (which dealt with the estates of deceased who were relatively wealthy) increased by 54 per cent. All the same, prominent residents in these maritime districts had political choices. County elections were usually rarer than borough elections because numerous voters often having to travel long distances meant huge expense. Yet Kent, like Surrey, went to the poll often. With about 8,000 voters, Kent was a large constituency but much of it was rural, so any reforming ideas from more industrialized Deptford and Greenwich were diluted. Kent's landed families dominated county politics and rivalry between them could be a distraction. They had modest holdings compared to clans in the Midlands and the North, where fewer landowners controlled great estates. The county of Kent had been firmly Tory in the 1750s but the next decade saw a political truce and its more active MPs held Whig principles. By the 1770s the picture had changed again: party divisions took a back seat as conflict with the American colonies encouraged voters to divide according to conscience on this major issue.

In the election of 1780, Kent voters sent a clear signal on their attitude to the American War: they returned, unopposed, two supporters of the

Opposition who were also experienced MPs. One was Filmer Honywood, whose family had been resident in Kent for generations. The other was Charles Marsham, son of politically independent Lord Romney, head of another family with substantial local influence. Romney's personal interests accorded with those of maritime trade. He had been a founder member of the Society for the Encouragement of Arts, Manufactures, and Commerce, and the first chairman of the Marine Society, the charity that sent poor boys to sea. Marsham, like his father, had advised a conciliatory approach to the American colonists and he voted against war. He opposed the ministry again in 1780, when presenting the Kent petition for economy in wartime expenditure, which broadly aimed to curb the power of the monarchy. In February 1783, Honywood and Marsham once more demonstrated their distaste for the American War, voting for the peace preliminaries negotiated by Prime Minister William Petty, Earl of Shelburne. But the peace terms were unpopular and defeated in the House. Later that year both MPs showed their support for extending the franchise when they supported William Pitt's proposals for parliamentary reform. The motion failed.

Kent was satisfied with the political direction Honywood and Marsham followed in spite of setbacks. In these years, the county took pride in its independence. Both men were returned to Parliament in March 1784, having publicly declared several times that they would vote with their conscience, not bend to party opinion. They kept their pledges.[23] Marsham, for example, supported the government rather than the Opposition on naval expenditure, believing that economy in matters of national defence was foolish. He held his seat until 1790 when effectively tricked out of it by Pitt. The ministry had fielded Sir Edward Knatchbull as its candidate, scion of another established Kent family and a firm supporter. What followed shows how national politics affected voters in Deptford and Greenwich. Shipwrights and dockyard employees qualified to vote generally supported government candidates. There was no secret ballot and those in need of government contracts naturally looked to their financial interest. Now the government's dockyard and maritime dependents helped to get Knatchbull elected. The poll record shows that the Deptford vote was overwhelmingly in his favour. William Barnard certainly voted for him. Knatchbull also got most votes in Greenwich, although there Marsham held on to a third of the vote – perhaps because Greenwich residents were less reliant on government contracts. Pitt's government took further steps to strengthen its hold on Kent during the long French Wars. In the 1796 election, both of Kent's elected MPs were government supporters.

The politics of Kent's borough towns had another dynamic. Canterbury enjoyed the status of a county, returning two MPs in its own right; its elections were entirely independent as no one interest dominated this market town. Kent had three borough towns, each with two MPs: Queenborough, Rochester and Maidstone. Queenborough had not changed much since Defoe described it as 'a miserable, dirty, decayed, poor, pitiful, fishing town'.[24] It was wholly controlled by the government because most of its voters worked for the Admiralty or the Board of Ordnance, responsible for arming British forces. Rochester was different. It had more shopkeepers and tradesmen than most Kent towns and was expanding under the influence of Chatham dockyard. Generally, it returned one MP in trade who voted with the Opposition, and another controlled by the navy who usually supported the government. (Substantial families in the neighbourhood looked to the navy for employment.) Maidstone had also split its vote for years, returning one MP likely to oppose the government and a second likely to vote with it. Yet after the 1768 election, its independent party, backed by a large Dissenting community, triumphed.

At grass-roots level, Kent politics offered a varied picture but broad trends are clear. Most of its MPs tended to oppose the American War. When that ended, pro-government candidates enjoyed more success. All the while, those who hoped for government favours, like Barnard and dockyard employees, dutifully supported naval or ministry candidates. In short, Kent valued its independence, but the county had groups of voters, dependent on government contracts or naval careers, who would always back the government.

In London, after the 1780 Gordon Riots the political climate changed; Wilkes himself became more conservative. In the 1784 Middlesex election, he stood successfully as a supporter of Pitt's government – easier for him, perhaps, as Pitt was promising parliamentary reform. Some claimed Wilkes owed his seat to illegal votes from Wapping.[25] William Mainwaring was elected alongside him, the first candidate with Tory leanings returned in Middlesex since Wilkes's triumph for the radical cause in 1768. Many disliked Mainwaring. As a magistrate during a period of inflation and high taxation, he had not been able to avoid unpopular decisions. At least he showed that prominent professionals in the eastern suburbs could succeed in becoming MPs without the help of the aristocracy. His political enemies derided him as the son of a bricklayer, although his father was the wealthy architect Boulton Mainwaring, designer of the London Hospital in the 1750s. Ignoring such jibes, in Parliament he represented local interests well, taking a special interest in law and order, and defending trade.[26] Both Michael Henley and John Perry voted for Wilkes and Mainwaring in the 1784 election, when the Opposition candidate, George Byng, was defeated.

Henley made sure that he was eligible to vote in elections for the City of London, where trading, financial and commercial interests were strongly represented. In 1775 he secured for himself and his son, Joseph, membership of the Farriers Livery Company. Farriers could vote in parliamentary and mayoral elections, unlike members of the Company of Watermen and Lightermen, to which Henley already belonged, which was not a livery company. In the 1796 City elections father and son chose the same four candidates. Several candidates claimed to have temporarily set aside their desire for greater 'liberty' because national security had become the critical issue in the wake of the French Revolution. William Lushington, one of the four elected, had been a member of the Society of the Friends of the People, demanding reform. Now he candidly stated that the revolution in France had changed his mind. The Henleys' choice accorded with the popular vote, with one exception. They did not vote for Alderman Combe, a Whig who strongly opposed war with France and who gained a seat. Instead, they chose Sir Watkin Lewes, a former Wilkes supporter, who trailed in last. He lost votes thanks to his alleged role in Pitt's unpopular proposals for augmenting the London militia. The outcome underlined that the radicalism of Wilkes was at an end, leaving no clear mandate for reform. Even so, strong, radical elements remained in London and Middlesex, which continued to press for parliamentary reform long after Pitt's enthusiasm for it waned.

An inquiring spirit

Riverside industries continued to be places of lively experimentation. At Deptford dockyard, there were trials over a long period of the best way to protect ships in tropical waters from the Teredo worm, which bored into hulls. In 1764, the *Tamar* was sheathed in copper, after the *Dolphin* was coppered a month earlier at Woolwich. The difficulties caused by electrolysis, given that the copper sheets had been fixed with iron bolts, were grasped when the ships returned two years later.[27] In 1769, the hull of the *Scarborough* was sheathed in chemically prepared paper and then extra planking before being sent out to the West Indies. The experiment was not a success.[28] There were more trials at Deptford involving copper sheathing throughout the 1770s. Even after copper was widely adopted, there were still experiments with other materials, including medicated leather.[29] The Admiralty oversaw other trials at Deptford, including attempts to convert seawater into drinking water, cook food for sailors using less fuel, and extract pitch from sea coal.[30] It rewarded an invention for measuring a ship's sailing speed and invited crowds to view a demonstration of a more efficient type of windlass.[31] It also constructed experimental flat-bottomed boats for landing troops, trialled models for speedy naval cutters, tested French warship designs that allowed for more cannon, built light boats of tin and cork for troops to cross American rivers, and sought new ways to season timber.[32] The Society for Encouragement of the Arts and Sciences tested whaling harpoons in Greenland Dock that could be shot from a gun rather than thrown by hand.[33] Towards the end of the 1780s there were early trials of steam-powered vessels on the river.[34]

This activity gave residents an interest in technology and scientific enquiry. It was, after all, an age of 'improvement' when towns across

Britain set up literary and philosophical societies. A Deptford landowner experimented with a new breed of sheep brought from the Bay of Biscay which produced fine wool (most likely the Spanish Merino breed).[35] Even the lecturer at St Paul's, the Reverend Dr Milne, was recognized for his interest in botany and published a botanical dictionary as well as sermons. Many clergymen, like naval surgeons, embraced the contemporary spirit of scientific discovery, being educated men. As lecturer, Milne helped the parish clergyman by reading and interpreting scriptures on Saturdays and weekdays to make sure parishioners heard as many homilies as possible, but this left him time to follow his scholarly interests.

Experiments were topics of conversation, and gave riverside people a sense of being at the cutting edge of progress. Locals themselves came up with inventions, such as a machine for rowing small ships (though it was too large to be practical), and an instrument to drag river bottoms for drowned persons.[36] Technological experimentation infused non-maritime manufactures, too. Henry Goodwyn, a brewer in Deptford, seems to have been alone in using a thermometer in the 1750s to improve beer quality. Later, he went into business with his son, also Henry, in Ratcliff Cross. An amateur mathematician, in 1784 Goodwyn junior was the first to install a steam engine in his brewery, the Red Lion Brewhouse near the Thames in East Smithfield.[37] Other brewers soon followed.

Over the years, maritime London became ever more strongly linked with voyages of exploration. The ships for James Cook's three Pacific voyages in 1768, 1772 and 1776 were all fitted out in Deptford. Its victualling yard grew experienced in provisioning these ventures. When Commodore Phipps's expedition set off for the North Pole in the *Racehorse* and *Carcass* in 1773, officials even thought to give him tea and sugar for the sick. In the 1780s, merchant voyages testing the viability of a fur trade with America's Northwest were provisioned at Deptford, and in 1791 George Vancouver's expedition to survey the northern west coast of America was also fitted out there. After Cook's discoveries, Sir Joseph Banks continued to organize expeditions from Deptford to collect undiscovered plants, trialling different containers and ventilation schemes to keep the plants alive during the voyage.[38] Returning crews had stories to tell of distant lands that fired the imagination.

Local manufacturers provided support for exploration and discovery in ways that have not always been appreciated. Deptford potteries, for example, supplied thousands of garden pots for botanical voyages. It was a centre for pottery, remarkable for having five potteries within a small area. Much local land was also devoted to market gardening, serving Londoners with fresh produce; the soil on both sides of Deptford Creek was especially fertile due to the sediment deposited by rivers. The concentration of potteries at Deptford was owing to the quality of local brown earths and nearby water transport to bring in other clays and to distribute finished goods for sale. It mostly produced plain and glazed red earthenware for everyday use in the kitchen or garden. Other typical wares included storage jars, cauldrons, colanders and chafing dishes for keeping food hot. 'Wasters', or defective items and broken fragments, were used in huge quantities locally as a construction material. They were dumped to consolidate the Thames fore-shore or to help with construction of shipyard ramparts and retaining walls.

When Captain Bligh set off in the *Bounty* from Deptford in 1787, with orders to transport breadfruit trees from Tahiti to the West Indies as a staple food for enslaved plantation workers, he took with him 796 garden pots manufactured in Deptford. Breadfruit does not produce fertile seeds and must be propagated from suckers. The trees had to be potted carefully in Tahiti and tended during the long voyage to the West Indies. The voyage famously ended in mutiny but Bligh was given a second chance. In 1791 he set off in the *Providence* to complete the mission, taking with him two botanist-gardeners. The more senior, James Wiles, chose to stay in the West Indies to cultivate breadfruit plants. He wrote to Banks asking for more pots: 'I therefore beg of you Sir, (if it is not improper) to send me out 500 or more Pots of the large breadfruit size as soon as possible.'[39] These, too, would have come from Deptford. On this second voyage, Bligh managed to transport the breadfruit trees safely to the West Indies. When he returned to London in 1793, he brought with him exotic plants destined for the royal gardens at Kew. They were taken upriver from Deptford in barges, and the pots as well as the plants found favour with royal gardeners. The account books for Kew Gardens confirm that Mrs Sarah Morris, a potter in Deptford, was still supplying plant pots in 1803. She had taken over the family business in Church Street after her husband died in 1800 and would have been glad of the contract.[40]

Deptford potteries also produced items for industrial use: chimney pots, pipes, tiles, crucibles, syrup-collecting jars and sugar moulds. In the last decades of the century, there were sugar bakers on Deptford Broadway and in Church Street. Before that time, the finished moulds and pots were transported by water to sugarhouses closer to the centre of London, notably off the Whitechapel Road. The new industry was booming as more and more Londoners drank sugared tea. Sugar was Britain's largest import by the end of the century and pottery linked Deptford to that trade.

Officials and regulation

Business leaders in London's maritime districts had to stay on good terms with key officials. It paid to keep in with Justices of the Peace since they took most of the local decisions and could help in disputes with employees. This was important to shipbuilders who often faced labour unrest in wartime. War brought inflation, and, while private yards could obtain naval contracts, there was government pressure to keep costs low, leaving shipbuilders to struggle with rising costs and wage demands. Justices also had political influence: they were appointed by central government and ministers liked to have trusted allies keeping the peace. Justices were in any case bound to be involved in national politics since their decisions affected the taxes voters paid. Many – such as Mawbey and Mainwaring – became MPs themselves. In the House they took sides on issues that directly affected local manufacturers. Henry Goodwyn and other Thameside brewers and distillers looked to Justices for support in 1799 when they called for a bill to prevent journeymen millwrights combining to demand higher wages. (Millwrights were essential to maintaining the machinery brewers used.) At quarter sessions and at assizes, Justices were usually on the grand jury, able to use the occasion to issue political statements to the county.[41] Mainwaring, for example, addressed the Middlesex Grand Jury in 1785, complaining about an increase in robberies and the high price of labour, and urging listeners to enforce the law and keep the unemployed out of alehouses.[42] In sum, leading manufacturers had good reason to align themselves with resident Justices, who were key figures in local networks of influence.

Other local officials included water bailiffs, employed by the Corporation of London's Thames Navigation Committee. They patrolled the Thames to stop fishermen using unlawful nets. They also made sure that riverside businesses did not encroach on the river or cause obstructions. The post was lucrative so could be purchased by auction: the annual salary in 1782 was £91 18s. 4d. but critics alleged that a bailiff could increase that to £377 13s. 4d. by extracting annual fees from tradespeople along the river. The bailiff collected a fee once he was satisfied that a business did not impede river traffic. The Ship Tavern in Greenwich, for example, paid an annual fee of £1 1s. Owners of timber mills, timber merchants, shipwrights and barge builders on the foreshore all paid similar sums. In 1783, the Thames Navigation Committee decided that water bailiffs should accept an annual salary of £60 plus expenses; special payments should cease.[43] Yet water bailiffs still found room for corruption: each had in his gift thirty-two watermen places and in wartime he could sell these for as much as £60 each, since watermen could obtain protections from impressment.[44]

Shipbuilding on the Thames was a very public concern. Given that the river was a major transport route, passers-by could estimate the business strength of a shipyard just by the number of ships being built. They could also pass judgement on each vessel. In 1769, when Barnard launched the *Morse* for the East India Company, his career received a boost when pundits judged it 'the largest and finest ship ever built for that Company's service'.[45] Newspapers carried regular reports on the state of warship building in Deptford's naval dockyard. In 1783, for example, the second-rate warship, *Impregnable*, was admired as the largest of its type ever built in England.[46] Publicity like this bolstered morale in wartime, elevating the status and self-esteem of shipwrights and other dockyard workers. The excitement of industrial activity along the river was also carried to a more distant audience. The marine artist, Richard Paton, chose a local industrial scene for his 1779 submission to the Royal Academy, *A View on the River Thames, with the breaming of a Ship in Dock, and the Iron Foundry at Deptford.* It conveyed Paton's enthusiasm for shipyards to hundreds of exhibition visitors, who presumably knew enough about shipping to understand that 'breaming' involved scraping a hull clean of weeds and barnacles.

But if the yards were key to innovation along the river, the other side to their practical experimentation was a drive from reformers to apply 'scientific' thought to standardize naval shipbuilding. In the 1770s, shipwrights resisted government officials who tried to analyse warship construction and divide it into elements that could be measured and managed. They baulked at attempts to privilege mathematicians in matters of ship design over shipwrights who had been trained on the job.[47] They jealously protected traditional skills, preferring to view naval architecture as an art and 'mystery' which they could control themselves. Their resistance to officialdom won some sympathy along the river: manufacturers of products subject to tariffs – soap, glass, tallow candles – were themselves affected by increasing standardization and regulation as government aimed to tax products as efficiently as possible.

London's status as a world city placed mounting demands on those living in its maritime districts. The capital was not only Britain's largest port but also a vitally important manufacturing centre. Glassmaking, sugar refining, soap making, brewing and furniture making all benefited from easy transport by water. Riverside industries thrived but owners found that the political and social networks associated with capital investment, government contracts and international commerce became ever more complex. Those who aimed to get ahead needed entrepreneurial skills of the highest order. London's maritime parishes also experienced conditions that made them a furnace of political activism and debate. Now, world events would soon put all residents to the test.

3

WAR WITH AMERICA

When the American Revolutionary War broke out in 1775, Benjamin Slade was extremely well placed. He could profit from it while making a loyal contribution to the British war effort. Appointed purveyor to the royal dockyard in Deptford five years earlier, he was now firmly established in the position. He had trained as a shipwright, and received the best instruction. He was apprenticed first to his grandfather Benjamin, master shipwright in Plymouth's royal dockyard. After his grandfather died in 1750, he was taken on by Thomas Slade, his grandfather's nephew, who filled the vacancy as master shipwright. Thomas became the most distinguished naval architect of the century. He analysed captured French warships and combined their best qualities with English shipbuilding traditions to make vessels that sailed wonderfully. He built the *Victory*, Nelson's flagship at Trafalgar, and became Surveyor of the Navy, the highest technical position in the service. In 1768, he was knighted. He was still in post when his former apprentice, Benjamin, secured the job of purveyor at Deptford, helped, naturally, by his family connections. But Benjamin himself was no slacker.

The post of purveyor carried great responsibility. It was the purveyor's job to survey the trees that could be felled for naval use. The tall trees needed for masts mostly came from the Baltic, though some came from New England (it was not economic to bring timber from Canada until the early nineteenth century). Most of the hardwood needed for hulls came from the private estates of British landowners and from royal forests. On Benjamin Slade's recommendation alone, the Navy Board spent thousands of pounds each year on timber for shipbuilding. The purveyor also inspected and priced many stores that the dockyard bought locally. His list of purchases might include buckets, anchors, shovels, pots, hourglasses, oil and sailcloth. He was an expert judge of the quality of a range of articles. At Deptford, which was close enough to the centre of London to be directly administered by the Navy Board, the authority to purchase technically came from the Board itself. The system for making purchases was designed to keep a tight control on costs. Slade was given an advance of money and had to ask for another each time he spent up to his limit. He submitted full accounts for each tranche of expenditure, listing items bought and asking for them to be received and checked off at the dockyard. Despite these restrictions, he had a great deal of freedom in the choice of supplier, and contracts might be continued for decades without again being put out to tender.[1]

The Navy Board needed to have full trust in their appointed purveyor. The records show Slade carefully building up this trust, because although he had held the same post at Woolwich, it had only been for a year. Early on, the Board instructed him not to spend more than £100 on any one item. It often happened that the quantity he was asked to source came to slightly more than that. Each time this happened, he wrote to the Board explaining that in accordance with their instructions he was asking for permission to spend over the £100 limit. Each time they replied that, although they had issued the instruction, nevertheless in this case he could exceed the limit set. On another occasion, when the Board asked him to find out how the price of bark had varied over the years, he explained that, rather than go to leather tanners (who got their tannin from oak tree bark), he would get the information from the clerk of Leadenhall Market:

The reason I did not chuse to go amongst the Tanners was I much fear'd it would awaken a spirit of curiosity and enquiry which would have prov'd troublesome from those sort of people, therefore thought it best to move as secretly as I could.[2]

The Board, who presumably wanted to make sure it was selling its bark for a good price, noted at the top of his document, 'His precaution approved'. Similarly, when asked to give out the yard's method of seasoning timber, he checked before releasing the recipe of the mixture used – a powerful concoction of saltpetre, alum and common salt.[3] Eventually, the Board had enough trust in him to increase his routine advance payments during the American Revolutionary War from £300 to £600 and even to £900. Enormous sums were now spent on naval stores and other items. The bill for fodder to feed the horses sent with troops to America was itself spectacularly high. Ingenuity was needed to source these supplies, and Slade had a network of contacts prepared to share information.

Several of the items Slade bought on the Board's behalf were supplied by members of his extended family. Fortunately, such contracts were long-standing and pre-dated Benjamin's promotion to the job. Presumably, too, there had never been an issue with the quality of the goods supplied. This may help to explain why he had no qualms about obtaining coal supplies from a relation in the trade, or getting fabrics, lace and binding from his aunt, Mary Slade, based in Deptford. But in this respect, too, he was prudent. He sometimes bought cloth for the navy from other suppliers – an indication that he impartially sought out the best deals.

Slade lived five minutes' walk from the dockyard, in King Street, Deptford, but he might be away for long periods surveying timber. It was better to schedule this work during the summer months when roads were passable. He rode across England to Essex, Suffolk, Norfolk, Hertfordshire, Somerset and Shropshire, and to counties in northeastern Wales. During the long days of summer, he could survey as many as 100 trees a day. On these inspections, he always kept in touch with the Board so that they were assured he was hard at work. For example, on 6 November 1770 he wrote from Norfolk to say that the trees were so widely dispersed, the days so short and the roads so bad from recent rain that he would not be finished until the middle of the following week. He asked the Board to forward any orders they might have for him. It was unlikely that officials did have anything else he could do in Norfolk, but at least he had explained why he was taking so long.

Benjamin Slade not only had respected forebears to live up to and living relatives who expected him to grease the wheels of their profitable dockyard contracts, he also had four young children to maintain. In due course, his sons might want a career in the dockyard themselves or access to government contracts. All these pressures made him circumspect. He had been well educated, wrote a beautiful, clear hand and knew how to present complicated accounts. Evidently, he had also been schooled by various family members in how best to handle the Navy Board. His letters are deferential while giving a clear steer to busy officials on the action best taken. During these years, he was a reliable employee who also served his family well. In due course his eldest son, Benjamin, went into business. Another son became a successful wine and brandy merchant.

As the dockyard's purveyor, Slade had extensive local influence. Dealers like the Weatheralls, who supplied the navy with beeswax by the hundredweight, and the Walkers who supplied red, white and blue thread by the pound, were eager to remain on good terms with him. When the Navy Board asked whether he thought the anchors of Mr Ambrose, a local supplier, were fit for purpose, Slade's favourable report was a matter of vital importance to Ambrose.[4] And when, in the same letter, Slade added that he could not find anyone along the river who could supply the large planks the dockyard wanted, many timber merchants would have been disappointed. Owners of private yards along the Thames were eager to curry favour with the dockyard in the hope of future contracts to build naval ships. For example, William Barnard offered the navy his surplus timber at market price in 1769 – perhaps no great favour since private yards were usually undercapitalized and could not afford to carry large stocks. Later Barnard used Slade as a go-between. When the navy was short of 3-inch oak planking, he told Slade that he could spare thirty or forty loads, so long as the dockyard did not pick through to choose the longest pieces. Wells's yard also offered about fifty loads of good planking.[5] In these negotiations, Slade was an essential broker.

Consequently, Slade could supply Navy Board officials with local intelligence. He also gained this by serving on the parish vestry for St Nicholas's, Deptford.[6] In 1770 he reported that there was so much work for caulkers that they could earn four shillings a day. The men, he explained, were reluctant to work for naval yards where pay was less. All the same, he had left cards at their favourite alehouses, inviting them to apply for work.[7] Doubtless Slade had opportunities to take backhanders from those anxious to supply the dockyard, but he was scrupulous, or at least never caught taking bribes. After all, he was earning a good salary. Actual dockyard wages had not increased since the previous century and were inadequate in an era of rising prices but, as in other areas of public service, incomes were made up to a reasonable level by a combination of official allowances, recognized perks and unofficial fees. A committee of 1786–88, reporting on the salaries of public servants, found that although the established annual salary for a purveyor at Deptford was £60, Slade made £263.[8] This put him firmly in the ranks of the middling sort, with money to spare for books and even paintings. To place his status in context, only about 3 per cent of families in England had an annual income of £200 or so in this period.[9]

During the American War, Slade certainly worked hard for his money. His role was vital to the war effort and he proved energetic and conscientious. It was up to him to source and procure every item the dockyard needed to continue working at full stretch. Tons of supplies were shipped from Deptford's victualling yard to British forces in America, unable to buy much food or fodder locally. Never before had a British government needed to provision an army 4,000 miles away, and although the dockyard's supply procedures were well tried, the pressure of work was enormous. While Britain's forces in America might be the front line as far as the land war was concerned, they depended heavily on the resources of maritime London.

War and poor families

The official beginnings and endings of wars are often arbitrary dates, linked to formal declarations of hostilities and the signings of peace treaties. According to this practice, the American Revolutionary War started on 19 April 1775 and ended on 3 September 1783. But fighting in the American colonies involving British troops had never wholly ended after the Seven Years War in 1763. There remained territories to secure against the French and scattered fighting with the American Indians. There were also increasingly violent protests from colonists themselves, who objected to British attempts to tax them to help pay for the cost of their military defence. In 1768 the government finally sent troops to North America specifically to deal with the political unrest of the colonists. Inevitably, troops and civilians needled each other until, in 1770, an argument ignited in Boston and shots were fired. The soldiers killed five civilians. It was a personal tragedy for the families of the dead but also a propaganda gift for American patriots, eager to stir up public opinion against British rule. The soldiers were arrested and tried, and two were found guilty of manslaughter. They were merely branded in the hand. The incident fuelled growing resentment at the quartering of British troops in the colonies.

The need to garrison Britain's overseas possessions also placed strains on the lower classes at home. Artisans and labourers might be pressed or might join the military out of financial desperation. (Debtors were known to enlist as a last resort to maintain their wives and children; the navy was happy to take them, though not other criminals.) Inevitably, there were men who joined to escape marriage, without trace, leaving wives wholly unprovided for. Such women were not mentally prepared for the strain of coping alone and lacked, in the short term, the support networks of those married to regular soldiers and seamen. With little understanding of how to access regimental relief funds or private charity, they turned to poor relief. Paupers were a financial burden, so those with no right of settlement in a parish were refused long-term help and dispatched to their home parish. Poor relief could be grants of money, fuel, food or clothes to the needy in their own homes, but parishes could require them to enter the local workhouse. In these institutions, the able-bodied worked, mostly without pay, in return for board and lodging. Those too old or ill to work were simply taken in. The rules within a workhouse varied from parish to parish but the regime was always strict, if not necessarily harsh. That said, conditions inside worsened later in the century as food prices rose with inflation.

To be seen in workhouse garb was a badge of shame. Clothing could easily be turned into ready money and women in particular were expert at judging its value, and therefore the status of the wearer. Workhouses preferred linsey for women's gowns (a coarse, plain-woven twill with a linen warp and a woollen weft). In the 1760s Greenwich opted for green linsey, but a bright colour was expensive and inferior greens looked dirty brown in candlelight. They were unpopular even among the poor, so by the 1770s most work-houses chose grey linsey for women's gowns. The material was hard-wearing, as was the checked fabric preferred for aprons, but workhouse dress, being uniform as well as cheap, was immediately recognizable. And if that were not shame enough, paupers were also meant to wear a badge on their arm.

In London's maritime parishes, workhouses had a distinctive role. For many households where men might be called overseas – whether as seamen or soldiers – the local workhouse routinely formed part of a family's support structure. If a woman's credit failed because her husband was slow to return or died abroad, she and her children depended on parish relief. Sometimes, the children alone might be admitted to the workhouse so that the mother could work. Transient populations also turned to the workhouse.

Ursula Gattey entered the Greenwich workhouse with three children in the winter of 1771; her husband, a breeches maker, had enlisted and been drafted overseas 'from Portsmouth or Plymouth', leaving her no money. They had come to London from Knaresborough in Yorkshire in search of a better life, leaving their eldest child, William, to be brought up in his father's trade. But there were just too many mouths to feed and too few customers. After a month in the Greenwich workhouse, Ursula was given a pair of shoes and sent away with her youngest child, James. The other children, Mary and Thomas, lived precariously in and out of the workhouse while the conflict with the American colonies took its course. Mary asked to be readmitted in 1772. Thomas ran away in 1779 and seems to have been urged back by his mother. She died suddenly in 1780, after which he came back of his own accord. There was some hope for Mary. In 1781, when she was fifteen, her Yorkshire brother William, now twenty-eight and in the tailoring business himself, asked the workhouse if she could be bound apprentice to him in Knaresborough. The workhouse paid him £2 to take her and supplied Mary with the standard two suits of clothes before she set off on her journey.[10]

Predictably, in wartime, there were more seamen's families needing charity as men were either pressed or willingly enlisted. On just one day in April 1777, five women with children whose husbands were serving on warships had to be admitted into the Greenwich workhouse. Sometimes, too, the house helped naval women to get their family to other ports where their husband's ship had docked. In 1773 Mary Giffin was allowed 5s. 3d. to travel to Portsmouth with her children, but the parish beadle was to make sure she was in the wagon before he gave her the money.[11]

Occasionally, seamen unable to supervise their errant wives chose to pay for their families to be maintained in the workhouse while they were at sea. In September 1777 William Smith of His Majesty's Yacht *Royal Charlotte* told the workhouse committee in Greenwich that his wife 'was such a Sottish Drunken Woman that she was incapable of taking care of herself or her Children' and begged that the workhouse would keep them.[12] He made over his entire pay to the house for their upkeep. Similar arrangements could continue when maimed or aged seamen retired to nearby Greenwich Hospital. The hospital had only a few positions for women, as nurses. When wives themselves grew infirm and needed the workhouse, husbands in the hospital were expected to contribute towards their maintenance, transferring a portion of their monthly allowance or their tobacco money to the parish.[13]

In wartime, more soldiers' wives who followed the drum and tramped with the regiment also turned to local workhouses. In 1778, the Greenwich workhouse agreed to provide out-assistance to one woman while she gave birth at a local tavern and until she was sufficiently recovered to march after her husband. In another case, it ruled that a soldier's wife could be admitted if she fell into labour before the regiment departed and was unable to go with him. It also provided a refuge for soldiers' wives who fell ill, as two did on returning from Gibraltar in 1779, but only until they could return to their home parishes. The burden of the poor rate fell heavily on maritime parishes in wartime because the cost of poor relief increased. Workhouse records also show that substitutes for the militia were routinely paid from the tax. At the same time, local officials understood that their work was supporting the domestic war effort.[14]

Divided opinions

There was a slow build-up to the official start of the American War in 1775. It had been the same at the outset of the Seven Years War in 1756. But in the maritime districts south of the river, a military presence had remained long after the social unrest of the late 1760s, partly to protect the dockyards at Deptford and Woolwich, partly because troops heading for the colonies often embarked from there. In 1769, dockyard workers in Deptford demonstrated their loyalty by burning an effigy of Wilkes on the anniversary of the king's accession, but civilians found the behaviour of local troops irksome.[15] In taverns, for example, groups of officers might commandeer rooms and joints of meat being prepared for other people's dinners. On the highway, they drew swords and caused injuries over minor traffic disputes. They even brawled in church.[16]

Occasionally, they proved a colourful distraction. In March 1770, soldiers destined to serve in America under Major-General Thomas Gage, Britain's commander-in-chief, marched through Deptford and Greenwich before setting up camp on Blackheath. Contemporary paintings show women, children, pet dogs and soldiers on horseback, all busy about the tents crowded near the windmills on Blackheath. A month or so later the king reviewed his troops there. Unfortunately, exciting military displays like this encouraged small boys to put real gunpowder in their toy cannon. After one fatal accident, the Justice of the Peace in Greenwich banned the making and selling of all fireworks.

In the summer of 1770 there was an international crisis. Spain and France seemed likely to contest British sovereignty of the Falkland Islands. In the absence of hard news there was much conjecture. Londoners scrutinized operations in the royal dockyard for signs of unusual activity or preparations for war. After a serious fire at Portsmouth dockyard that July, security was stepped up in other yards in case enemy agents were tempted to try sabotage. Rumours were rife, and it was said that a letter threatening to torch Deptford dockyard next had been sent to the Admiralty. In the end, France decided not to back Spain over the Falklands and the tension diffused. All the same, the incident gave a foretaste of British sailors' likely attitudes to war. When a press gang tried to seize men from a merchant ship near the Pool of London, a sailor fetched some pistols from below deck and shot its officer dead on the spot. A newspaper printed a letter, said to be written by a seaman, claiming that unfair distribution of prize money made men unwilling to serve. The letter-writer showed little respect for naval officers: 'Numbers, as well as myself, will never consent, at the hazard of our lives, to enrich the most arrant fools the world ever produced, under the notion of serving their country.'[17]

Then, as now, there were probably many who knew little about national issues and who cared still less, unless directly affected. Some stood to gain financially from an increase in military operations, and dockyard workers were among them. At the time, their families were suffering hardship: work had slackened off in naval dockyards at the end of the 1760s. When war seemed likely in 1770, Deptford shipwrights petitioned for higher wages, claiming they could not manage on their pay. Probably they hoped to capitalize on the need for their services in wartime, but their petition was refused. In the harsh winter of 1771, Deptford shipwrights who had been sent to work in Portsmouth begged to be returned. They could earn more at home and had received word that their families lacked fuel and food because tradesmen would give them no more credit. A month later the sailmakers at Deptford dockyard tried petitioning for extra work to bolster their pay: the cost of food was rising and many had large families. By 1773, London newspapers were reporting that numbers of shipwrights, caulkers and other specialist dockyard workers had no work at all; they were as destitute and miserable as the Spitalfields weavers had been in the late 1760s. All these waged workers were desperate to earn more money.[18]

As Britain geared up for war with the American colonies, the build-up of troops and warships in maritime London could disrupt life at many levels. In May 1774, the *Cumberland* man of war, just launched at Deptford, met easterly winds that stopped its progress downriver. Food supplies ran low; its sailors ravaged local market gardens in the evenings, filling sacks with vegetables and stealing pigs and fowls from farmers' yards. Eventually, local constables managed to arrest some of the men and confined them in watch-houses. Afterwards, about 300 sailors from the *Cumberland* armed with crowbars, hatchets, staves and cutlasses seized their chance to come ashore in order to rescue their shipmates. A disgruntled local mob joined them, brandishing weapons taken from a blacksmith's and cleavers from a butcher's shop, swearing to hang any magistrate or constable they could find. The crowd rioted in Greenwich for some hours. Then, rumours that a company of guards from the Tower was marching towards them drove the sailors back to their ship. The daughter of the local Justice of the Peace had meanwhile fallen into fits and was said to be in a bad way. The *Cumberland*'s officers, prevented from taking action against the seamen while a local mob swelled their numbers, captured the ringleaders on return. The men were later publicly whipped in Deptford Broadway for the losses inflicted on local gardeners.

Government critics stoked sympathy for the rebellious colonists. They pointed out that the Thames was crowded with transport ships loading grapeshot, howitzers, hand grenades, bombshells and other instruments of death destined for the North American colonies, at the same time as merchant ships from these very colonies were anchoring in the river, laden with corn to relieve the hungry metropolis.[19] In London's maritime districts, merchants fearing disruption to their trade formed a vocal group opposed to war. The dispute with the colonists opened up differences of opinion at many levels. The conflict was not the usual battle for territory between nation states but more of an internal disagreement about the extent and nature of the authority of government. Close links between Britain and its colonies meant that many regarded hostilities as a civil war. The last American colony had been founded in living memory. On 17 November 1732, the social reformer James Oglethorpe and a load of ex-debtors had set sail from Deptford in the 200-ton ship *Anne* to found Georgia. Oglethorpe aimed to provide a new life for the 'worthy poor' and many English tradesmen and artisans had been happy to join him. In the 1770s, much popular sentiment focused on the need for reconciliation. As one amateur versifier exclaimed, 'Let Britons meet again, / Nor be one Brother by another slain.'[20] The poem was judged to have sufficient appeal to warrant newspaper publication.

The trouble was that although even-handed commentaries on the situation were available, it was all too easy to cloud the discussion with emotional appeals to ideals of freedom and liberty. Patriots in the colonies, who increasingly aimed at nothing less than independence, used the same rhetoric of liberty as did commentators at home when upholding the British constitution and Parliament's right to tax colonial subjects. This shared language made it harder for supporters of the government's position to denounce colonial opposition. Long before ministers had finished mismanaging the situation, the clear-sighted saw that American independence was inevitable. The more discerning even feared that the real enemy lay elsewhere:

Can it be supposed, by any Man of Common-sense, that the other Powers of Europe will remain quiet Spectators of a great Empire dismembering itself, without taking a share in the general Wreck? . . . We are running to our Ruin faster than they could drive us.[21]

Those anxious that France and Spain would take advantage of the situation were soon proved right.

In the first few years of the war, diverging public opinion placed additional strains on towns bearing the brunt of mobilization. Since London's maritime districts provided daily evidence of wartime preparations, they were at the heart of conflicted views about the American rebels. Londoners who objected to sending troops to the colonies were especially outraged by the sight of military operations in Deptford, where transports were loaded in full view of people on the northern bank of the Thames. Some newspapers even larded their reports of Britain's naval preparations with expressions of support for American independence.[22] Others warned darkly that this latest government expenditure would increase beyond all bounds the vast national debt carried over from the Seven Years War.

The conflict led to heightened activity all along the river. By July there were twelve 'houses of rendezvous' in Wapping, Rotherhithe and the Borough, where seamen could enlist. The atmosphere grew tense. In August, sailors due to man the transports for America rioted in Wapping, demanding more money; soldiers were sent from the Tower to disperse them and one man was wounded. Ten transport vessels lay off Deptford with food and stores for the soldiers in America; three more were anchored by the Tower, loading gunpowder and weapons. By September, the number of transports heading down the Thames had doubled. Bakers of ship's biscuit in Wapping and Rotherhithe were making additional supplies for the navy. The government had also contracted with Peter Mellish, a wholesale butcher in Smithfield Market, to supply oxen and 14,000 of the largest and fattest sheep that could be got. Four thousand were to be sent across the Atlantic immediately and soon hundreds of sheep were being ferried noisily downstream to be heaved, alive, onto ships bound for American ports. (Mutton does not salt well.)

No one in Parliament had more experience of the Admiralty than Lord Sandwich. Returned as First Lord for the third time in 1771, he at once tried to put the navy on a better footing, ordering six frigates from private yards along the river.[23] Some warships, hurriedly built during the Seven Years War from unseasoned timber, had rotted. Now he established annual dockyard inspections and aimed to build up the fleet with royal support, shrewdly getting George III – who had a technical brain – interested in the intricacies of shipbuilding. By the autumn of 1773, two new 70-gun ships were on the stocks at Deptford. Yet even Sandwich could not long withstand urgent calls for economy and a reduction in the national debt. He was forced to make savings. In 1774, on the eve of war, naval shipwrights were laid off. So, when war in America was finally declared, these workers at least rejoiced at the prospect of certain pay. Soon naval dockyards were so busy repairing warships and keeping them at sea that they had only limited capacity to build new ones. One solution was to try to make shipwrights more productive.

Dockyard reforms

In the dockyard, a working day varied with the seasons but routinely lasted eleven and a half to twelve hours. Men started work at first light, had half an hour for breakfast, and looked forward to their dinner around midday. Single men went to the nearest public house to eat. Married men went home, or their wives brought food to the yard. The dinner break lasted one or two hours, according to season. These rest breaks were rooted in traditional practice and officials found it hard to adapt work patterns to make them more efficient. Men did overtime if there was a rush on, as in August 1777 when orders came down for ten 20-gun ships to protect the Channel, but worked no more than five extra hours, making a seventeen-hour working day.

The yard's impressive clock tower, topped with a weathervane, helped to regulate procedures, reminding men of the Navy Board's authority and power over their lives. Of course, there were corrupt practices. Clerks – whose own inadequate wages were bolstered by fees – could be bribed to mark a worker as present when he was moonlighting. But generally, the ability to tell time accurately subjected people to a stricter working regimen. The clock tower also indicated the national importance of their work. When the dockyard was demolished in the twentieth century, no one could quite bring themselves to jettison the clock. It was towed downriver and now stands, improbably, in Thamesmead town centre.

Dockyard work was hard and men stuck together. Accidents were frequent, which is why each dockyard had its surgeon. Men fell from great heights, drowned, strained themselves lifting heavy loads or were crushed by falling timber. Those escaping sudden injury were still liable to suffer rheumatism and asthma as they worked outside in all weathers, with little protection from the wind as it swept across the river. Workers were on a daily rate but were often paid long in arrears; in April 1771, for example, workers finally received their wages up to the previous Christmas. This helped to justify the right of more privileged workmen to 'chips' or bundles of wood. Pay day was such a rare occasion in naval dockyards that it was reported in newspapers. But in the private yards, shipwrights were paid by task work, usually every two or three weeks. Their jobs were less secure and they might work longer hours, but they earned more money, especially in wartime. Now Sandwich set about imposing task work in the naval dockyards.

There was trouble at once. Britain had been at war with its American colonies for just a matter of weeks when, on 14 June, shipwrights in Portsmouth dockyard went on strike. They knew that their services were vital in wartime and, having failed to get a pay increase four years earlier, they seized their chance to gain the upper hand. Sandwich had not managed to explain his plans in detail to the more distant yards. The men feared change. They also saw that the new system would penalize the old and the less experienced workers. Inevitably, too, there was valid dispute about how long individual tasks took to complete and how much each task was worth. Shipwrights easily coordinated strike action because naval dockyards cooperated with each other and had regular lines of communication. But the strike divided communities. The Deptford yard had a good relationship with the Navy Board: the dockyard was close to central London and Sandwich visited often. Deptford shipwrights had taken trouble to build up trust with this important official, scrupulously thanking him for minor favours. Now they were inclined to approve his plan for piecework: the rising cost of living was acutely felt in London and they needed the extra money. On task work, some could earn a shilling more a day than on the

old system, even with overtime. Sandwich rewarded Deptford's shipwrights
by allowing two apprentices to each company of sixteen grouped for task
work. They drew lots for these trainees – the lucky ones effectively adding
to their wages since they collected their apprentices' money too.

Although Sandwich was forced to make task work voluntary, the strike
continued because shipwrights now demanded more money: a daily wage,
before overtime, of 2s. 6d. rather than 2s. 1d. (Their wage structure was
complicated: in summer they received 2s. 8½d. for a longer day and any
overtime was on top of that, but now they based their demands on the
basic daily rate.) The shipwrights also wanted strike-breakers to be
dismissed. Other dockyard trades stood ready to stake their claim if the
shipwrights won the day and leaders tried to keep the strike solid. In July,
it was reported that men from Portsmouth, Chatham and Woolwich had
agreed to meet at Chatham and march in a body to Deptford to prevent
shipwrights there from working. Strikers had support from their communities. Publicans, for example, offered credit at the rate of £10 per man
until they were paid again. The authorities grew uneasy. Not only were
these key workers vital to mobilizing the fleet, but also bands of strong
men on the march or idle in alehouses were likely to disturb the peace.
When rumours reached London of a full-scale riot at Woolwich dockyard,
Horse Guards were hastily dispatched from Whitehall, given the talk –
unfounded as it turned out – of plans to set fire to shipping and stores.

The strike was of national importance. It put maritime affairs in the
spotlight and increased public understanding of how much shipwrights
were paid. They pleaded their case in several newspapers, prompting wider
discussion that helped to pave the way for dockyard reform. Some thought
it would be a good thing if a wage increase could buy out men's right to
'chips'. The entitlement should have been worth 4d. a day but the volume
of wood men took home cost the navy much more. Low wages also encouraged pilfering.[24] The Admiralty took a hard line with strikers, announcing
that it would never again employ them and advertising for replacements.
Meanwhile, compliant riggers and caulkers from Deptford were drafted to
Portsmouth to help prepare the fleet. The entire episode served to intensify

public divisions at the outset of the war. Arguably, it also compromised Britain's mobilization. In the summer of 1775, the Navy Board had orders to get ten warships to sea but there were few shipwrights willing to work on them and no crews to man them. As if to heighten the navy's difficulties, newspapers that August reported the launch of a fine new ship for the Jamaican trade built at William Barnard's private yard. In a display of commercial confidence, dignitaries were entertained afterwards at the Mile End Assembly Rooms and a glittering ball was put on for the ladies.

The Admiralty had broken the strike by August but labour relations in the private yards became volatile in turn. One indication is that in 1776 sawyers got together to demand higher wages and to punish those working at a lower price. With rough justice, they tied up one terrified man, put him on an ass with his face to the tail, pinned a label on his back saying 'Working under price' and paraded him through Wapping.[25] Law officers swiftly arrested the ringleaders and sent them handcuffed to Newgate. During this troubled time, Captain Cook was still able to set sail from Deptford on his third Pacific voyage in July 1776. His chief task was to look for the Northwest Passage – a shortcut for shipping between the Atlantic and Pacific Oceans that people hoped existed in the Canadian Arctic. Deptford was by now firmly linked to voyages of exploration and had experience of adapting and provisioning ships for these expeditions, yet it is a wonder that the dockyard managed to fit out Cook's ships in wartime given the shortages of labour and materials. That said, when Cook arrived off Hawaii in December 1778, he had cause to complain bitterly in his journal about the quality of naval stores issued to him. Still, officials in the victualling yard learned useful lessons from Cook's voyages. On earlier expeditions, he had found sauerkraut a good protection against scurvy and now vast quantities were prepared in Deptford for the use of the British army in America.

By the summer of 1777, dockyards and shipyards along the river were working at full stretch. Even private yards had no spare capacity, being busy with naval contracts. But life was still hard for local people. There was regular work but also food shortages and inflation. The price of rice, for instance, had almost doubled since the war started. Family life was often disrupted. Dockyard workers, like seamen, had to be prepared to leave home for long stretches of time, shuttled between naval dockyards, depending on where the demand for labour was greatest. In January 1777, shipwrights from Deptford and Woolwich were drafted to Portsmouth and Plymouth to repair warships due to a shortage of skilled workers. Young volunteers were even sent to Nova Scotia in Canada. The demand for their skills was such that by 1779, ordinary carpenters, with extra instruction, were carrying out shipwrights' work at Deptford. Pensioners were even taken out of Greenwich Hospital to help fit out warships. Naval dockyards were soon a real target for sabotage. The arsonist John the Painter was hanged in March 1777 for setting fire to the rope house at Portsmouth. After this, security was stepped up at other yards and extra watchmen and alarm bells were provided. In this heated atmosphere, speculation about conspiracies and foreign spies persisted. In 1779, men were arrested at Deptford, accused of being in the pay of the French government and selling information about British masts and rigging to the enemy.[26] The riverside parishes became places of rumour and suspicion.

London's maritime populations also witnessed the distressing sight of wounded soldiers and sailors being landed from service overseas. Many of the soldiers were bound for Chelsea Hospital but holding areas were set up for them and local help was needed with nursing. Communities providing large numbers of men for the sea knew at first-hand the human cost of military service. In July 1774, a Mrs Jane Axstone married a lighterman near Rotherhithe. It was her third husband and, remarkably, as one newspaper noted, the three men had but two legs between them. Her latest husband had lost a leg while serving in the navy, though this did not prevent him working on the river. Double amputees were a common sight and, being less able to earn a living, were recommended as objects of charity.

Manning the navy

As soon as war was formally declared, seamen abandoned merchant ships in the river, afraid that press warrants were about to be issued. Vessels that used to be constantly employed in the American trade were moored uselessly in the Thames; navigation became almost impossible in the crowded river. It was almost a relief when officials from Deptford dockyard targeted thirty empty ships for transport duty to America. The need for transports increased at an unprecedented rate. While shipowners like Michael Henley stood to benefit, more vulnerable seamen paid a price. It was extremely difficult to find crews for transport vessels, even when they were offered high wages. Throughout the war, the navy and the transport service would compete for seamen, with men being pressed from transport vessels.[27] The easiest way for the navy to recruit competent men was to force those on returning warships to re-enlist. They might have been away for years but had no chance to visit their families. Typically, when the *Adventure* was paid off in Deptford in August 1775, a party of guards with fife and drum was there to persuade the crew to go to America. Men had a poor choice: enlist or be impressed.

In 1775, sailors eagerly backed proposals to find a way of manning the navy without impressment. On 26 October, around 500 set out from Wapping to deliver their loyal petition to the king. At the same time, men with experience of the sea and likely to be targeted by press gangs took precautions. Despite the bounty money on offer, naval recruitment was having only limited success. In October 1776, Sandwich got permission to impress seamen for the navy's guard ships – reserve vessels which could be mobilized quickly if invasion threatened or an enemy fleet was sighted. Arguably, the measure was overdue but it was unwelcome news to riverside parishes.

On 28 October 1776, there was a 'general press' on the Thames. About twenty manned boats came upriver from Deptford and Woolwich. Press gangs boarded merchant ships and took for the navy every member of the crew except the master, mate and boys. Over 1,000 men were said to have been pressed in this one exercise. No wonder the Thameside parishes were in uproar when, on 8 November, the King issued a royal proclamation that called for the return of any seamen serving foreign countries and, worse still, granted rewards for anyone informing on sailors who hid from the press. That November, a large hospital ship was moored off the Tower to receive volunteers and pressed men. There were violent struggles with press gangs in which women often played a prominent role. Even so, there was a serious shortage of experienced seamen; transports bound for America were stranded below Gravesend for lack of men to sail them.

Sailors working for the East India Company, armed with bludgeons, broomsticks and cutlasses, crowded outside its London headquarters and demanded protections from the press.[28] Local people mostly sympathized with the sailors.[29] In Southwark, a press gang 'headed by a black fellow with a naked sword' was chased by a mob into a tavern yard where its leader was wounded. A woman, rushing into the brawl to find her husband, was stuck on the head with a cutlass and killed on the spot.[30] Tempers ran high. In Wapping, locals helped three sailors from an East Indiaman repulse a nine-strong press gang in August 1777. Men were impressed from as far away as Leicester and brought to London heavily ironed, which yielded sarcastic commentary about Britain's claims to be a land of liberty. Pressed men were held in tenders (holding vessels) moored near the Tower. Some who could swim made daring escapes on the ebb tide.

Merchant seamen were reluctant to join the navy because they had no idea when they would be discharged. They also knew that press gangs would create a shortage of seamen along the river and that eventually ship-owners would have to put up wages. No one liked impressment; it was just that the alternatives seemed impracticable. In March 1777, a bill in Parliament calling for a registry of seamen and a system of manning the navy without impressment got much publicity. It had the backing of Wilkes but even so the bill was defeated. In this crisis, people chose to put their faith in tried and tested methods of manning the navy. By now the pressing fear was that the French and Spanish fleets would be ready to put to sea before the British, especially since most available hands seemed committed already to the transport service and to operations in America. If there was sympathy for sailors among the lower orders in the maritime parishes, wealthier citizens feared for national defence. Leading residents in Greenwich, Woolwich and Deptford met in the Mitre tavern at

Greenwich towards the end of 1777 to open a subscription with the aim of raising 1,000 men for the king. Finally, government accepted the urgency of the situation and, in January 1778, Sandwich got Cabinet approval for a general press.

Accelerated impressment brought new tensions. Press gangs now regularly caused violent affrays. Their battles with seamen and coal heavers, and the injuries that all sustained, were well reported. There was at least one occasion, as in August 1781, when returning seamen strongly resisted being pressed in the Thames. One crew clambered aboard the tender but refused to join other pressed men below because they were owed wages. Instead, they grabbed the helm, drove the tender on shore and ran off. Whenever men in sailors' clothes committed violent robberies, they were usually presumed to be members of a press gang. Thugs certainly posed as press gangs, extorting money from victims by demanding a bribe to release them. But in these hard times, soldiers also turned to robbery. The army was more likely to include criminals anyway because the navy was reluctant to take them.[31] So, the riverside parishes were plagued by desperate men – some evading capture, some making strenuous efforts to press them, some taking advantage of the situation to commit crimes.

By now, even men who had protections (such as watermen and certain seamen) were being pressed, prompting some to argue that government should reimburse any money they might have paid for protections.[32] Private shipyards had to contend with press gangs snatching skilled workers. In response, the Navy Board authorized shipyards to issue certificates of protection to shipwrights engaged in naval work. Merchant ships were delayed in the Thames while their owners got protections for their crews; only sailors in the coal trade were routinely protected. Even so, in October 1779, Michael Henley wrote to the Navy Board asking if he could delay his contract to supply coal because his crews had been pressed.[33] That year, too, William Barnard had to write to the Board about two of his shipwrights who had been wrongfully impressed because they were working on warships for the navy. Merchants complained that with so many men being pressed from returning ships, it cost them extra to hire men to get ships with expensive cargoes safely up the Thames. At the end of 1781, returning East Indiamen found there were no pilots to guide them upriver, seamen were so scarce. By 1782, sailors were routinely pressed as soon as they entered home ports, while scenes of troops boarding transports for America had become a familiar occurrence.[34] London's maritime districts were at the sharp end of resourcing of war and counting its human cost.

A war of survival

Britain's dispute with its American colonies had long affected trade. Angry colonists preferred to deal with other European nations and boycotted British traders. Those merchants in turn were tempted to sell to rival powers instead. After the outbreak of war, merchants found means to recoup their losses. In 1776, several privateers licensed by government to capture enemy ships sailed from Deptford with provisions for eight months. They had instructions to patrol the coasts of North America and to stop colonists trading with foreign powers.

From the start of hostilities, ministers kept a wary eye on naval preparations in France and Spain. France had long been supplying the American colonies with arms and ammunition, and in February 1778 it recognized an independent United States of America. Britain promptly declared war on France. Even now, there were reports of warships waiting in the Thames, ready to go to sea but lacking sailors to man them. In 1779, Spain entered the war against Britain. Newspapers claimed that two-thirds of its fleet had been built by British shipwrights, enticed to Spain on promise of double wages during the strike of 1775. The combined fleet of the two powers threatened to invade Britain in the summer of 1779, causing widespread panic, until sickness and delays caused the fleet to withdraw before autumn's bad weather set in. In December 1780, the government declared war on the Dutch in order to stop them supplying the French. Britain was now engaged in a war for survival against three European nations; the American colonists were no longer the real issue. In British newspapers, patriotic verses started to appear alongside idealized descriptions of loyal, honest 'Tars'. There was less criticism of press gangs; instead they were credited with seizing useful sailors or helpfully clearing them from brothels.

All the yards along the Thames worked overtime. Advertisements appeared for sawyers, guaranteeing them full employment in all weathers at salaries from 40s. to 45s. a week. London yards even offered to pay travel costs to sawyers from other counties.[35] Deptford's dockyard was enlarged with more storage: its capacity to provision fleets was obviously vital. It advertised for supplies ranging from hammocks and hospital bedding to forges for use in military camps, so the economic impact on supply trades up and down the river was marked. Some tradesmen benefited when the Admiralty sold off old stores – though the Opposition pointed to this as another waste of public money. In this emergency, the East India Company, which had ships building at various yards along the Thames, donated three 74-gun ships to the government's service.

Yet the nation was still divided. Constant fears about growing public debt led to demands for economy, though amid general anti-war protest this was an attack directed at the Crown, already judged to have lost America. In April 1780, numerous constituencies petitioned Parliament for an inquiry into public expenditure. Westminster's petition, backed by Opposition figures such as Wilkes and Fox, was expected but Kent's, where many were profiting from wartime expenditure, struck home: 4,000 citizens had signed. It prompted a counter petition in Kent, which further split local opinion. This time, signatories objected to the kind of county association that had produced the first petition, complaining that those who presumed to dictate to government risked dangerous outcomes. Among those who signed the counter petition were members of the Slade family.

Opponents of the war, playing on fears of invasion, saw that naval administration and dockyard efficiency were easy targets. In 1781, the Opposition forced a parliamentary debate on the state of the navy. One MP complained about scandalous negligence in Deptford dockyard. Men, he claimed, were supposed to work until noon but always downed tools at 11.30 a.m. The bell called them to work at 1 p.m. but not a stroke of work began before

3 p.m.[36] This debate intensified a long-running argument about the efficiency of naval dockyards compared with private yards. Dockyard performance was now a matter of common conversation and political urgency. Dockyard workers were portrayed as lazy, ill-disciplined and unproductive. Shipwrights become a political football in a moment of national crisis. The Admiralty redoubled its efforts to manage public opinion and noticeably more bulletins appeared in newspapers describing swift progress on ships under construction in naval yards. All this effort produced spectacular results. In October 1781, during a week of high autumn tides, the Thames sometimes saw two launches a day. At the end of 1781, the Admiralty ordered another 500 shipwrights to be hired immediately, of which 70 were to work at Deptford. Whether or not such numbers could be found, they were sorely needed. When a large warship had to be finished quickly, 500 shipwrights might be assigned to that vessel alone.[37]

As Britain reached a critical point in this unequal war, one crucial measure gave the navy an advantage. In 1778, the Admiralty had taken a decision to sheath the hulls of all warships with copper to protect them from the Teredo worm. The policy was aggressively pursued and the work mostly finished by 1783. It succeeded better than could have been imagined: the copper plating also made ships faster since it deterred marine growth, and the dockyards' great effort to complete the programme paid off. The other decision to make a difference was that warships were given more firepower: lighter carronades that could be carried on an upper deck. In time, the obvious strength of the British fleet, compared with the navies of other European powers, won public confidence.

British forces in America were forced to surrender at Yorktown in 1781. American ships sailed into the Thames flying flags with thirteen stripes even before the British government authorized peace negotiations with the colonists in March 1782. An angry reception caused them to leave off the practice, for the time being. Newspapers continued to list British warships under construction but now made pointed comparisons with the intimidating French navy, stoking nationalistic rivalry and calming public fears by turns. Four warships were on the stocks along the Thames in August 1783, each a three-decker. This had never been seen before and observers gained new confidence that Britain might emerge victorious.

Portraying dockyard work

If critics described London's dockyard workers as time-serving idlers, dock-yard hands were fortunate in having artists among them who could represent their labours in a heroic light. Deptford shipwright John Cleveley was a talented, self-taught artist. Born in Southwark in about 1712, he specialized in dockyard scenes and painted ships on the stocks or being launched along the Thames. His work benefited from first-hand observation and technical knowledge, and had a ready market. He repeated his compositions, sometimes slotting in different vessels to please patrons, and made slightly different versions of his paintings, most likely for local sale. Many of his best works can now be seen in the National Maritime Museum, Greenwich. He was a great promoter of Deptford dockyard. High-level officials there seem to have supported his artistic career by giving him a succession of easy posts that allowed him to paint while also being employed. (He would have found it hard to earn his living by painting alone.) They made use of his drawing ability, sending him to other yards to take the lines of ships. His wife, Sarah, who died in 1793, described him in her will as 'late Carpenter of his Majesty's ship, Victory'. The ship was held in reserve in Chatham and not commissioned for sea service until after his death, so he would have been spared regular work in that post.

Some of Cleveley's work suffers from the circumstances in which he had to paint. Even his most impressive painting, a large canvas depicting the launch of the *Cambridge* at Deptford in 1755 and including – fictitiously – the impressive *Royal George* at the same event, has strange proportions and curious omissions. Some figures seem too small in relation to others and the men rowing a small boat on the river lack oars. Critics have speculated that such oddities result from his painting by candlelight, perhaps with a reflector to maximize the flame. As he moved the pool of light from one area of the canvas to another, he would have had little opportunity to view the image as a whole. Did Cleveley mostly work at these pictures in poor light, outside work hours? Perhaps he set up his canvases in a room at the top of his crowded house near the dockyard in King's Yard Row, Dogg Street (now Prince Street).[38] We know from his wife's will that the house had two rooms to a floor, but they had five surviving children: three sons and two daughters. And the house may only have been enlarged in the 1770s when much of the street was redeveloped. Yet the evidence of his dockyard career suggests that he did not always do a full day's work as a shipwright, so oddities in this piece may indicate that he painted the ship from a model.[39]

Two of Cleveley's sons were also marine artists, and arguably better ones. Their paintings are more fluid and atmospheric because they had some formal training. Yet both also worked in the dockyard. John Cleveley the Younger was a shipwright like his father, while his twin, Robert, was apprenticed to a caulker, though he detested the work; he was teased for working in gloves – presumably not to spoil his hands for painting – and soon gave it up. Aged twenty-three, in 1770, Robert was fortunate to secure a place as a clerk to Captain William Locker, who liked the arts. Later he became a naval purser, in charge of the stores and accounts on a ship. It was a position that carried some risk, as all provisions (though supplied by government) were charged to his account at fixed prices. Pursers had to submit strict financial records to get paid but had ways of making a profit. These methods were generally suspected of being at the crew's expense, so pursers were rarely popular on board.

James, Cleveley's youngest son, could also draw. He sailed as a carpenter on Cook's third and final voyage, making watercolours in the Pacific which his brother John later worked up into oil paintings. Some have questioned John's stock pledge of authenticity (that his paintings were based on sketches 'taken on the spot'), because they include features typical of Western-trained artists who had never seen the Pacific. Yet clearly he had access to the visual material resulting from Cook's voyages. And John had worked in this way before: when he created a watercolour of the ships *Racehorse* and *Carcass* forcing their way through Arctic ice in the 1773 expedition, he based it on a sketch by a crew member. This dramatic image was engraved and helped to fire popular interest in the Arctic.

As well as the Cleveley twins painting dockyard scenes and enjoying access to travellers' sketches, thanks to their maritime contacts both also went to sea. John sailed with Sir Joseph Banks in the summer of 1772 as draughtsman on an expedition to Iceland. Robert was based in American waters from 1773 to 1777 as clerk on the warship *Asia*. He used first-hand knowledge of the coast to depict some of the battles of the American Revolutionary War. As a war artist, John seems to have responded to the conflicted sensibilities of viewers at home. For example, his watercolour of the opposed landing of British troops in New York in 1776 depicts four warships bombarding the town but this act of aggression is balanced in the work by the flat-bottomed boats carrying troops inshore, looking horribly exposed.[40] The war in America was just as finely poised: British troops captured New York on 15 September but lost a battle to Washington and his army the next day.

The Cleveleys' paintings were not only patriotic, they also helped to link maritime scenes to economics, visually bringing home to people that riverside trades supported British imperial power. The paintings by the Cleveley twins were designed to be engraved to reach a wider audience. Sandwich, a friend of Joseph Banks and keenly interested in exploration, saw in Deptford skilled workers who could both contribute to voyages of exploration and help to promote new discoveries. Yet the artists' dockyard scenes also helped to raise the profile of shipwrights themselves. Shipwrights were already respected artificers but the Cleveleys connected them to wider culture. John Cleveley the Elder was a member of London's Free Society of Artists, exhibiting at its annual exhibition from 1764. His son John was also a member; Robert exhibited at the prestigious Royal Academy from 1780.

The younger Cleveleys were especially well placed. Their personal circumstances gave them huge opportunities for visual communication in an age when the sea was regarded as Britain's natural element and maritime pictures were popular. 'History painting' – scenes from classical mythology, the Bible, or Greek and Roman history – might have been regarded as the highest form of art but people of the day were interested in current affairs and much news revolved around war at sea. In dockyards, the Cleveley brothers could study and depict the most advanced technology of their age: ocean-going vessels. They had the chance of foreign travel, witnessed momentous events, and had access to first-hand sketches of exotic landscapes which they could work up. Towards the end of the eighteenth century, scenes from recent history – including large battles – duly received the status of history painting. The Cleveleys were not artists of the highest stature, but they helped to win greater recognition for maritime art. Their work brought out the heroism of ordinary people's lives. It also brought them personal success. John Cleveley the Elder managed to leave his illiterate wife a small annuity. When Robert died, his wife inherited nearly £2,200 in government bonds as well as the money owing to him as a purser.

The Cleveleys had links with other marine artists north of the river in Wapping and Shadwell, partly through membership of the Society of Artists. These included Robert Dodd, who painted river and dockyard scenes before also turning to the American and French wars, and Francis Holman, who was fascinated by the shipbuilding programme along the Thames during the American War and who depicted its momentous battles. Holman's prolific apprentice, Thomas Luny, also lived in Wapping and then Ratcliff until 1790. All these artists helped to communicate the unique identity of maritime London and its importance to Britain's commercial and military success.

War's aftermath

If some profited from the American War, others did not. Contractors and shipowners in the transport service were resentfully credited with profiteering, 'rioting in luxury and wallowing in voluptuous pleasures for many years at the expence of their country'.[41] Newspapers claimed that in Wapping there were contracting butchers, bakers and carpenters lounging in coaches. They were said to own servants in livery, country seats and even hounds and hunters. Some merchants made money from privateering. In contrast,

William Barnard's father went bankrupt in 1781. Since government finances were stretched, the Navy Board changed the way it paid private yards for building warships: there was no advance instalment when the contract was signed. Instead, the first payment was made only when the builder assured the Board that he had enough timber to start building. Even then he was paid in post-dated navy bills. If he took these to a bank, for cash to cover materials and labour, bills were discounted at rates of up to 11.25 per cent. Yet the naval contract contained no escape clauses to cover wartime inflation and included a penalty clause of up to £5 per ton for late delivery. After his father's bankruptcy, William was responsible for completing the warship for which his father was contracted. His letters to the Navy Board around this time, asking for more work, mention the increase in the price of materials and show signs of stress and even paranoia. He nearly suffered financial disaster himself. When the war ended, he had two 74-gun warships on the stocks. The Board said it would put off the launches of both ships until 1785. At the end of a war, it was standard practice for the Navy Board to keep newly completed ships on their slipways: they would only begin to rot, if launched. This meant Barnard's final payment for the warships would be delayed. He would have to find wages and materials to complete them but, without payment, would not have money to buy timber for his next ships. Nor would he be able to fulfil other contracts as his building slips were occupied. To make matters worse, the insurance on both warships would expire before a new launch date. William's pleas to the Board fell on deaf ears for weeks. Eventually, it allowed him launch the vessels but only on condition that he accept late payment.

The Treaty of Paris formally ended the war in September 1783 but seamen were being demobilized from April. Foreign sailors, prepared to work for less, started taking merchant vessels to sea. British seamen angrily petitioned the navy for outstanding wages and complained about the injustice of using foreign crews when they themselves had no work. Magistrates were put on alert in case seamen caused disturbances. For the time being, shipwrights were kept fully employed on warships still under construction. Private yards had even been allowed to repair smaller frigates from early 1783, freeing up naval dockyards to work on ships of the line. But by February 1785, significant reductions in the number of naval shipwrights were rumoured: at Deptford, 150 men seemed likely to lose their jobs. It was an anxious time because government always reduced the navy when war ended. Yet by June it was clear that the men would be kept on. Newspapers reported that this was because rival French, Dutch and Spanish navies would be only too happy to employ them.[42] In fact, the new prime minister, William Pitt, had realized that Britain's military defences needed a thorough overhaul. Dockyard workers were set to work, repairing the existing fleet and inspecting naval stores. Unwanted ships were sold off but large warships were ordered.[43]

London's maritime districts saw improvements to their built infrastructure as a result of the war. In Deptford, after a period of little growth, hundreds of new houses were built between 1770 and 1792 – an indication of the prosperity war brought to some. Many houses were substantial, of local brick and roofed with plain pantiles from local potteries. John Thompson, a dockyard carpenter who led a consortium of tradesmen as his own career developed, built several of them. He became master house carpenter at the dockyard in 1787. Probably, the introduction of piecework in the yard encouraged this kind of diversification but Thompson was also responding to a demand for housing as Deptford's population grew.[44] At the victualling yard, expanded facilities were completed by the end of 1786, making it the best equipped in Europe. In future, the Navy Board centred all its baking, slaughtering, curing and storing in the capital at Deptford, creating new jobs. In Wapping, where so many businesses had been contracted to supply goods to the navy, residents successfully petitioned to have key streets widened so that wagons could pass. Roads were paved and lit to improve transportation, a process that was unfortunately helped by disastrous fires in Wapping, notably in 1779, when about fifty properties were consumed.

The American War had been a confusing, traumatic and brutalizing experience for many, whether working at home to the point of exhaustion or fighting overseas. Demobilization further aggravated tensions within communities. Sometimes riots broke out when warships were paid off and men came ashore. Pubs were boarded up for safety. By 1783, Wapping was thought to have upwards of 1,500 unemployed foreign sailors. Gangs of British seamen paraded the streets to warn foreigners against any attempt to undercut their wages by entering merchant ships for lower pay. A year later, Wapping still had crowds of unemployed seafarers and handbills were put up to dissuade them from entering the Dutch navy. There was friction in Deptford dockyard, too. In October 1786, soldiers were posted there, ostensibly to guard against smuggling. In Rotherhithe, that same month, Thomas Massett, a shipbuilding supervisor for the East India Company, was shot in the stomach as he walked home one evening. He died the next day. People speculated that he was the victim of a personal grudge or mistaken for a customs officer since no money was stolen. The American War had helped to bring about a fractured society, and crime in London's maritime districts was reaching new heights.

4

CRIME AND PUNISHMENT

On the night of 12 April 1775, the moon was almost full. It would set in the early hours. Four Revenue officers, Joseph Pierson and three others, stood on Deptford Broadway near some elm trees not far from the watch-house. They had information that smuggled tea and other goods would be brought overland to London and stood ready to intercept the gang. In their belts were loaded pistols.

Suddenly, they heard footsteps and voices. Men were coming towards them. As the voices drew closer, the officers saw that there were just two, seemingly the worse for drink. The closest, unsteady on his feet, stumbled against Pierson and slurred, 'How many of you are there?' 'What's that to you?' retorted Pierson. 'Be on your way.'[1] The two made off towards Blackheath; the officers continued to wait, nervously. It was now past midnight. In the dark, they heard a shrill whistle. A signal from the gang? They hurried in the direction of the sound, but could see nothing. Then ten or twelve men came along the road, armed with bludgeons, seemingly on their way to an early shift at work. The officers quietly asked the watchman if he knew who they were. 'Riggers from Woolwich' was the reply. Pierson thought that the men bringing up the rear were the same two they had seen earlier, but they trudged by. Less than an hour later, the gang returned, hats down to hide their faces. The men turned into Church Street, then spotted the officers. 'Here they are!' Giving what was later termed a loud 'war whoop', its leaders fell on the officers with fury.

Outnumbered, the customs men split and ran. Two raced off towards Blackheath. Pierson and William Anchor headed for the nearby watch-house. The watchman had gone on his rounds and they were soon surrounded. 'Keep off, or we'll fire!' they warned. 'Blast ye, you dogs, we'll sacrifice you,' was the retort. More of the gang came up, all smelling of drink. The two officers frantically pushed past them and ran down Church Street. In the dark, Anchor stumbled against the railings outside Trinity Almshouses. He felt blows raining on his back. 'This way!' yelled Pierson. 'I know a way round.' Anchor struggled free and tried to follow but Pierson had disappeared into the darkness. At Deptford Green, Anchor turned right and soon sensed that the footsteps behind him were fading.

Pierson had mistakenly headed into a narrow lane called Hughes Fields. There the gang clubbed him to the ground. He cried for mercy, pleaded for his wife and four helpless children, but the men did not spare him. Windows began to open in nearby houses. Residents heard the leader say, 'Now, my lads, give him one blow apiece for me. And another, for liberty!' There were four or five more violent blows. One witness later said it sounded like men threshing, stroke after stroke. Pierson's groans ceased. A neighbour called down, 'What goes on there?' 'Stay out of it,' the men warned, 'or we'll break every window in your house!'

As the gang made its way back to the home of the ringleader, Gipsy George, it fell in with two labourers going early to work and invited them to share a glass of gin. These workers later testified that Gipsy George (George Bride) gave each in the gang half a crown, except one called Henman, who received three shillings. Half a crown was the sum that highwaymen generally gave to the hired drivers of hackney coaches and post chaises when instructing them to drive on after a robbery. It was more than a day's earnings, and bought silence. After the drink Gipsy George said, 'Now you may go, but you'd best go down the road and pick up the dead. Damn such fellows, there's no sin in killing a hundred such.'

The men returned to fetch Pierson but took fright and ran when they saw him. Neighbours were already up and about. A waterman living at the bottom of Hughes Fields carried Pierson to his house with the help of two others, and sent for a surgeon. He refused to come, so neighbours summoned the local surveyor, a customs official, who took one look at the wounded man and fetched the surgeon himself.[2] Afterwards, Pierson was taken by boat to the London Hospital. His skull was exposed and beaten in, his chest mangled, and his right arm so badly broken that it had to be laid open to the shoulder. His wife was sent for and was given permission to stay in the hospital to help look after him. He died on 10 May.

On hearing of Pierson's death, one of the gang, Samuel Whiting, presented himself to local churchwardens and turned evidence. He said that Gipsy George had called the men together that night, plied them with gin, and encouraged them to give the revenue officers a good beating. They had filled an old tea sack with straw and carried it with them to cause suspicion and encourage the officers to stop them. Following his testimony, three men, Thomas Henman, Benjamin Harley and Joseph Bland, were arrested. Gipsy George could not be found, though the custom house offered a £50 reward for information that led to his capture or to the arrest of others in the gang.

Pierson had died in Middlesex, so the case was heard at the Old Bailey though the crime had taken place in Kent. At their trial in May 1776, all the accused protested their innocence. Elizabeth Tomb, a woman at Harley's lodgings, swore that Harley was at home that night, and called upon their landlady to confirm it. She did, but unfortunately called Elizabeth Tomb by the name of Elizabeth Harley, and though the landlady swore it was an unfortunate slip of the tongue, it weakened her evidence. The court decided there was no case against Bland but Henman and Harley were found guilty, hanged and their bodies sent for dissection.

In July, two more gang members were picked up at Portsmouth: Robert Harley, Benjamin's brother, and Edward George. At their trial, several respectable people in Deptford swore that they had known the defendants for years and confirmed their honesty, industry and humanity. A newspaper noted drily, 'It is very remarkable that every one of the witnesses examined concerning the character of the prisoners, declared on oath, that they were never known to be concerned in smuggling.'[3] The verdict went against them all the same. They were executed at Tyburn that September. It was reported that the crowd was not so numerous as was usual on such occasions but that many known offenders were present. Before the bodies could be cut down from the scaffold and sent for dissection, a woman climbed the ladder to be stroked by the hand of one of the dead men, as a remedy for a wen on her breast.

The manhunt continued, since the custom house was determined to make an example of the case. In January 1777, others were picked up and brought to trial. An incident that had been a talking point for almost two years was gradually put to rest. But why was such a large swathe of the community apparently complicit in such a crime? One factor may have been that those involved had known each other since childhood. At the trial of Harley and George, one witness said, 'I was bred and born in the same place they were; they were all people of Deptford.' The exception was Gipsy George, and he had lived there eighteen years. Even Whiting, who turned evidence against them, said, 'We were all children brought up together.'[4] Another factor might have been the attitude towards authority of the labouring classes. When Gipsy George called upon the gang to give another blow for liberty, he was appealing to a certain mindset. This was 1775. If the colonists in America were claiming that there should be no taxation without representation, working people in Deptford might well have felt the same.

A broadside that was being circulated in London around this time declared:

They, who have *no* Voice nor Vote in electing of *Representatives, do not enjoy* Liberty, but are absolutely *enslaved* to those who *have* Votes, and to their Representatives: For, to be enslaved, is to have Governors whom *other* Men *have set over us*, and to be subject to laws *made by the Representatives of Others.*[5]

Few adult males in Deptford had the vote, as it was restricted to those with wealth and substantial property. The two elected Members of Parliament for Kent were not actively involved in local affairs, though prompt to enforce justice.[6] While the gang may not have been given to debating what constituted liberty, they would have been aware of the rhetoric of the times, which seeped into sermons, newspapers and broadsheets. And one aspect of that rhetoric was that the law itself needed to be subject to restraint, lest it become tyranny.[7] Customs officials were liable to be regarded as interlopers, appointed to uphold unjust as well as inconvenient taxation. Others in this decade argued that the law preserved liberty only if it had been passed with the consent of the people. The Pierson case therefore gets to the heart of contemporary debates about liberty. Triggered by smuggling, it also prompts questions about the limits of law enforcement in maritime London and the levels of everyday violence.

In southeast England, as in other regions with coastlines, smuggling was carried out on a massive scale. This was organized crime, with networks from coastal towns to the capital. Many larger gangs used extreme violence and intimidation to make sure that no one informed against them. Few condoned such brutal tactics but the general feeling was that evading tax was hardly a crime. Many were content to deal in 'duty-free' goods. Backed by public opinion, smugglers viewed their activities as somehow innocent and, when caught by customs officials, saw the use of violence as a legitimate way to defend their 'just property'.[8] And in London's maritime districts, there were rich pickings on a local, manageable scale. Smuggling was routinely linked to the pilfering from merchant ships all along the Thameside quays. Residents of Deptford and Greenwich had unique opportunities because returning East Indiamen, crammed with tea and exotic goods, often lay off the Isle of Dogs, just opposite.

All levels of the community were implicated. In 1769, for example, a chaise and pair, driven by two well-dressed men, was stopped in fashionable Croom's Hill in Greenwich. Customs men seized India silks and other materials of great value. The chaise and horses were also forfeited to the Crown for having carried smuggled goods.[9] Yet small-time criminals could be intimidated by networks of more distant professional smugglers. The defendants in Pierson's murder trial claimed they were afraid to drag Gipsy George away from the victim in case other smugglers came up and turned on them. Their brutal ringleader may have had dangerous contacts that helped him to maintain his hold over the gang.

In 1784, on the advice of Richard Twining of Twining's Tea Company, Prime Minister William Pitt introduced a bill to reduce tax on tea from 119 per cent to 12.5 per cent. Almost overnight, the Act put an end to smuggling tea. There was so little difference between the price of smuggled and legally imported tea that no one cared to endanger their life for so little profit. Less smuggling meant more tax revenues, given that trade was expanding. That same year, another bill removed duties on rum and spirits imported from the West Indies, which reduced the smuggling of brandy. But before these sensible changes to the law, smugglers had a field day. When no dealer who paid the duty on rum could afford to sell it at less than eleven shillings a gallon, licensed retailers in Rotherhithe and Deptford were knocking it out at 8s. 6d. a gallon.[10] Even local Justices were hostile to excise men and often reduced the fines officers imposed on people for selling ale or spirits illegally.[11] Customs officers never had the resources to stamp out illicit trade but from time to time they did step up their searches for contraband. Successful customs raids prompted violence. It was as if their victories rankled and justified armed resistance.

In the years leading up to the attack on Pierson, customs officers had made notable seizures in Deptford. A breakthrough seems to have happened in the autumn of 1772 when a child gave information about twenty-two Deptford households hiding smuggled goods. Officious customs men even stopped poor sailors bringing a pound of tea ashore, duty free. Such zeal paid off at Rotherhithe when they searched a man with a child of about seven years and found yards of lace hidden under the child's clothes. Retaliation followed: just before Christmas that year, the body of a customs officer was taken out of the river near Deptford. His hands were tied behind him and his throat had been cut.[12] In 1773 there were no fewer than six seizures, two of which netted hauls worth several hundred pounds. Goods ranged from fine Indian cottons and arrack (alcohol from South and Southeast Asia) to Brussels lace. In one case officers got information from a servant by making him drunk. In 1774, a waterman who had helped to ferry goods from a ship tipped them off about Indian silks and taffeta worth £500 in a house at Deptford. That same year officers seized twenty-six sacks of tea hidden under shavings in a cart coming to town. These were considerable losses to local smugglers and tempers ran high. When three men from Deptford were stopped and searched without licence, there was fighting and one officer suffered a fractured skull. The year 1774 ended with a smuggling cutter, laden with tobacco and cambric, being seized and burned at Deptford.[13] To many it represented a terrible waste. Others were conflicted: at Deptford dockyard, fast coastal boats were being fitted out to patrol against smugglers, providing legitimate work for some.

The Pierson affair seems to have dampened ambitious smuggling in Deptford for a couple of years, although goods were seized in a house on Deptford Bridge in 1776 when a waterman's boy suffered a beating from his master and promptly informed on him.[14] Officers stayed vigilant. In July 1777 they even stopped a hearse on the Deptford Road, perhaps remembering a case five years earlier when contraband goods worth £100 had been found in a coffin. This time the coffin contained a dead child. As they told the driver to leave the coffin with them, this too caused indignation.[15]

The 1784 Acts lowering taxes on tea and spirits reduced the volume of contraband goods on the road, but East Indiamen moored in the Thames were a continuing temptation. In 1786 a bloody fight broke out in Deptford when officers tried to search one house near the river. Two customs men were killed and several residents wounded.[16] Eventually, in 1787, customs officials insisted that to prevent smuggling, East Indiamen would have to unload articles of private trade in Long Reach, near sparsely inhabited Purfleet. By 1791 they had to unload completely there rather than at Blackwall or Deptford.[17] But smugglers now had their own troubles: they were reported to be holed up in Guernsey, too afraid of being pressed for the navy to come up the Thames.[18]

Rising crime rate

Smuggling apart, crime was in any case regarded as a problem in London's maritime parishes. It was related to the numbers of seafaring men and prostitutes living there. Crime rates routinely soared at the end of every war, when men were demobilized and unable to find work. Crime also went up during economic and financial crises, especially if there were food shortages. In the second half of the eighteenth century, as much as 85 per cent of crime in London's maritime districts was theft. North of the river, where Old Bailey trial records give reliable data, only 11 per cent of prosecutions for theft involved violence, while 10 per cent were burglary. But violence was more likely to occur during crime waves, when burglary also increased, particularly after 1784 once men had returned from the American Revolutionary War. Wapping was the most crime-ridden of the northern maritime parishes. It had over twice the number of prosecutions as Shadwell, which came next. South of the river, there was a much higher percentage of violent theft, accounting for as much as half of all theft. Most of this was down to the footpads and highwaymen who infested the roads leading into London.

The 1780s saw a massive increase in theft across London. Newspapers reported several cases a day, making readers nervous and suspicious. Even the eagle-eyed Michael Henley could not avoid being cheated – in 1781 one of his men, employed to deliver bagged coal to houses in Wapping, was prosecuted for stealing it and selling it cheap on the side.[19] South of the river, even communion plate and surplices were stolen from church vestries. Soon, theft was considered a pressing social problem and people called for an overhaul of the criminal justice system. But the crime wave was caused by several factors and there was no easy solution: real wages had fallen by 11 per cent,[20] there were poor harvests in 1782 and 1783, the stock market dipped and high food prices made life hard for working classes. And when the American War formally ended in 1783, around 130,000 soldiers and sailors were demobilized. Ironically, overseas trade was doing well.[21] But towards end of decade there were again financial difficulties, which culminated in the economic crisis of 1788. That winter, the frost lasted from November to January 1789, and the Thames froze over.

The increase in theft during the 1780s was entirely down to men; prosecutions against women fell by the end of the decade.[22] Either the authorities targeted unruly men home from the war or women preferred to seek relief from workhouses and other charities. But theft by women was soon on the rise again. Prosecutions for crime north of the river shot up in 1794, when women accounted for over half, and rose again in the early years of the nineteenth century. Violent crime also increased south of the river in the early 1790s. There are plausible reasons for these increases. In 1792, after a bad harvest, the price of corn was nearly 25 per cent greater than during the previous year. The financial crisis of 1793 was the worst of the century and port towns, where trade had been booming, felt the blow hardest. Declaration of war against France that year pushed up prices. Bread riots followed in 1795 and 1796. Yet when crime figures peaked in 1794, male theft did not reach the same level as it had in the 1780s. Perhaps this was because it coincided with the beginning of a war, not the end, and desperate men simply enlisted or got jobs as labourers in maritime-related industries. In contrast, female theft that year was much higher than it had been in the mid-1780s, presumably because women did not go to war.

In this criminal underworld, women could be as active as men, a fact that may be related to the number of female heads of households in the maritime districts. Prostitutes solicited sailors and then robbed them, often with female accomplices, either in bawdy houses run by women or in lodgings. In 1775, two women lured Alexander Hanna, an American colonist on his first visit to London, to their basement in Saltpetre Bank, Wapping. They 'began to use some freedoms' with him, and having distracted him somewhat by unbuttoning his breeches, they seized the money from his pocket and ran. It was more than £54 and they knew at once that they needed help to evade the law. Crossing the river, they sought out Ann Palmer, a known receiver, in Deptford. She passed on some of the coin for them, buying cloth. But her servant turned informer. The women were arrested, tried and sentenced to death but the jury recommended mercy – perhaps because Hanna, in desperation, had previously accused other women of the crime.[23]

Whenever there were peaks of violent theft, more women worked in groups to accost sailors on the street, prepared to add brute force to persuasion. They also committed burglaries, sometimes in mixed gangs. In such cases, if men were found guilty then their female accomplices were usually acquitted. But women were not passively conned into helping men to commit crimes. It is true that some who witnessed fraudulent wills to get seamen's belongings, or who signed letters of attorney to get seamen's prize money and wages, professed, when caught, not to have understood what was being asked of them when they gave their signature. But women initiated daring crimes of their own. In 1776, two women were caught red-handed in Golden Lane, Smithfield, stealing 300 lb (136 kg) of lead from some houses belonging to St Bartholomew's Hospital. One, in her defence, claimed her husband was gainfully employed in Deptford as evidence that she had no motive to steal. But she was found guilty and straightaway branded on the thumb with a 'T' for theft.[24]

Women who ran pawnshops and grocery shops often dealt in goods pirated from the river, buying stock cheap with no questions asked. Women were also routinely tasked with pawning stolen goods – it was presumed that they were better at getting a good price. But it would be wrong to suppose that those prosecuted for receiving were mostly women. Prosecutions for receiving stolen goods went up whenever theft increased but, in maritime parishes north of the river, 51 per cent of these cases involved women. And receiving accounted only for just above 5 per cent of all prosecutions against women. The acquittal rate for women prosecuted for receiving was just over 75 per cent (and over 50 per cent for men). This is much higher than the acquittal rate for female crimes generally. Either it was hard to pin the crime on them, or they gained more sympathy in court. For example, Rosa Samuel in 1765 called character witnesses who testified that she was a good mother, and was acquitted.[25] But in general there is no evidence that women were more lightly punished than men for comparable crimes.

Women were often involved in coining, which became widespread as trade increased, especially towards the end of the 1780s when there was a shortage of coin. They were skilled at 'ringing the changes', or exchanging counterfeit for genuine coins. Their skills helped them to infiltrate gangs of coiners, which may explain why women also acted as paid informers – luring gangs of coiners into the hands of constables. This was the trade of Bridget Lewis whose husband was a pensioner in Greenwich Hospital. She sold apples in summer, was a washerwoman in winter and, having herself been a 'smasher' (someone who passed base coin into circulation), she snitched on others who made a similar living.[26]

Partly owing to the shortage of coin, much of society ran on credit. Women with husbands at sea were especially dependent on female borrowing networks to meet short-term needs, as were the wives of dockyard workers who were always paid late. But maritime districts did not necessarily house a happy sisterhood. There were misunderstandings (perhaps conveniently) about what female employers or acquaintances had agreed to lend. Women might pawn goods that had been 'lent' to them and, if they did not return the goods when the owner expected them back, could be accused of stealing. When prosecuted, the accused might claim that they fully intended to redeem the items but were not always believed.[27] Or, in an alcohol-fuelled environment, neighbours simply fell out and took each other to court. Female pawnbrokers and moneylenders unscrupulously acquired property below market value by appropriating houses left as security. Afterwards, they earned still more by renting them out.[28] These people were not operating a charity.

In desperate times, desperate people took every opportunity to get money. Unscrupulous women decoyed young children and stripped them of clothing, without much sympathy for either the mother's feelings or the infant's.[29] Women who let out rooms had to be cautious – poor tenants were not above pawning the bed linen. Old Bailey cases suggest that many thought they were entitled to do so, as long as they meant to redeem the items. These same trials indicate that landladies were ready to take prompt action and prosecute as soon as goods were missed. The reason is obvious:

if they became known as a soft touch, they would have been cheated time and again. But in 1791, a woman of St Paul's, Deptford, due to be transported for this crime, was reprieved thanks to a local petition claiming that she had been brought up in the parish, her husband and small children were sick of the fever, and she had always intended to return the goods.[30]

Whenever theft peaked, the top two items stolen were money and clothes, followed by a mixed haul of both these together with watches or jewellery. Mixed goods were most often netted through street robbery or burglary. Men and women stole differently. Able to range further afield, men had greater access to industrial workplaces. In prosecutions for theft in maritime parishes north of the river, all stolen goods that might be defined as 'industrial', such as wood, tallow or rope, were taken by men. Because women were less mobile, they were more likely to steal from people they knew, including employers and landladies.[31] But the great thing about the maritime districts was that the world – in the form of hundreds of seamen – came to them. And as the women did not necessarily know these victims, they had more options when defending themselves in court. They could easily cast doubt on the testimony of a drunken sailor, newly landed, who claimed that he could identify the woman who robbed him.

Apart from industrial items, both sexes tended to steal the same things. In fact, more men than women were prosecuted for stealing clothes – reflecting the value of clothing and the ease with which it could be used as currency. Prosecutions for stealing money or household goods were almost the same for both sexes, though there were slightly more cases involving women. More men than women stole cloth (probably reflecting the fact that men could more easily steal cargo from ships on the river). But women were more likely to rob from shops – goods disappeared into their aprons or muffs while they side-tracked the shop assistant – and they also stole pewter items from alehouses.

It is difficult to comment on value of goods stolen since not all of them were necessarily included in a prosecution total, which might be massaged to lessen the punishment due. But, in maritime parishes north of the river, it is noticeable that women were ambitious thieves, particularly when men were at sea. If stolen goods are grouped by value, then women stole more than men in every category, except within a narrow range valued between 20s. and 40s. So, either maritime women were smarter thieves or they had better opportunities for theft.

While some thieves stole from necessity and others may have been spurred to rob the rich by blatant social inequalities, others ignobly preyed on their own. Familiar sights of poverty also made some heartless. To counter this, publications aimed at the middling sort regularly encouraged charity. One such tale focused on a seaman's widow from Wapping, with a child at her breast, who collapsed from hunger in the street. Nearby women thought this might be a ruse to gain money and were prepared to walk by. A young sailor stopped to help. He and a gentleman took the widow to her lodging, and a doctor was called who recommended wine. The sailor at once volunteered to pawn his necktie to buy her a glass.[32] The tale reflects the distress that sailors' widows might be reduced to, living hand to mouth; the hardness that operated in some female relationships, when so many were seeking alms; and the ease with which clothing could be turned into cash. During the French Wars, too, sailors were increasingly used in stories like this as models of spontaneous good-heartedness.

Fighting crime

In eighteenth-century London, law enforcement was a haphazard affair. Each parish paid for a watchman from the public rates who patrolled the streets at night. He was recruited by the beadle, a minor church official, salaried by the parish, who kept an eye on public order: removing vagrants, apprehending prostitutes and reporting people who traded on Sundays. The beadle's wage varied with the wealth of the parish. In 1777, for example, Greenwich paid its beadle £25 annually with a bonus payment of £2 10s. a quarter. He was doing the work of two men, the other beadle having been sacked for misbehaviour, and had complained that he no longer had time to supplement his income with odd jobs. In contrast, a beadle's salary in St Nicholas's, Deptford, was just £19 12s. a year in 1787.[33] There were constables in each parish who oversaw the work of the watchman. At first, they were unpaid and elected annually from local responsible householders. But it was a difficult, time-consuming job and those chosen for office often preferred to pay a fine or hire a deputy. By mid-century, most constables were hired and some served for several years, effectively as professional policemen. Constables interrogated suspects taken up by the watchman and decided whether or not they should go before a Justice of the Peace.

Justices were not paid either, though they could charge a fee for their services. This led to accusations of corruption. Justices were expected to be among the leading men in their locality, suited by birth and education to arbitrate in local affairs. Yet in urban areas particularly, it became hard to get people to serve and the role devolved to merchants and tradesmen. In heavily populated built-up areas, busy Justices attracted abuse from criminals and had to spend a great deal of time listening to distasteful cases. They had no comfortable estate but lived on the profits of their judicial trade. These 'Trading Justices' were the kind that served in London's maritime districts.[34] They were accused of being susceptible to bribery and even of drumming up business to maximize income, though many were hard-working.

Justices of the Peace determined whether defendants deserved summary punishment for such minor offences as drunkenness or selling bread at short weight, or whether they should be tried by jury. Some cases, such as bastardy examinations and hearings to decide whether a pauper was entitled to parish relief or would be removed to another parish, had to be heard by more than one Justice. So these and other small offences came before Magistrates' Courts or Petty Sessions, sometimes held in church vestries. Most people who encountered the law did so through these lesser courts, which were essential to the administration of local government. If the penalty was more than a fine, Justices sentenced criminals to a house of correction – usually for a whipping or hard labour.

Serious crimes north and south of the river were dealt with differently. In the City of London and Middlesex, people accused of felonies were tried at sessions of the peace, and the most serious cases were referred to the Old Bailey courthouse. Before trial, they would be held at Newgate, greatly feared as a place of rampant disease, or at the Marshalsea, a debtors' prison also used for smugglers and pirates. Whenever Newgate became excessively overcrowded, prisoners might be sent to the 'New Gaol' in Southwark, which served Surrey, or to the New Prison in Clerkenwell, which served Middlesex, transferring to Newgate before trial.[35] South of the river, those arrested for felonies in Surrey and Kent would be held in county jails in Southwark and Maidstone before standing trial at the quarter sessions – local county courts held four times a year.[36] From here, the most serious crimes were referred to the assizes.

The assize court judges were appointed by the monarch and travelled around the country on circuits, holding trials twice a year. Surrey and Kent fell within the Home Circuit, which also contained Hertfordshire, Essex and Sussex. So, the Lent assizes for Kent took place alternately at Maidstone and Rochester, while the summer assizes took place at Maidstone. This was over 30 miles away from Deptford, or a four-hour ride at a good trot. By the 1770s, thirty coaches a week left London for Maidstone but the legal process could be expensive even if travel became straightforward. A Greenwich surgeon testifying there in 1772 claimed 10s. 6d. a day for his expenses over five days.[37]

The assizes were a major event. In British constitutional thought, the right to trial by jury was a fundamental element of liberty. The judges' procession to open proceedings was part of the ritual associated with the performance of justice. In July 1768, for example, newspapers reported that judges Lord Mansfield and Mr Baron Smythe had passed through Southwark on their way to Maidstone. They were attended by the High Sheriff and his officers as far as Deptford, where they were received by the High Sheriff of Kent and a 'grand Cavalcade of Gentlemen' who conducted them to Maidstone. After dining, the judges attended church, where the clergyman tailored the sermon to the opening of the assizes. Meanwhile, nineteen felons accused of capital offences waited to be tried.[38] After trial, local petitions might be got up to ask a judge to lessen sentences for convicted criminals. These, some judges felt, were too easy to procure and 'in no wise to be depended upon'.[39]

From 1750, London had a small team of 'runners' (essentially 'thief-takers'), made up of constables and ex-constables, paid for from the public purse and based at Bow Street. Here magistrates were available throughout the day for pre-trial hearings to speed up the justice system.[40] In the 1760s, the arrangement was copied in other parts of London and, whenever trouble was likely, the eastern parishes were patrolled more heavily than those in the west. In 1785, there was a plan to extend the system to the city of Westminster, Blackwall, Deptford, Greenwich and Lambeth. The City of London, keen to preserve its independence, opposed the idea.[41] It permitted a less ambitious plan in 1792, when seven offices were set up in addition to Bow Street. Each had three salaried magistrates and six constables (who, on twelve shillings a week, still relied on rewards to make up their pay).

The maritime parishes had an office in Lambeth Street (which ran north–south between today's Commercial Road and Hooper Square in Whitechapel), and another in Shadwell's High Street, a continuation of Ratcliff Highway. Property owners appreciated having constables nearby, although constables were not above planting stolen goods on innocent victims in order to share the rewards of prosecution.[42] Before this development, Wapping had been a place where criminals could disguise themselves as sailors and easily go to earth. A shipowner, writing to *The Times* in 1792, put the case for better policing of the eastern parishes, perhaps with some exaggeration:

> In that neighbourhood there are some of the greatest receptacles for thieves of every description—(viz.) *Saltpetre Bank, St. Katherine's, Nightingale-lane, Gravel-lane,* and some parts of *Wapping*. I live in Wapping, and am in the habit of passing through all those places almost every day, and I know that were it not that a runner may be got in a few minutes, it would not be safe to pass through either of those places in the middle of the day, much less at night.[43]

Although Southwark had an office, the arrangement did not extend to other parishes south of the river. Still, by 1797, Bow Street operated a patrol, sixty-eight strong. It was organized by parish but could unite to deal with major disturbances. To quell violent crowds, the authorities relied on the army or on London's militia.

The justice system was improving but there were still loud calls for reform. In 1790s Greenwich and Deptford, for example, there were complaints that constables used the office for their own profit, locking up poor vagrants on the least complaint, then escorting them to Maidstone's court at the public expense 'for the pleasure of a ride'. One constable, a trader in spirits, penalized innkeepers who refused to buy his alcohol by billeting soldiers on them. When glaziers, carpenters and painters were elected churchwardens, they tended to overcharge for unnecessary repairs to the local church. To prevent abuse there were calls for annual elections and a barring of unprincipled tradesmen from office.[44]

London's maritime parishes were associated with important milestones in the development of its police force. In 1756, Joseph Cox, High Constable of Blackheath and resident in Deptford, exposed a diabolical scam in which thief-takers conned victims into committing robberies. They apprehended the 'criminals' themselves and claimed the reward.[45] The crime that proved their downfall took place on the Deptford to Greenwich road, close enough to Greenwich to allow them to claim the £40 reward which that parish was offering for the prevention of highway robbery. The villains were sentenced to seven years' imprisonment and each was to be pilloried twice. The fury of the mob was so great that one prisoner was pelted to death. Although Cox sanctimoniously declared that whatever punishment they deserved from the law, no one deserved to be killed through the rage of the populace, this public display of justice was vital to restore confidence in the honesty of the runners.

The maritime parishes are also linked to the development of London's river police. Theft from the river was a growing irritation. As most river workers were complicit and turned a blind eye, thieves stole cargo from vessels even in daylight. In 1785, workers unloading ships were stealing such high volumes that the East India Company turned to the runners, who caught three thieves red-handed. They also arrested a woman for receiving stolen goods, discovering more than eight hundredweight of saltpetre in her house.[46] In 1798, a Thameside police office was finally opened at Wapping New Stairs. The office had magistrates, eight constables and a force of sixty-two surveyors who patrolled the river and quays. West India merchants contributed over £1,500 to the running of this new office but formal legislation was needed to ensure officers were regularly paid.[47]

In communities where street fighting was all too common, there was an element of self-policing. Late one night in July 1768 a Thames waterman came ashore at Deptford Creek with some other men who appeared to be sailors. They broke into a storage house, occupied only by a woman and her female servant, and did great damage. They beat the women, smashed windows, plates and bottles, and destroyed liquors. Luckily some fishermen heard the noise and rushed to the house, giving the intruders a severe drubbing and forcing them to run off. The fishermen also seized the gang's boat and in it found a fine gammon of bacon, which the mistress of the house dressed the next day for their dinner with some beans. Yet such incidents, where justice seemed to be served, were far outnumbered by violent robberies when highwaymen or footpads got clean away.

Crimes might also be detected by watchful neighbours. This was an era when local reputation counted for much. Trust was essential in borrowing networks; many small businesses depended on credit. Neighbours were observant. This was how in 1794 bodysnatchers operating between Deptford and Mile End were caught. Residents grew suspicious when time and again coaches stopped at a house to unload sacks and hampers. When constables stormed the place, they found occupants drinking tea on a bench; at the other end were the corpses of two children. Six adult bodies were in another room, 'besides which the floor was strewed with limbs in a state too shocking for public description'.[48] Those detected in crimes were sometimes punished by the populace, as when a pickpocket was doused in a tar barrel in Deptford dockyard and then stuck all over with prickly burs (a traditional dockyard punishment by its workforce).[49]

Highway robbery

In maritime parishes south of the river, people suffered disproportionately at the hands of footpads and highwaymen. While many certainly attended clubs and social events in the evening, sparsely inhabited roads remained dangerous. Robbers could find easy pickings. In 1774, when a highwayman stopped a man and his wife in their carriage on the Deptford Road, he made off with £200 in rings, watches and cash.[50]

Some victims fought back. On 11 April 1771, at about nine o'clock at night, Colonel Desaguliers of the Royal Regiment of Artillery was heading home to Woolwich in his light, sporty chariot. He had just passed the toll gate on the Deptford Road and was nearing the Five Bells Inn at New Cross when a single footpad came onto the road in front, pointed a pistol at the coachman and yelled at him to stop. As the man pulled up the horses, the robber demanded the colonel's purse. It contained forty shillings and the robber paused to stow it safely in his pocket. But this was no hired coach, and the coachman was loyal to his master. Seeing his chance, he leapt from the box, fell on the thief and tripped him up. The footpad was a strong man, about twenty-five years of age. He managed to struggle up and aimed a blow at the coachman with the butt-end of his pistol. But the colonel had jumped out of the carriage and drawn his sword. In the scuffle, he wounded the robber. The noise brought two other young men on the road to the scene. At the same time, the colonel's footman came up – he had stopped at the turnpike to pay the toll. They got the footpad into the carriage and carried him to an inn in Greenwich where he was put under guard until fit enough to go to prison.[51]

There were known crime hotspots. The 5-mile stretch of Deptford Road, between Shooters Hill, over Blackheath, and through New Cross to the Old Kent Road and London, was notorious. In the 1780s there were some periods when not a night passed without incident. Numerous robberies happened between the Five Bells Inn at New Cross and the Half-Way House tavern, 3 miles out of London, where Kender Street now meets the New Cross Road. One Sunday evening in 1780, two highwaymen robbed no fewer than thirty carriages here. Sundays offered mostly non-commercial traffic but some highwaymen favoured that day because fewer constables were around. Another place that struck fear into travellers was the Peckham Gap, sometimes called Devil's Gap, half a mile farther west. Here, in the spring of 1771, the Greenwich stage was often robbed, even at six or seven o'clock in the evening. In both these locations, highwaymen could ride south, down narrow tracks to escape into countryside.

The Lower Road, which ran through marshy fields between Rotherhithe and Deptford, close to the river, was more suitable for footpads. Their haunt was another Halfway House, at the junction with today's Plough Way. The Dog and Duck tavern, just by the river there, was also a dangerous place for strangers after dark.[52] Footpads usually blacked their faces and some used clothes as well as face-blacking to disguise themselves – often wearing the kind of linen smock associated with tradesmen like tallow chandlers. Some, using knowledge gained from sea travel, invented novel ways to rob the public; in 1775 a gang of pickpockets on the Lower Road first lassoed their victims with a strong rope to prevent them making any resistance.[53]

No one wanted to be robbed, but highwaymen got more respect than footpads. A highwayman tended to be from a slightly higher social rank. The horse he rode was a kind of status symbol. It was expensive to maintain and he risked being identified by the animal, but highwaymen had to be well mounted in order to escape if pursued. Stories proliferated representing highwaymen as intelligent, witty and even urbane. In the summer of 1773 two gentlemen travelling in a post-chaise over Shooter's Hill, Blackheath, were stopped by a highwayman on a good-looking grey horse. He accosted them with the usual, 'Your money or your life!' adding that whatever money they gave him had better be good. He carried a pair of scales in his pocket and would not be imposed upon with light coinage. The gentlemen immediately gave him three guineas and he rode off. As soon as he could, the highwayman weighed the money and found each coin more than two shillings below value. He turned back and soon overtook the chaise between Deptford and London. He swore that if this was the best money the two men could produce, they could have it back again. They solemnly declared that it was, so the highwayman returned it, saying he was too honest to be

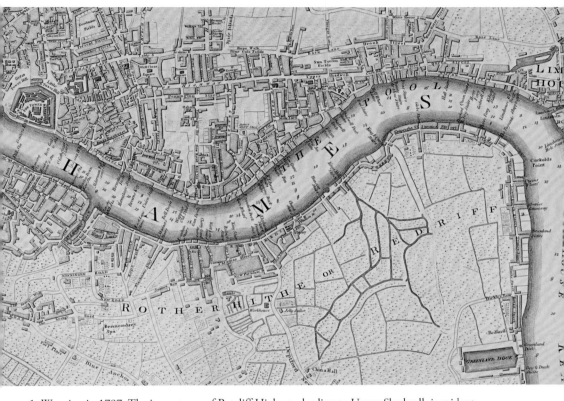

1. Wapping in 1797. The importance of Ratcliff Highway, leading to Upper Shadwell, is evident. Wapping Wall, crowded with wharves and warehouses, follows the line of the river; central Wapping still has orchards and market gardens.

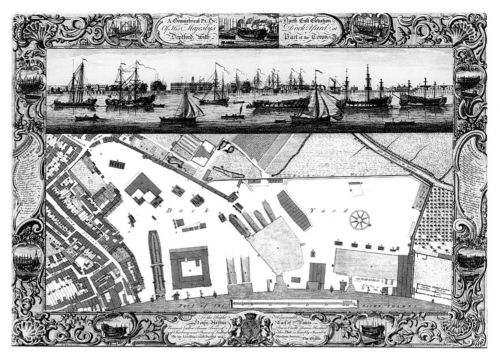

2. Deptford dockyard in 1755, one of a series of views of Britain's six royal dockyards which depicted them as efficient industrial centres. The border vignettes show the stages of building a ship, with its launch as the headpiece. They were probably drawn by John Cleveley, shipwright and artist.

3. The *St. Albans*, a 60-gun warship, is shown being floated out of her building dock at Deptford dockyard in 1747. The building to the left is the master shipwright's house. Built in 1708, it is still standing. The building to the right, with the clock tower, is the Great Storehouse.

4. St Nicholas's church, Deptford, in 1790. Its tower dates from the fourteenth century and the death heads at the entrance gate are still imposing. Charles James Bromley produced this engraving from an earlier study for the part-work *Old and New London*, 1873–78.

5. The Salutation Tavern on the Greenwich riverfront around 1800 (now Cutty Sark Gardens). Fishwives and oysterwomen land the catch amid flirtatious scenes. The tavern sign advertises an 'ordinary' or public dinner on Sundays at two o'clock.

6. London's custom house, 1753. Cargoes had to be registered here as duties were levied on imports and exports. The first custom house was built around 1275 and rebuilt several times. This building, designed by Thomas Ripley, was completed in 1725 and destroyed by fire in 1814.

7. This porcelain punch-bowl, made in China for export, is decorated with drawings of half-built merchant ships copied from European books on shipbuilding and set in an imaginary Chinese landscape. Inside is the inscription 'Success to Mr Barnard's Yard'. It is the only bowl of its type known to have been dedicated to a merchant builder.

8. Oval miniature portraits, 7.5 cm high, of William Barnard. Left, he wears a brown jacket, white lined stock and his own hair, powdered. The miniature is set in a gold frame with blue enamel, seed pearl and hair plait on the reverse. The other portrait of Barnard, right, is by the same artist.

9. The encampment on Blackheath, Greenwich, 1780. Blackheath was often used for military reviews and entertainments. This print shows that women and children travelled with soldiers.

10. The Five Bells public house on the New Cross Road, 1840. The inn was one of many catering for travellers on the busy road from London to Dover. A toll gate operated at New Cross from 1718 to 1865.

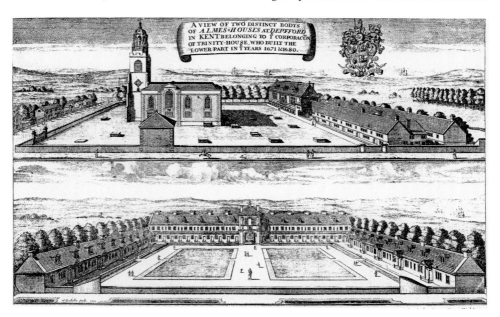

11. Top: Trinity House almshouses near the river and St Nicholas's church (Deptford 'Lower Ground'). The first almshouses on this site are said to date from the fifteenth century. Bottom: Trinity's later, more imposing almshouses in Deptford Church Street (Deptford 'Upper Ground'). From 1866 these fell into disrepair until Trinity House let the site in 1875.

12. Once the American colonies declared independence in 1776, Britain could no longer send convicts to Maryland and Virginia as cheap plantation labour. In this crisis, old vessels were converted into prison hulks. Several were moored on the Thames where convicts, manacled, were put to work.

13. William Bligh's wife, Betsy, by John Webber, 1782. On Cook's third voyage, Webber was official artist and Bligh was master on the *Resolution*. They were present in Kealakekua Bay when Cook was killed. Bligh married Elizabeth in 1781 shortly after *Resolution* came home to London. It has been suggested that this painting was a wedding present from Webber.

14. This portrait of Elizabeth Cook in dignified old age by William Henderson, 1830, was probably done from an earlier drawing or painting. It shows her in a silk calash (collapsible bonnet), ruff and shawl.

15. The Easter fair at Greenwich filled the park and streets of the town until the authorities banned it in 1857 as bad for public order and morality. Among the attractions shown here is a boxing match, within the circle to the left.

16. The 110-gun *Queen Charlotte* was launched at Deptford dockyard in 1810 to the sound of a military band playing 'Rule, Britannia!' and loud cheers from thousands of spectators. The First Lord of the Admiralty christens the ship with a bottle of wine.

17. This watercolour shows the Old Roman Eagle public house and assembly rooms in Deptford Church Street, 1841. It was a popular venue for political meetings, business transactions, dances and other entertainments.

18. A small shipyard, most likely on the Rotherhithe waterfront. This painting commemorates the launch of the vessel on the slipway, centre right, It appears to have the letters 'PO' in a cartouche at the stern and to be destined for the Post Office packet service.

19. An ox has been goaded into running amok on London Bridge, upsetting the Greenwich and Blackheath coach. It is pursued by a mob armed with clubs and dogs. The masts of ships in the river are visible behind.

20. By 1800, Deptford was on the way to becoming an industrial centre. This factory, clad in weatherboard, is typical of local building and shows the scale of early industries near the river.

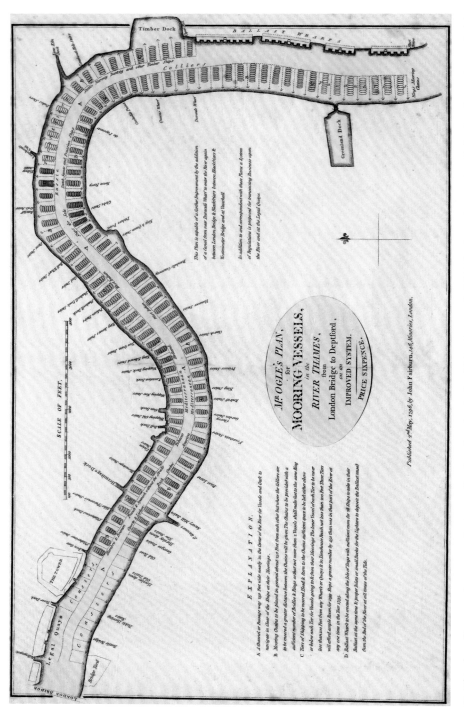

21. This chart illustrates the range and volume of trade to London in the 1790s when nearly 3,500 foreign-going vessels sailed to London each year. Ogle's plan was an attempt to solve the problem of overcrowding in the river.

22. A bird's-eye view of the Brunswick Dock, part of Perry, Wells and Green's shipyard in Blackwall. The mast house in the foreground was a crane for masting ships. In the yard below, horses move shipbuilding timber.

23. This hand-coloured print of 1803 shows the layout of the new London Docks at Wapping. Ships are moored in tiers on the river; the dome of St Paul's is dimly seen in the distance, left.

24. The West India Docks in 1810, showing warehouses at the quayside and West Indiamen moored alongside. Extensive warehousing was needed for thousands of tons of cargo, including sugar, rum, molasses, coffee, spices and hardwood.

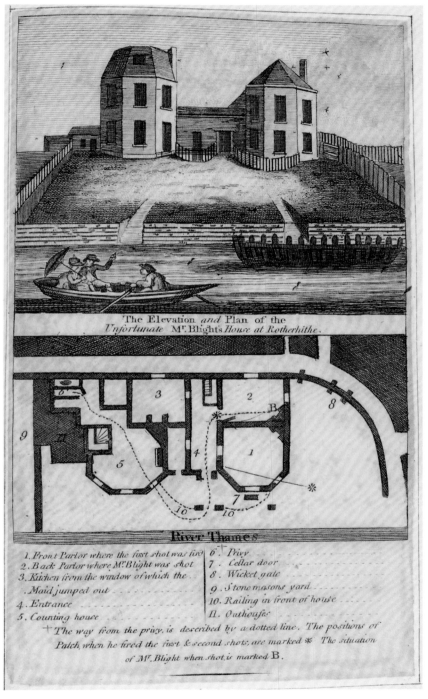

The Elevation *and* Plan of the
Unfortunate Mr Blight's *House at Rotherhithe.*

River Thames

1. Front Parlor where the first shot was fired
2. Back Parlor where Mr Blight was shot
3. Kitchen from the window of which the
   Maid jumped out
4. Entrance
5. Counting house
6. Privy
7. Cellar door
8. Wicket gate
9. Stone masons yard
10. Railing in front of house
11. Outhouses

† The way from the privy, is described by a dotted line. The positions of
Patch when he fired the first & second shots, are marked ✳ The situation
of Mr Blight when shot is marked B.

25. In 1805, shipbreaker Isaac Blight was shot in his parlour. A surgeon summoned from
Guy's Hospital could do nothing for him; Blight died in agony some hours afterwards.
This elevation and plan of his house in Rotherhithe was a response to public interest in
the trial of his murderer.

26. A scene below decks on an East Indiaman. A sailor loads a young woman with contraband goods (tea, rose oil, cognac) which she will smuggle ashore under her clothing.

27. King George III and Queen Charlotte, escorted by horse grenadiers, bowl past the Centurion public house at the junction of Deptford High Street and the Broadway. In a satiric dig, the sign above their carriage advertises the Learned Pig. Trained to answer questions by picking up cards in its mouth, the pig was a sensation in the 1780s.

hanged for being both a clipper and a highway robber – the point being that bogus coin was so rife that rogues would not risk their lives for it.[54]

Highwaymen needed a base. One taken in 1775 had a wife and home in Deptford.[55] Inns sometimes sheltered them and publicans might be associates. Francis Place, the radical tailor, wrote in his autobiography that as a boy in the 1780s, he often saw two or three horses at the door of the Dog and Duck in St George's Fields on a summer evening. People hung around, waiting to see the highwaymen mount, and 'flashy women' came out 'to take leave of the thieves at dusk, and wish them success'.[56] A daring servant regularly borrowed his master's horse for some moonlighting as a knight of the road. The ruse was discovered only when he was wounded one night. A maidservant heard groaning in the kitchen and came downstairs to find him sitting in his greatcoat, stained with blood. At first he claimed to have been hurt while seeing off intruders but then the horse was discovered in the stable, still tacked up, with the saddle all bloody. The man was taken to Guy's Hospital, where he pretended to be more severely wounded than he was so that, when his woman came to visit, he got clean away in the clothes she smuggled in for him.[57]

Perhaps because of the aura that surrounded highwaymen, few victims seemed prepared to tackle them. A vigilant coachman might spot footpads and whip up his horses to get past. It was harder to evade highwaymen. In many cases, they needed to use little force to encourage travellers to give up their valuables. They usually wore black crepe masks to protect their identity, and some managed to evade justice for years. John Martin terrorized roads in Kent from Rochester to London for three years before being taken in 1771.[58] Footpads could not rely on intimidation and had to resort to physical violence.

Newspapers turned robberies into juicy narratives and included details that might help potential victims. Reports indicated where dangers lay, the kind of carriage most easily assaulted, the most vulnerable passengers and the kind of rapid action that might offer protection. Men escorting women were at more of a disadvantage than men travelling together. Footpads targeted light, one-horse carriages, which were less able to thunder past than more powerful vehicles. For those determined to guard their property, a blunderbuss, often carried by naval officers on warships, was a good precaution. It was effective at short range but because the shot dispersed, it tended to wound rather than kill. One footpad who held up a post-chaise on the Deptford Road with a horse pistol quickly made off when the passengers presented a blunderbuss. The gun could also see off highwaymen.[59] But armed, nervous passengers could make mistakes. A man had his brains blown out with a fowling piece when he approached a coach near Deptford and asked it to stop. It turned out he was only trying to get a lift.[60]

In 1775, after a spate of successful robberies, law officers set a trap and travelled, weapons ready, down the Deptford Road. When two footpads stopped their coach, they jumped out and secured them.[61] That same year, four stout sailors took vigilante action against a gang of footpads on the Lower Road. They pretended to be drunk and wandered near the Halfway House to lure the footpads out. A battle ensued in which the sailors captured two of the robbers and sent them to Borough Gaol.[62] In the 1780s, there were nightly horse patrols on the Deptford Road. These began to have some effect, seizing notorious footpads, but residents were unwilling to pay to protect travellers who were simply passing through, so a regular horse patrol was not established until 1805.[63] Luckily, in 1790 the chief magistrate at Bow Street, Sir Sampson Wright, set up a permanent foot patrol in London during the hours of darkness, and this also operated south of the river. Foot patrols stationed themselves near pubs like the Five Bells. It was said that they guarded roads around the metropolis so effectively that criminals returned to its centre, where their presence marred the reputation of 'the first city in the world'.[64]

Convict hulks

In 1776, the Lord Mayor of London chose as his motto, 'Justice is the ornament and protection of Liberty'. This was reported in the press, with no apparent irony, just above a report about uproar in the maritime districts over the pressing of seamen. It was followed by an account of convicts, employed to raise ballast from the Thames, who had escaped from their convict hulk by seizing the arms chest, holding pistols to the jailers' heads, forcing them into the hold, and then making their escape in a longboat which accomplices had brought alongside.[65]

That year, prison hulks for men were set up on the Thames at Woolwich Reach. War with the North American colonies meant criminals could no longer be transported there. In any case, people were beginning to feel that criminals should be punished in ways that were more productive. An Act of 1776 allowed judges to sentence men to hard labour on the Thames and women to hard labour in houses of correction.[66] There had long been calls to dredge the Thames at key locations. Silting at Deptford, for example, limited the size of ships that could be launched there. The public was also hopeful that convict labour might improve the safety of shipping in the river by removing shoals. Some of this ballast was conveniently intended for building and repairing roads. Shipwrights in the naval dockyards were soon tasked with adapting superannuated vessels to make prison ships. By October 1777, there was capacity for 1,200 convicts on the river. It was even reported that a prison hulk for women would be stationed at Blackwall. They would pick oakum and spin yarn for the navy.[67]

Conditions for those sentenced to work as ballast-heavers were severe. They were given only coarse cuts of meat – ox cheek or shins of beef boiled into a greasy soup – and had nothing to drink but water or weak beer. They wore a squalid uniform. No one could visit them except with the permission of the overseer, and whoever gave them the least relief could be fined forty shillings. The expense of these convicts was covered by government, not parish, funds. Relieved of the financial burden of their maintenance, people went to see convicts working and they became something of a tourist attraction. Some escaped to commit robberies locally. Others died in the attempt. Whenever there were serious civil disturbances, naval vessels were sent to guard the hulks in case they were stormed and the prisoners released.[68]

In the early 1780s, a hundred or so convicts who had served their time were simply freed with no provision for how they might get their living afterwards. Naturally, they contributed to the increase in crime that decade. Two were said to have committed a daring robbery on the Deptford Road on the very day of their release. One correspondent wrote to the newspapers asking why such men were not pressed for the navy. It would be doing them a service, he thought, since at the end of a voyage ex-convicts only had to say they had been in the navy to get a job, whereas no one would employ them straight from the hulks. But thieves were the very sort of men the navy did not wish to take, and there was no demand for extra hands in peacetime.[69] Gangs of footpads in the 1780s could be large. When one thief was captured and gave evidence against others, he described a gang of twenty-eight. Soldiers went in search of them and arrested seven, all of whom had recently been released from the hulks. Others in the gang included sailors from ships moored at Deptford, although sometimes footpads dressed as sailors in order to pass without notice.[70]

Before the American Revolutionary War, Deptford residents would have seen convicts from various prisons being ferried out to waiting ships for transportation to the colonies. Wartime disruption meant that such convicts languished in jail for years because their sentence could not be carried out. West Africa was briefly tried as a place for convict settlement: it proved more expensive because convicts could not be sold for labour there. Also, they died in droves from the climate. In 1784 a petition was got up for John Wood, just twenty years old, convicted of highway robbery and sentenced to be transported to West Africa. His health had already suffered from two years in overcrowded New Gaol at Southwark and relatives wanted to save him from what amounted to a death sentence. The petition was ignored.[71] Prisons and hulks became desperately overcrowded but it was only in 1786 that the government finally decided to ship convicts to Botany Bay, Australia. The 'First Fleet' of convict transports sailed in 1787.

There were distressing scenes as convicts were brought to Deptford by river and by cart, often shackled, to await transportation. The government, keen to build up its colony, was against sending women to Australia who were past childbearing age.[72] Many of the women were therefore young and had their children with them. Most had been convicted of petty crimes or streetwalking, and they often arrived wet and miserable. Each had their own sad story. John Nicol, a sailor serving on the *Lady Juliana,* which transported 225 women to Australia in 1789, was particularly struck by one girl, 'as kind and true a creature who ever lived'. She had borrowed a mantle from an acquaintance who later prosecuted her for stealing it. But the same shipment included Mrs Barnsley, a noted shoplifter. She boasted that for a century her family had been swindlers and highwaymen, and her brother, 'a knight of the road as well dressed and genteel in his appearance as any gentleman', often visited her on board before the ship sailed.[73]

Deptford locals may have felt a personal tie to the Australian scheme. Deptford shipwrights repaired and adapted vessels for transporting the convicts; butchers in the victualling yard slaughtered and salted thousands of animals to supply them on the voyage.[74] Afterwards the yard sent tons of supplies to maintain the new colony. At least one resident, the shipwright Daniel Paine, spent part of his career there.[75] There was money to be made from the transportation system, which led to notable hypocrisies. The banker William Curtis, son of a wealthy Wapping biscuit maker and Sheriff of London from 1788 to 1789, criticized the harsh treatment of convicts on the voyage but was himself an investor in the First Fleet. He was part-owner of the *Lady Penrhyn*, which shipped out most of the female convicts, observed to be largely naked and filthy when they embarked.

Securing a conviction

In Deptford, there was more recorded crime in St Paul's parish than in St Nicholas's, which was hemmed in by the river, smaller and poorer. But the naval dockyard near St Nicholas's church suffered huge amounts of petty theft. Wives bringing food to dockyard workers during breaks, and permitted to gather offcuts of wood ('chips'), regularly left with iron spike nails concealed in their baskets. Labourers, with less to lose than better-paid shipwrights, routinely filched timber, iron and bags of nails. Some, working in gangs, got away with much more: they were caught stealing slops (sailors' clothing), old rope and even sails and anchors.[76] Theft also occurred in the private yards. Two brass cannon were stolen from a naval vessel being repaired in the yard Frances Barnard owned in 1799.[77] The widow was beside herself in case the navy refused to give her further contracts. She told her foreman to do all he could to find the culprit and a man was duly convicted. Local petitions were raised claiming that he was just a passer-by who happened to be near the cart in which the stolen cannon were concealed, but the judge thought such petitions 'easily procured' and let the sentence of transportation stand.

It could be difficult to secure a conviction for stealing naval stores. Jurymen at the assizes often came from Deptford; many in the community would give the accused a character reference.[78] A death sentence might readily be reduced to transportation. But there was increasing intolerance of embezzling naval equipment. In 1800, local petitions to reduce the sentence of a seventeen-year-old shipwright's apprentice, convicted of stealing copper, were unsuccessful. In 1805, a widow and keeper of a chandlers' shop found guilty of receiving stolen copper, and with a previous conviction for the same, was refused mercy despite being more than sixty years old. She was transported for fourteen years.[79]

The river offered a quick transport route for burglars. At first light on 29 April 1774, four armed men rowed upriver with the tide and landed at Deadman's Wharf, Deptford, just above the victualling yard. One was left in charge of the boat, another set to watch in Grove Street, which ran between open fields and Dudman's shipbuilding yard. Two men broke into a house on the street. They stripped the lower floor of all the most valuable things and then tried to go upstairs. As they forced open the door to the stairs, they rang the bell fixed to it and alarmed the mistress of the house. There was only a wainscot between her house and the next, and now she rapped against it sharply. The man next door anxiously asked if a fire had broken out. 'Thieves!' she cried. At once, he leapt out of bed and threw open his sash window. Spotting the fellow in the street at watch by the front door, he discharged his pistol at him. The fellow made off groaning and certainly wounded. The sound of the pistol shot brought the two thieves out of the house. Each fired back at the neighbour in the window but missed him. The mistress of the house slept with a loaded gun in her chamber, and seeing that the thieves had shot at her neighbour, she opened her window and fired her gun at them. She aimed too high and the shot went through the glass of the house on the other side of the street, narrowly missing a young lady just opening her shutters to see what was the matter. The men got clean away with their booty, rowing swiftly in the direction of Limehouse Reach.[80]

This well-planned burglary reveals a number of things. While local houses might be two storeys, and equipped with locks and alarm bells, many were only wooden-framed and residents were used to little privacy. Also, Deptford people had goods worth stealing: when the house of William Jacobs was burgled in 1775, thieves made off with plate and other valuables worth £300.[81] In comparatively secluded areas, householders took precautions and armed themselves. Women, like men, had no compunction about firing guns, though perhaps could have done with more practice. In September 1774, a corn lighterman living near Deptford similarly discharged a blunderbuss from his window at four ruffians who were trying to gain entrance to his house. One of them was thought to be mortally wounded, crying out 'by G—d he has done for me'. The forces of justice seem to have been fully on the side of this householder, too.[82]

When crimes were judged to be particularly heinous, the authorities framed punishments calculated to shock and deter others. In 1773, Elizabeth Herring of Wapping was sentenced to death by burning for murdering her husband. He was an abusive waterman and she stabbed him in the throat during a quarrel in a public house. Burning was the specified punishment for women guilty of treasonable acts, such as coining, or (as in this case) reversing the normal social hierarchies, but only seven women received the sentence in this half-century. She was taken from Newgate to Tyburn in a sledge drawn by four horses. Having been hanged for twenty minutes, the faggots piled beneath were set alight and her body was consumed to ashes. In another shocking case, William Passmore, who set fire to his Deptford house for the insurance money but destroyed properties either side, was hanged in 1789 on temporary gallows set up in Butt Lane at the site of his crime. Passmore was so loathed that residents pelted him in the cart as he was taken to the place of execution.

The extraordinary thing is how people coped with so much daily violence.

5

SPIRITED WOMEN

On 19 August 1789, Captain William Bligh, wrestling with the heat and humidity in Timor, Southeast Asia, finally sat down to write to his wife, whom he had not seen for over a year. The story he had to tell was of mutiny and failure. It was also a tale of desperate survival. His right-hand man, Fletcher Christian, along with other disaffected crew members, had seized his ship, the *Bounty*, and set him adrift in the ship's launch, together with the men who stayed loyal to him. His mission to carry bread-fruit plants from Tahiti to the West Indies had ended in utter humiliation. Yet he had managed to sail the open boat some 3,900 nautical miles to the island of Timor. His sailors suffered agonies of hunger and thirst but all landed alive, except for one killed by islanders on Tofua, their only stop. It was an important letter – both on a personal level and as a record of events. He focused all his powers on getting it right:

My Dear Dear Betsy

I am now in a part of the world that I never expected, it is however a place that has afforded me relief and saved my life, and I have the happyness to assure you I am now in perfect health . . . Know then my own Dear Betsy, I have lost the Bounty … Christian having the morning watch, He with several others came into my Cabbin while I was asleep, and seizing me holding naked Bayonets at my Breast, tied my Hands behind my back, and threatened instant distruction if I uttered a word.[1]

The letter took six months to reach England. What must have been Elizabeth Bligh's feelings as she sat down to read and reread this news in Wapping, struggling to take it in, contending with London's street noises outside and the racket of her nursery inside? Already, she had five daughters: the oldest was eight and the youngest, twins, just over a year old. Her domestic responsibilities were intensified by constant anxiety. Yet despite the new fears Bligh's long letter brought, it allowed her to support his account of the mutiny until he could put his case in person. She would also reassure her young family that their father was well and on his way home. Over time, this and similar trials would damage her nerves and physical health.

Seamen's wives

Women had many relationships with seamen: as wives, cohabitants, land-ladies, mistresses and prostitutes. Traces of their lives emerge from private letters and public sources, such as newspapers. All, in varying degrees, were economically dependent on sailors, but different ranks of women, attached to different kinds of seamen, could look forward to different prospects. Most shouldered responsibility for the home; some also worked. A few achieved public notice. Their stories, with those of other women along the river, help to build a picture of women's work and life chances in maritime London. Here, as across Britain, there were more women linked to seamen in the second half of the eighteenth century than ever before. During the American War, the British navy grew from about 10,000 men at the outset to around 100,000 by 1780. During the French Wars from 1793 to 1815, an estimated 600,000 served in the navy, perhaps more.[2] Trade also expanded. Career sailors like James Cook and William Bligh often moved between the merchant and naval service, depending on whether the country was at peace or war.

For women in relationships with long-distance sailors, the year was regulated by seasonal arrivals and departures largely determined by winds blowing in distant parts of the world. In London, more than half of all ship departures took place between October and February. Most returned between June and November. This was the pattern followed by vessels trading to Jamaica: captains aimed to avoid the worst of the Atlantic hurricane season from August to October. Those in the tobacco trade with the American colonies aimed to get to the Chesapeake by June when the crop was packed. East India Company vessels left the Thames between December and April. Their return, and the rich cargos they carried, were eagerly anticipated from June if they sailed from India, and from September if they were coming from China.

During the months when seamen were away, their women shouldered most of the domestic burdens, turning to relatives, friends and neighbours for support. Women kept in touch with their menfolk as best they could, exchanging letters and obtaining news from seafaring networks. It is notoriously difficult to estimate literacy levels but between 1700 and 1790 it seems that literacy remained steady at 60 per cent for men, and rose in women from 40 to 50 per cent.[3] The poor with access to charity schools would be taught to read the Bible and, if unable to write, could usually find someone to scribble a letter for them. Communication with absent seamen might be irregular but their letters were highly prized, not least because information at first-hand usually proved more reliable than newspaper accounts.

Women whose menfolk were in the coastal trade, rather than long-distance trade, saw them more regularly. If married to shipmasters, women might also take on added financial responsibilities. Whilst most sailors were paid at the end of a voyage, some arranged for part of their wages to be paid monthly to their families. In port towns, masters' wives often took on this task, alongside local tradesmen prepared to give credit. These women might keep pubs, or businesses that supplied the shipping industry, so they had the ready money to pay allowances to seamen's families. The shipowner reimbursed them later. But the system could break down: a captain might stop a crew member's allowance if he feared a mutiny. And if a man deserted, his money was stopped at once. Sometimes the system was simply not set up correctly. Families suffered, perhaps with no means of knowing exactly what had happened.[4]

In 1797, John Allden, a seaman on one of Henley's ships bound for Gibraltar, wrote to his wife to ask if his 'deal gall' was getting her monthly forty shillings. The spelling gives an indication of his Suffolk accent. He was worried because a shipmate had got a message from his wife in London complaining that she had not been paid; the paperwork had not been properly endorsed. He addressed his letter to himself, to be left at a tavern called the Ship in Pakefield, Suffolk. It somehow reached his wife. It is now filed in the archives with a note from his captain to the Henleys confirming that Allden's behaviour was satisfactory (and therefore that the allowance should be paid). The captain also asked the Henleys to pay the wives of several other crew members, some of whom wrote messages to friends and relations at the bottom of his note.[5] But Allden's wife, who presumably could read but not write, now had to seek help from another source. Eliza Graham of Pakefield wrote to the Henleys:

> Gentlemen I take the liberty of addressing you in behalf of a distressed woman and three children, to grant them the favour if you have any correspondents at Lowestoft, Beccles, or Yarmouth, to transmit their monthly pay as they are at two great a distance to come or send for it and it is their only support – Be pleased to pay into the hands of the Bearer the months pay that is due, and beg a line by the same person informing me if it is possible to have the money conveyed to her, and her children as it will greatly relieve them.[6]

This story shows how seamen's women managed to get by, relying on others to help overcome problems of distance and literacy.

The housewifely duties of some women with husbands at sea or in seagoing trades extended to providing clothes and equipment for the boys employed by their husbands and under their care. In 1780, Michael Henley's wife, Mary, went to a slopseller and bought clothes, two knives and two combs for one of her husband's apprentices to take on board.[7] The wives of naval carpenters clothed their husbands' assistants. Even the genteel wives of naval captains could be asked to procure caps and jackets for the boys on their husbands' ships. The clothing was packed into the regular parcels they sent to husbands at sea.[8] All such purchases helped to knit seamen's wives into the local maritime community.

The government slowly woke up to the fact that seamen's women were an important social group. Britain certainly depended on naval wives as well as on the navy itself for defence and trade protection. Women made it possible for men to serve at sea for long periods; the government had to make regular provision for them. The 1758 Navy Act allowed seamen overseas to send money home on a yearly basis, six months in arrears. Fewer than 5 per cent of them did so. In 1795, a Navy Act enabled men to allot part of their wages to dependants every twenty-eight days. This system was more effective. If a man died in service, his wife or mother received his outstanding wages and prize money in a lump sum. Interestingly, the amount was always much more than soldiers' wives could expect and sometimes allowed seamen's families to join the lower ranks of the middling sort.[9]

Elizabeth Cook

James Cook's wife lost her naval husband not in war but in pursuit of imperial power through exploration. Her trials as a seaman's wife were extreme, and prolonged through fifty-seven years of widowhood. In 1762, towards the end of the Seven Years War, Cook had returned with £291 19s. 3d. in back pay and a firm resolve to get a wife. He had left the coal trade for the navy at the beginning of the war, risen to the rank of master and won recognition for his surveying and charting skills. Largely self-educated, a man who had mastered astronomy, Euclid and map-making in his limited leisure time at sea, he was formidably single-minded and on an ambitious path. On 21 December, he married Elizabeth Batts in Barking, then a fishing port about 8 miles east of Shadwell. Elizabeth was attractive, intelligent and, at twenty-one, thirteen years his junior. They probably met while she was visiting her mother in Shadwell but, as Cook had only ever spent short periods in London between ships, it must have been a brief romance. There was no time for the banns.

It was a respectable marriage. He was clearly a competent officer with a promising career. She came from a family that was good with money and fairly well-to-do. Her mother ran a tavern in Execution Dock and other relatives in Bermondsey were curriers (leather workers). Crucially, she was self-reliant and could be trusted to run a home in his absence. During their seventeen-year marriage, they lived together for four years, and never more than a few months at a time. Elizabeth obligingly got pregnant whenever he returned and gave birth to six children: five sons and a daughter. After a few months of married life, Cook departed in April 1763 for North American waters to survey Newfoundland. The work was well paid at ten shillings a day and he was soon trusted with extra responsibility. He returned towards the end of November, when he saw his eldest son for the first time. This was to be the pattern for the next few years: summers spent surveying overseas, winters spent at home, perfecting charts.

At first, the couple rented in Shadwell where Elizabeth could be close to her mother. Then, in 1764, with wages from his last voyage, Cook purchased a sixty-one-year lease on No. 7 Assembly Row, facing the Mile End Road. It was a typical narrow-fronted, Georgian terraced house, next to a gin distillery and certainly not the grandest in the street. But given that so many Londoners lived in overcrowded, rented rooms, and when even better-off shopkeepers chose to live at ground level and rent out upper floors, this eight-roomed family house delighted Elizabeth and signified that Cook was doing well. Before leaving for his summer surveying in 1764, he insured it for £200 with the Sun Fire Office.

In 1768, Cook was chosen for an arduous voyage to the Pacific. He was to record the Transit of Venus across the face of the Sun from Tahiti. This, astronomers hoped, would help them calculate the distance of the Earth from the Sun, and improve navigation. Cook was also given secret instructions to search for an undiscovered continent that experts reasoned had to be in the southern hemisphere to balance the mass of Europe and Asia. On 23 June 1768, he reinsured his house for £270 before sailing. Increasingly prosperous, he added to his policy goods worth £200, clothing worth £50, plate worth £25 and a timber shed behind the house valued at £10. Elizabeth could take some comfort that her husband was doing what he could to protect her welfare when absent.[10]

With her two sons and a daughter, Elizabeth was now left to carry out the usual role of a sailor's wife – maintaining the house, bringing up the children and looking after her husband's interests. She had a garden; there were fields nearby. The area was more respectable than others closer to the river but, tied as she was to small children, and given the dangers of travelling too far alone, even with servants, her life was circumscribed. Separation was harder to bear because communication with the Pacific was less certain than with Europe or the British colonies. It was normal to hear nothing for six months or more. Cook would have given her the names of naval officials whom she could turn to. She had family nearby in Shadwell and in Bermondsey. Cook had also taken her relation, Isaac Smith, with him – a favour that gave her an additional claim to support from relatives. Their help was needed. A third son, Joseph, was born and died in 1768 without Cook ever seeing him. Elizabeth's mother, who lived in Star Street, Shadwell, died in January 1771. In April, a daughter, who had been just one when Cook left, also died. Elizabeth had to cope with all these bereavements without her husband.

Cook returned in June 1771, after an absence of nearly three years, bringing home exotics from the South Seas: Tahiti barkcloth (tapa), shells and other items he had collected. There would have been an awkward period of readjustment as he took up his role as head of the house. Now he could advise Elizabeth on his sons' education – there were some well-established schools in Stepney. As both boys were destined for the navy it was understood that when the time came he would get them places at sea.

He was at home for barely a year before leaving on a second Pacific voyage. While he was away, Elizabeth had to endure the death of a fourth son. Yet Cook's second voyage was another triumph. In July 1775, he returned a hero, to be feted at court and by learned societies. He was still a busy man, transcribing his journal for publication, but fixed at home. In August, he was offered a position at Greenwich Hospital with a comfortable salary. He was being honourably pensioned off; Elizabeth dared to hope that her happiness would last. But he could not reconcile himself to the prospect. He wrote to an old friend in Whitby:

A few Months ago the whole Southern hemisphere was hardly big enough for me and now I am going to be confined within the limits of Greenwich Hospital, which are far too small for an active mind like mine.[11]

A third voyage to the Pacific was mooted, nominally to return Omai, an islander brought to London on Cook's second voyage. But chiefly the expedition was to search for the Northwest Passage – this time from the Pacific side, since Commodore Phipps's 1773 voyage from the Atlantic had produced no results. Lord Sandwich, First Lord of the Admiralty, knew that Cook was best qualified to command the expedition. He also knew it would be unfair, after two gruelling voyages, to ask him to lead a third. In January 1776, he invited him to dinner with other members of the Admiralty, ostensibly to take his advice about the new venture. It seems that in the course of the evening, Cook – fired with enthusiasm for this latest voyage – offered to lead it himself. He may have been pressured into doing so, but he was not ready to take a safe berth. His wife's feelings can easily be imagined. For the remainder of his stay at home, he was occupied with preparations for the expedition as well as his publication. James Boswell, who now met the couple, was amazed to think that such normal-looking people could be linked to such extraordinary feats: 'It was curious to see Cook, a grave steady man, and his wife, a decent plump Englishwoman, and to think that he was preparing to sail around the world.'[12] The explorer departed in July 1776, less than two months after his fifth son was born.

Cook was killed in 1779 by Hawaiians. His bones, scraped clean and charred, were returned to his ship, along with part of his scalp and his hands, which identified him. They had been preserved in salt. The body parts were buried with full honours at sea. News of his death reached England in 1780 and George III immediately called for his widow to be given a pension. Although financially secure, Elizabeth was devastated by her husband's death. When in 1782 a biographer asked for details of her husband's voyages to enliven his account, she turned pathetically to Dr John Douglas, Canon of Windsor, who had helped Cook to prepare the journal of his second voyage for publication. 'I am not able to write a single Word upon so very distressing a subject. Indeed I can recollect no particulars', she wrote, asking for his help to do what she could not do herself.[13] The tapa waistcoat she had been embroidering for Cook remained unfinished.[14]

More tragedy followed: she was to see all her surviving sons die in succession. Nathaniel was lost at sea aged sixteen in 1780. Her youngest, Hugh, destined for the church, caught scarlet fever at Cambridge University and died in 1793 aged seventeen. James, her eldest, drowned aged thirty-one in 1794. His boat overturned as he was returning to his ship. He had been advised to wait for calmer weather but the achievements of his father put pressure on him to act boldly. At this point, Elizabeth burned all Cook's letters. Some thought it was because nothing else could efface painful memories. Yet perhaps she was determined to keep something of her husband to herself; she had already lost so much to public service.

Elizabeth went to live in Clapham, sharing a house with her cousin, Admiral Isaac Smith, who had sailed with Cook on his first voyage. The admiral retired from the navy in his fifties, having contracted hepatitis in the East Indies. Later he inherited property in Merton, after which the two of them spent winters in Clapham and summers in Merton. Elizabeth lived in an age when the tittle-tattle of provincial ladies could break a reputation. She guarded her respectability. Every Thursday at 3 p.m. she held a sedate dinner party for her friends; she fasted on the anniversaries of the deaths of her husband and three sons, spending these days meditating and reading the Bible. She lived to be ninety-three and always wore mourning and the ring with her husband's hair in it. She treasured the coffin-shaped memento containing locks of his hair that the crew of his final voyage had made for her. She hoarded the curiosities that Cook had brought home, but in old age gave many items away as marks of esteem. Her physician of later years received the superior edition of Cook's second voyage awarded her by the Admiralty.

To the end, she guarded her husband's reputation. When pressed to comment on reports of him being severe and reserved, she always emphasized his benign qualities as a husband and father. In accordance with her wishes, she was buried in Great St Andrews, Cambridge, near two of her sons. In an eleven-page will, she bequeathed £60,000 to relations, friends and charities. Cook's gold Copley medal went to the British Museum. She left money to the Royal Maternity Charity; she knew about childbirth in difficult circumstances. In some ways, her life was typical of women who married sailors – seeing her husband at rare intervals, having (and burying) children in his absence, and outliving him after his sudden death in service. In other respects, she is highly unusual – a diffident public figure who became wealthy, pensioned and a resource for folk who wanted to know about Cook.

The labouring poor

In busy maritime parishes, women were highly visible in the world of work. True, much of their labour was low-paid and unskilled: women worked in domestic service, in making or mending clothes, nursing and midwifery, victualling, shop keeping, street vending and textile production. Typically, seamen's wives might have seasonal jobs, take in plain sewing, or work as washerwomen when their eyesight failed with age. To make ends meet, they turned to kinship and borrowing networks in their husbands' absence. Some, as we have seen, chanced the workhouse or resorted to criminal activity. Workhouses did not always take in women if they were capable of work. They might supply clothing and even small sums of money so that women could subsist as street hawkers. In April 1777, Elizabeth Beazley was dismissed from the Greenwich workhouse with a pair of shoes and a shilling to buy periwinkles (the shellfish, in season from March to October, were popular with courting couples and others who liked a leisurely meal). Mary Barker, claiming out-relief in December 1778, was allowed four shillings to buy a basket and sprats to sell. In the parish of St Nicholas, Deptford, the workhouse gave another woman five shillings in 1781 to buy greens to peddle on the streets.[15]

Whenever it seemed a parish might recoup such funds, they were treated as loans, which also left the poor some self-respect. In 1783, Jane Leach was dismissed from the Greenwich workhouse with 3s. 6d. to buy silk for knitting purses and trinkets to sell; she promised to repay the money from her profits at the rate of six pence a week. Similarly, in 1790, Ann Mitchell was allowed four shillings to set herself up in the fish trade, agreeing to repay the loan at four pence a week. (Wartime inflation meant that the same stock cost six shillings in 1797.)[16] Workhouse records help us to understand the range of female employment on the margins of society, and the kind of choices facing poor seamen's women. They also show the trades that workhouse committees chose to support when aiming to keep the poor from vagrancy, promote industry and maintain order in the neighbourhood.

The poor valued the medical attention available in the workhouse, which formed part of their local support network. In 1796, for example, the surgeon in the Greenwich workhouse responded to the pleas of one of the nurses working in Greenwich Hospital and undertook to cure her daughter of venereal disease. The cost was one guinea, and he agreed it could be paid in two instalments.[17] The community sent into the workhouse women who miscarried in the street, foreign seamen who arrived in port ill and even lone victims of street crime. Still, women who were forced to place their children in the workhouse knew it was not always a safe refuge. Young girls were apprenticed 'upon liking' to local tradesmen and it was not unknown for them to be raped. Workhouses did sometimes press charges, in spite of legal costs. In 1771, the Greenwich workhouse paid the expenses of its surgeon, churchwarden and several witnesses when they gave evidence in a rape case at the Maidstone assizes.[18]

The dangers that faced young girls were related to the social status of poor, single women. Low-ranking sailors who left sweethearts behind might well have worried about their vulnerability. A tragic event sheds light on attitudes of the time. In September 1751, a young maidservant working for a prosperous tradesman in Deptford's Union Street (now Albury Street) seized her chance when her master was away from home to invite friends into the house. The deception was to prove fatal. As a newspaper later reported, the group was fooling around in high spirits when one of the men – said to be her lover – spotted a rusty sword and a flintlock pistol in the room. He picked them up with a flourish. Pointing the pistol at her head, he felt for the trigger and fired. The pistol was loaded and he killed her instantly. According to the newspaper, he hadn't suspected any danger and the episode had driven him frantic.

Readers would have brought a range of common perspectives to the case, the most obvious being that young servants were no better than they should be and needed supervision. Left in sole charge of a house, domestics tended to abuse their position. (The maid was clearly not entertaining her friends in the servants' quarters.) It was not unusual for a wealthy tradesman to have a loaded weapon in his home, next to a naked (if rusty) blade. Weapons were easily available; levels of street violence and the risk of burglary meant that it was prudent to have them to hand. But the master of the house had not thought to tell his female servants that he kept the gun loaded – the fun-loving girl had no idea that the pistol was primed or she could have shouted out a warning. Some newspaper readers would have shaken their heads over the tragic incident. Others would have commented that it showed the danger of the lower classes exceeding their station: the servant was 'romping' on Sunday with her 'favourites' in a way that no well-brought-up young lady would.

The tone of the report reveals much about the position of young servant women even in this parish, mostly comprising skilled workers. The woman's fate was not considered a particularly important story. In an age when choice news items were repeated word for word in different newspapers, it appeared just once. It carried no suggestion that the young man would be held responsible, let alone brought to justice. His version of the story was not, apparently, called into question. Quite simply, the woman's death was 'a melancholy accident'. This account was followed by yet another factual report, in the breathless manner of newspapers of the time without any headline to signal a pause: a new ship for the East India Company, just launched near Deptford, was shortly bound for China. In the second half of the eighteenth century, London was already a trading centre of worldwide importance. In this global context, the fate of an indiscreet maidservant was of passing interest.[19]

The mishap took place during a period of disruption and social unrest after the War of the Austrian Succession (1740–48). There was rapid demobilization, unemployment, food shortages and even fears of a moral collapse.[20] But such turbulence was a recurring problem in a century wracked by wars and mounting prices. The Gordon Riots during wartime, in 1780, show that violent unrest could be quite unrelated to demobilization. Women, like men, could be unruly, and the riverside neighbourhoods were not short of gangs of young females. In 1786, a group lay in bed all week in the Greenwich workhouse, refusing to work. They were clogged with a piece of hardwood weighing several pounds fixed to the ankle, fed only bread and water, and publicly whipped in the workroom by the beadle. Another truculent group in 1797 beat their clogs on the floor, abused the old women and smashed crockery. Summoned before the workhouse committee, they swore roundly, refused to be cowed and were very impertinent. The committee ordered them to be placed in straitjackets, fed on little and kept in separate rooms well away from each other. A fortnight later their clogs were removed for good behaviour. Probably, what really quietened them down was that their ringleader had to be put under the surgeon to be treated for venereal disease, contracted during one of their escapes over the workhouse wall.[21]

The girls' aggressive stance before the committee was rash, but violent punishment had become the norm, albeit behind closed doors. A woman who absconded over the wall might be stripped naked to the waist and whipped by the beadle until her back was bloody.[22] At the lowest level, life for seamen's women in this environment could be a brutal experience. In 1781, a group of women ferociously attacked the warden of Deptford dockyard when he stopped them picking up wood at the gate.[23] Spirited women were not afraid to join bread riots or denounce crimp houses (informal recruiting houses where men were held against their will). In August 1794, women played a major part when rioters tried to pull down London's most infamous crimp houses. The disorder was widespread, reaching Wapping and Deptford.[24]

It was safer for women to stay within a support network of neighbours, tradesmen who might give credit, and local pawnbrokers, rather than follow their menfolk's ships to different ports. The choice was emotionally difficult. At ports, there were often sailors' women – real and feigned – begging for money and complaining that they had been left behind when the fleet sailed.[25] As ever, some commentators tried to deflect these harsh and degrading aspects of Britain's maritime power by using humour. The figure of the 'Wapping Landlady', for example, circulated in prints, literature and dance pieces for the stage. She was depicted as a rotund brothel keeper, who cheerfully overcharged seamen for sex and drink until their money ran out, then urged them back to sea. The phrase was soon used flippantly to describe a type of dishonest tavern keeper. The predatory situation behind the image, in which young women as well as men were cruelly exploited, became blurred as part of normal life in maritime districts.

Women in business

Higher up the social scale, the wives of tradesmen, skilled workers and ship's masters were women of substance and a force for stability in maritime communities. Some worked alongside their husbands; others had their own businesses. In this period, a married woman had no separate legal identity and her husband had ownership rights over her property. But marriage, if amicable, did not restrict a woman's enterprise. Anyway, if a husband could legally take his wife's profits, he was also liable for her debts.[26] Affluent families might draw up marriage settlements so that husbands had no rights over a woman's inherited wealth. The lower middling sort made these precautionary arrangements too. At the end of their lives, such women independently willed money to friends and relatives as they saw fit.

Jane Weatherall, whose father supplied stores to the navy, inherited properties in Flagon Row, Deptford (provided, while underage, she married with the consent of her mother). When she did marry, a settlement was drawn up to protect her inheritance. A lease of 1768 gives an insight into Jane's business interests. That year, she let one of her shops to a spinster for an annual rent of fourteen pounds, stipulating that her workmen would inspect the property twice a year to make sure it was properly maintained. When it was sold to a shoemaker in 1801, its description gives a vivid picture of the responsibilities shopkeeping involved. Fixtures included:

> All the Counters, Glass Cases, Desk and Drawers & Shop Fittings in the shop, and the Binns Dressers and Fixtures in General in the Leather Cellar – the lead water pipe from the main, brass cocks, Lead Cistern & Sink, one Glazed Cupboard in the Kitchen, all the Grates and Stoves, the Copper and Dresser in the Kitchen, Water Butts & Border Boards in the Garden, all the Interior Locks on the Rooms and Closet doors – the Bells as hung the Festoon laths to the Windows and other trivial articles Window blinds etc.[27]

The purchaser also had the option of taking the floor cloths and carpets at a fair price. All the fixtures were sold for £80.

Intelligent, well-connected women could make substantial sums of money in retail and property. The business environments of London's maritime districts gave them scope to succeed and to enjoy a display of their wealth. Mary and Elizabeth Slade were in the haberdashery business together and shared a house in Deptford. Neither married. This was a period when specialist haberdashery boomed as more people imitated the latest fashions.[28] The sisters also prospered from government contracts – supplying material to the dockyards for upholstery and flags – and from renting out the property they accumulated. The royal barges were kept at Deptford, which perhaps explains why their nephew Benjamin, purveyor of the dockyard, was placing orders with his aunts for quantities of green damask, green lace, the making and stuffing of cushions, and quality binding, as well as for stronger types of cloth.[29]

The sisters' wills not only show what they bought with their money, they also reveal their sense of family obligation. Elizabeth died first, in 1786. She willed the two local houses that she owned to her sister. She left her government bonds to her nephews, and the interest on them to her sister during her lifetime. Perhaps their business was partly financed by this regular investment income. The value of these bonds is unclear since, apart from specific bequests totalling £160, Elizabeth simply divides the remainder of her investments equally among male relatives. All her bequests were to be paid on the death of her sister, Mary, except one to a female relative for £30 which was to be paid when she became twenty-one, presumably to contribute to her dowry or independence.

Elizabeth left all her clothes, furniture, plate, silver, china and household goods to her sister. After her sister's death, members of the family were to receive key pieces. These bequests indicate the possessions Elizabeth valued and the quality of life the sisters shared. They clearly bought valuable silverware that advertised their status whenever they entertained friends and acquaintances. This show was good for business, too, as the value of their possessions indicated robust finances. The eldest son of their nephew Benjamin was to get two silver candlesticks, a pair of silver snuffers and a silver snuffer stand. Benjamin's younger sons were to receive silver-handled cutlery and tableware. His daughter was to get a silver tea kettle and lamp. Tea kettles, with their stand and burner, were the most expensive part of any tea service and could be richly decorated. The spirit lamp kept water hot for topping up the teapot. No other woman of the period living in the maritime districts mentions a tea kettle and lamp in her will, so Elizabeth's must have been a prized object. She left her younger relatives a range of silver tableware. For example, the daughter of another nephew, William, was to have Elizabeth's largest silver waiter (a tray, on which china cups might be laid out on a dresser) and her small rose diamond ring. Rose-cut diamond rings were slightly old fashioned since the 'brilliant cut' gave more fire and was in the ascendancy throughout the eighteenth century. That said, nothing could beat diamonds for candle-lit evening events. They were a prime indicator of prestige and economic independence when worn tastefully.[30]

Elizabeth's major beneficiary was a third nephew, John Fisher, who came from a family of tallow chandlers. He got her best rose diamond ring; a silver coffee pot and waiter; a silver medal of King George III, probably commemorating his accession in 1760; and a silver-plated candlestick and snuffers. Fisher was also to have all her books, prints and drawings, and (after her sister's death) the household furniture, china and silver, family portraits and a drawing of the *Royal William*. This 100-gun warship was unusually long-lived and very popular. Launched in 1719 it had served in the Seven Years War and had brought General James Wolfe's body back to England after he died taking Quebec in 1759. Local artist John Cleveley the Elder had made an oil painting of the ship in 1760 and this drawing may have been an early study or a copy of the work.[31]

Mary Slade died in 1795, reputedly aged ninety-four. Her detailed will – nearly seventeen pages long – shows her to have been surprisingly wealthy. In addition to her plate, furniture and jewellery, she left thirty-three houses (three of them held leasehold), a stable, 3 acres of pastureland, legacies in government bonds totalling £6,650 and the interest on a mortgage of £700. Most of the houses were rented out to widows and men of standing, including a surgeon and a sea captain. They generated income but also show Mary's role in the district's infrastructure. Whereas Elizabeth in her will had carefully left valuable personal objects to her relatives, Mary singles out no favourite possession. She focuses instead on distributing her property and investments. Her books, clothes, linen, household goods, plate, jewels, china, pictures and furniture all go to the same nephew to whom Elizabeth had left her goods: John Fisher. The impression given by Mary's will is of someone less sentimental and more hard-headed. She also comes across as a person of her word, a vital quality in business. She states that she 'verbally engaged' to pay the costs of a nephew's board and lodging during the time he was apprenticed to a shipwright in Sheerness. The nephew had come into an inheritance that ought to cover his expenses but, if not, she directs that any shortfall should come from her estate so that the shipwright is not out of pocket.

Clearly Mary had strong views about female education and independence. Several bequests to female relatives are specifically willed to them alone, not to be touched by their husbands. For example, Elizabeth Slade, wife of a coal merchant, was to receive the rents on six houses and interest on bonds worth £800 'for her own sole separate and particular use and benefit' while she lived. The money was to be wholly free of her husband's 'engagement control or intermeddling'. Mary also left money to another female relative by marriage, the widowed sister of naval officer John Inglefield, who presumably would or could not provide for her. (Inglefield's father, Isaac, was a Deptford shipwright and family friend, mentioned by name in the will.) Mary bequeathed £50 in bonds to her maidservant, if she were still in her service at the time of her death. This was a generous sum but not enough to keep the servant: a codicil revoked the legacy. Another codicil revoked a bequest to one of Benjamin's sons, James Young Slade. He had been due to get the house and stable that he occupied already. Instead, Mary gave the property to James's daughter. The rental income from the house was to be used for the girl's maintenance and education until she reached the age of twenty-one.

Mary's will indicates that local women of standing had their own business networks. Mary had bought her 3-acre field from Jane Weatherall, whose family was also in retail. She had purchased one of her houses from another local woman. The Slade sisters entertained decorously in their home as a way of consolidating these connections. Mary's bequests also indicate a growing imperial network. Some of her properties were to be held in trust for the use of the wife of a surgeon in the East India Company, who was based in Bengal.

Of all Mary's properties, her 'new built freehold brick' houses on Butt Lane took pride of place. A brick house cost £100 or more to build and had more status than a timber-framed one.[32] She proudly bequeathed those on Butt Lane to favoured relatives. Nephew Benjamin got the one he occupied already. John Fisher got the house next door where Mary had lived with her sister. She had good reason to be proud of them. She had bought freehold land, commissioned and paid for these houses herself and there were few larger ones in the whole of Deptford. Known as Slade's Place, the terrace comprised ten houses (now 104–122 Deptford High Street). It was built between 1775 and 1785, when a wave of housing construction took off in London. The houses are not entirely symmetrical, so did not meet the strict standards of the most fashionable architecture, but their size alone indicated prosperity.[33] The project helped to develop rustic Butt Lane into a proper street linking Lower Deptford, on the river, with Upper Deptford, near the main London to Dover road. At this period, the process of building houses was changing. A London directory of 1768 pointed out that master house carpenters had taken to calling themselves 'builders' because they costed up the entire house-building project, then employed their own masons, plumbers and smiths. Before, a gentleman or merchant had gone to each trade in turn and effectively managed the project himself. This explains how a woman, with presumably little knowledge of the building trade, could commission ambitious building projects.[34]

Slade's Place was designed for a genteel and aspirational market. Mary and Elizabeth lived in the largest, number 110. It had a 30-foot (9-m) frontage and a huge garden leading to a small field on which there was a stable and shed. Most of the other houses in the row were only 18 feet (5.5 m) wide. Even so, all had three storeys and a basement, front gardens and views across the fields to London. There was much panelling and wooden construction inside but crucially the houses were of brick, not weather-boarding, which made them stand out. Mary was not just a shopkeeper: she was a businesswoman and a developer. The Slade sisters' tea and supper parties would have been prominent in Deptford's social round. Yet because Mary bequeathed her property to numerous relatives, her wealth was largely dissipated in the next generation. This helps to explain, perhaps, why the role of such women has had scant recognition.

Cross-dressing women

Many women had direct experience of the sea. Hundreds of prostitutes were ferried out to the British fleet at anchor and some may have been smuggled aboard on voyages. Warships also carried women officially. The wives of some warrant officers (boatswains, carpenters and gunners, who stayed with their ship even when it was out of commission) could sail with their husbands. In battle, they often served bravely, helping the surgeon or carrying gunpowder from the ship's magazine to the guns. Captains sometimes brought their wives on board although it was against Admiralty rules – it saved the expense of keeping house. The newly married Captain Matthew Flinders tried to take his wife with him when he sailed in 1801 to survey the coasts of Australia; their plans were discovered and he was ordered to put her ashore. Tragically, he was imprisoned by the French on his way home and she did not see him for nine years. And there were other women who disguised themselves in men's clothes to go to sea. Improbable as it may seem given the crowded conditions, some worked at sea for years apparently undetected. There is no way of knowing how many women chose this route, but several cases made the headlines. In 1779, for example, sailors joining a privateer in London discovered one of their number to be a woman in men's clothes. She had already worked in disguise as a bricklayer, and was one of at least three women found trying to join the military that year alone.[35]

There was concern in the 1770s about the weakening of gender boundaries, as usually happened when war threatened. (The topic is treated in more detail in Chapter Seven.) In fashionable areas of London, elite men drew disapproving looks as they sported absurdly flamboyant, even effeminate French costume. Women who wore riding habits of a masculine cut triggered unease, though it was a fashion of long standing. During the American Revolutionary War, satirical prints targeting army officers

143

depicted scenes where men and women swapped roles. *An Officer of the Light Infantry, Driven by his Lady to Cox's Heath* (1778) is just one example. It shows an overweight army officer sitting in his carriage, sleepily resting on his sword. His lady, in military dress, stands upright beside him. She whips the horses vigorously into a smart trot towards Coxheath, an army training camp where, in the summers of 1778 and 1779, large mock battles were fought.[36] But however much the wealthier classes enjoyed or drew criticism for gender-bending behaviour, poor women who donned men's clothes and went to sea were probably making a calculated life choice. After all, many were used to manual labour. Eighteenth-century domestic equipment was heavy, maidservants carried buckets of water up and down stairs, female street hawkers set off each morning with weighty loads. A key difference between this drudgery and working at sea in male disguise was that a sailor's life promised adventure and freedoms. And there were well-publicized accounts of other women who had done it before.

One such woman was Mary Lacey. Her story is simple in outline. She grew up in a village in Kent, turned out to be a difficult teenager and in 1759, aged nineteen, ran away dressed as a boy. A naval carpenter in Chatham took her on as his assistant and she sailed with the fleet. Four years later, she left the navy and trained as a shipwright at Portsmouth dockyard, still dressed as a man. Later, she seems to have worked in Deptford dockyard.[37]

Lacey claimed that rheumatism, brought on from exposure and wearing wet clothes, forced her to give up hard physical work and reveal that she was a woman. She may just have been found out. Amazingly, she obtained a naval pension despite having disclosed her sex. She had a case for payment, having completed her seven-year apprenticeship. And local shipwrights who had collective bargaining power chose to support her. Afterwards, she married. We know all this because in 1773 she published her life story, *The Female Shipwright*. It was unusual enough to have been interesting even in her own time. Lacey claims to have written a factual account, but she may have coloured events to appeal to a market and probably had help writing the book. The public loved titillating stories about cross-dressing women so it was an instant money-spinner. The interest was not that she had been a woman at sea – there were plenty of them – but that, when dressed as a man, she had been expected to behave like one.

Lacey's story is fascinating for what it tells us by implication about life in maritime London. With her regular, independent income, Lacey was a good marriage prospect. Her husband, Josias Slade, was also a shipwright (though no relation to the purveyor Benjamin Slade), and they probably met in Deptford dockyard, where both worked. Josias did not fear jibes that he allowed his wife to 'wear the breeches'.[38] The newspapers announced the birth of their daughter, Margaret, in 1773 and they went on to have at least five more children. Only the oldest and youngest seem to have survived into adulthood. Lacey died in 1801, having helped to ensure that her family prospered. When Josias died in 1814, aged seventy-four, he left their two children £150 each in 3 per cent consoles (government bonds) and an equal share of his house, 50 King (now Watergate) Street, Deptford.

Lacey, in a remarkable transformation, became a respectable member of the community. In her book, she is careful to draw a clear contrast between her own values and those of people in her old life who could damage her by association. As the wife of a shipwright, and one qualified to vote in elections, she makes sure that she condemns the common-law wife of the carpenter to whom she was once apprenticed. This woman could never be considered respectable. She disturbed her neighbourhood with her fighting and cursing. She drank so much that her husband could not pay her debts and went to prison. Lacey also pointedly contrasts the boys whom the Marine Society sent to sea with the unruly naval boys who picked fights with her. Set up in 1756 at the start of the Seven Years War, the Society had equipped 10,000 urchins for the navy by the end of it. Some grumbled that the navy needed skilled men, not boys with no experience of the open sea, but prominent members of the Deptford community were keen supporters. The Society's boat was moored for long periods off Deptford, a visible reminder of its work. Some boys transferred to the merchant service at the end of the war, and the charity was held to be of such national importance that it was incorporated by Act of Parliament in 1772, just when Lacey was writing. She also criticizes violent male behaviour. Her experience of cross-dressing allows her to critique both male and female conduct and so contribute to emerging standards of urban sociability.

Lacey's claim to 'middling sort' credentials is found in the detail of her account. Offered a basin of tea at her master the carpenter's house, she comments how much she had missed the refreshment on the road. Even the working classes had managed to adopt this polite beverage by the 1770s; Lacey resolutely signals that she was used to drinking it. Her book includes the letters she supposedly sent her parents, indicating that she understands polite forms of letter writing. She also states that she learned arithmetic at sea, underlining her intellectual credentials. Throughout she demonstrates her capacity for hard work and unwillingness to contract debts. While she depicts the brutal violence of port towns, she insists that she always avoided licentious company. Given the titillation in her book, Lacey may have found it hard to escape all community criticism. Still, it says much that she could trade on her reputation as 'the female shipwright' to lobby dockyard officials at Deptford on her husband's behalf. She petitioned that he might have an apprentice. In time, this was granted.[39]

Respectability and reputation

Women were energetic petitioners for their rights, and seamen's women were active because they often headed up households. Petitioning was pervasive at all social levels since it was the only acceptable way to address local and national authorities when seeking redress or advancement. Seamen's women petitioned for their husbands' pay and pension, or for charity. As we have seen, women also petitioned if their menfolk were convicted of crimes. Mary Randall, wife of a Rotherhithe shopkeeper dealing in old rope, lobbied unsuccessfully on his behalf in 1790 when he was sentenced to transportation for receiving a stolen foresail. The couple had six dependent children.[40] Effective petitioning could involve winning the support of local politicians, church officers and respectable tradesmen. It needed initiative, powers of persuasion and a good reputation.

Not all seamen's wives who stayed at home managed well. The wife of one of the Henleys' seamen became pregnant while he was at sea, so they stopped her allowance. She also got him into so much debt that he faced prison on return.[41] Women who became pregnant while their men were away faced a difficult decision. Some attempted suicide rather than face returning husbands. In 1775, a young woman went to the Castle pub in Deptford, treated people to a drink, then drowned herself in a great butt of water in the back yard. She was six months pregnant.[42] The number of children killed at birth in such circumstances is unknown. Infanticide was a capital crime and associated in the legal mind with single rather than married women, but women tried for murdering their newborns were mostly acquitted in the eighteenth century, particularly if they could show that they had bought childbed linen and prepared for the birth. Either juries were sympathetic or just uneasy with the harsh penalty. Maidservants were notoriously vulnerable. Masters regarded them as fair game but if they fell pregnant they could lose their place. There are several reports of female servants killing their bastard children and throwing them down the privy.[43]

At neighbourhood level, there were still powerful forms of social policing, mid-century. One woman might publicly announce that another was a whore; she in turn would accuse her of slander. Such cases were resolved by informal arbitration or prosecution. As urban populations increased, community policing faded away. Women and the middling classes thought it hardly respectable to scream insults at each other in public, particularly in cases of sexual immorality. Reputations were still important and gossip still feared, but class, occupation, business contacts and church membership became the preferred means of establishing respectability.[44]

In a notorious case, one naval officer trashed the reputation of his own wife. Captain John Inglefield, whom we have met before, accused his wife of adultery with his black servant, John Webb, in 1786. The divorce proceedings absorbed the public's attention for months. Inglefield was the nephew of naval architect Sir Thomas Slade. His mother, Dorothy Slade,

147

had married a promising shipwright in Deptford dockyard who in the end failed to get promotion. Inglefield, helped in his naval career by his Slade connections, nursed social pretensions and was sensitive about his father's lowly rank. In 1773 he married Ann Smith, a spinster whose family owned cottages in Greenwich, only to find that her modest fortune was settled on her children and so was out of his reach. They had four children but the marriage became strained, not least because Ann, a modest, shy woman, did not possess the social skills that Inglefield thought would advance his career.

During the American War, Inglefield served in the West Indies and leapt to fame in 1782 after the wreck of his ship, the *Centaur*. The British fleet had won an important victory at the Battle of the Saints in April that year. Sailing home, towards the end of the fighting season, the fleet was caught in an autumn hurricane. The *Centaur* took in water fast but Inglefield managed to escape with eleven officers in the ship's boat. After fifteen punishing days and the loss of one man, they made dry land. News of the fleet disaster was a terrible blow after the recent victory. Partly to compensate, Inglefield's escape was published as a heroic narrative.[45] A court martial cleared him of blame. Although today we might consider that he saved his own skin, taking a few officers and leaving the rest of his crew to drown, at the time people admired his manly determination to survive. Abandoning ship was viewed as a continuation of his fight against the elements, just in a smaller boat. Readers would have known, though it was never mentioned, that a substantial proportion of the *Centaur*'s crew was black, as in most vessels sailing to and from the West Indies.

Back home in Greenwich, the new hero festered ever more deeply under the banality of his marriage and sought a way out. Eventually, Inglefield accused his wife of adultery with John Webb. Enslaved in Africa, Webb had entered the captain's service in the West Indies, worked at sea, then been welcomed into the Inglefield household. His legal status was uncertain: people believed that slavery was illegal in Britain but the law was not clear and Inglefield held sway over him. The African swore an affidavit supporting Inglefield's claim, saying that Ann had repeatedly tried to seduce him over eighteen months when the captain was at sea. Later he retracted his testimony, claiming that Inglefield had forced him to make it because he wanted to be rid of his wife. Both husband and wife had reputations to lose. Each fought their case in public, publishing vivid accounts that delighted scandalmongers. The story was even serialized in *The Rambler* magazine, which offered juicy extracts from Webb's original testimony:

> As the deponent [Webb] was alone with her [Mrs Inglefield], and dressing her hair, which he constantly did, she put her hand under his apron and unbuttoned one of the flaps of his breeches, and began handling or playing with his privities, and the deponent immediately drew himself from her and buttoned up the flap of his breeches, and she then burst into a laugh, and told him to finish her hair.[46]

The piece was illustrated with three suggestive prints entitled 'The Hair Dressing Scene', 'The Kissing Scene' and 'The Chamber Scene'.

The divorce case hit a nerve because it was bound up with conflicting attitudes to the slave trade, with contemporary pornography involving white women and black men, and with cultural trends that encouraged men to assert their masculinity through sexual behaviour as opposed to other expressions of male identity. This led in turn to anxieties about sexual performance. This powerful context inclined sections of the public to sympathize with Inglefield but respectable friends of his wife, married to naval officers, stood by her. She was fully exonerated in court.

The verdict in her favour points to changing views of women – or at least of decorous women. They were increasingly seen as a force for civilizing society rather than as the weaker sex with a predisposition to irrationality and unrestrained sexuality. There remained fears of mixed-race relations involving lower-class women, particularly in maritime districts. Women were thought more liable to give vent to their carnal appetites with blacks (also considered to be naturally more sensual). While the court case was going on, the authorities were trying to rid the London streets of the black poor, many of them 'loyalists' who had fought on the British side in the American War for a promise of freedom. A scheme was afoot to resettle hundreds in Sierra Leone.[47] It is testimony to the power of the English law that, in this context, Ann got a fair trial. She was presented as patriotically fulfilling the role of a naval wife in wartime: faithful to her husband and shouldering domestic duties. In contrast, it seemed that Inglefield had cynically attempted to exploit contemporary prejudice and anxiety about black males of the Atlantic world to be rid of her. Even so, the judge looked for a way to avoid blaming Inglefield. He ruled that adultery had not taken place, but vilified Webb as the cause of discord between husband and wife, even though in the end Webb had honourably put truth above his own interests.[48] Inglefield gained custody of the children and his career prospered. He and his wife never lived together again.

Defending absent husbands

Some seamen's wives were not just competent domestic managers but called upon to defend, intelligently, their absent husband. Charlotte Whitford, who kept a shop in Back Lane (now New King Street), Deptford, letting out an upper floor to lodgers, had to step in when her husband was accused of deserting his ship. He regretted having enlisted. Conditions were terrible in the North Sea and he had already been away for two years. 'You may depend on this I shall take the first chance I can to escape from this floating hell', he wrote.[49] When he and others were tempted to abscond, they were put in irons. A severe flogging was imminent but Charlotte contacted relations and asked them to intercede with her husband's captain.

Few were as assiduous in their husband's defence as Elizabeth, wife of William Bligh. The couple met in 1781 on the Isle of Man where her father was Receiver-General of Customs. They married after a whirlwind romance: Bligh had served under Cook on his third voyage to the Pacific and was expecting a new commission. He returned to sea just ten days after the marriage. Betsy, as Bligh always called her, was a Glasgow-born, vivacious woman who dressed with verve and style. She was well educated, fluent in French and Italian, and wrote confident letters in a bold, italic hand. She was also well connected. Her maternal grandfather was principal of Glasgow

University, chaplain to the King, and friend of leading figures in the Scottish Enlightenment. Her uncle, Duncan Campbell, was a wealthy merchant. He owned a fleet that traded with the West Indies and was contracted to ship convicts to Britain's American colonies. Later, he managed convict hulks on the Thames. Bligh benefited from these connections.

After the American War, when Bligh faced the prospect of maintaining his family on naval half-pay, Campbell employed him as a master sailing to the West Indies. As Betsy said, 'a Rum and Sugar Capt may be as well off as any other'.[50] In fact, rather better. When in 1787 he took the captaincy of the *Bounty* to transport breadfruit from Tahiti to the West Indies, he took a salary cut from £500 to £50 a year. Whether Bligh ever captained slave ships is doubtful, but he did not baulk at working in the shadow of the slave trade. Breadfruit was intended to provide cheap food for slaves on the sugar plantations.

Bligh was notoriously thin-skinned and exacting. He had an explosive temper. While he has been unfairly blamed for the mutiny on the *Bounty* – it was his misfortune rather than his fault – there is no doubt that his ability to curse and swear was extraordinary. He was court martialled for it in 1804 and he must be one of the few British naval officers ever to be ordered to moderate his language at sea. The more surprising, then, to find that his letters to Betsy were models of affection and politeness. They were devoted to each other. Some have claimed that Betsy was Bligh's only companion since his character was so unsuited to making and keeping friends. They had six daughters, the last suffering from epilepsy and learning difficulties. They also had twin sons who died soon after birth.

Like many naval husbands, and with such a large, female household, Bligh learned the trick of shopping for foreign wares whenever opportunity presented itself. Having been sent to convoy East Indiamen from St Helena in 1800, he wrote to Betsy off Dover regretting that he had missed the chance to buy her an Indian shawl. Still, he had obtained dress material, fine china and good tea. He asked for advice on how to convey his purchases home, assuring her that if any were unwanted, she need only say and he would sell them instead.[51]

When Bligh was at sea he readily gave Betsy power of attorney, and her letters to family members about contested legacies and legal matters show that she was both able and decisive. She was a good financial manager and conscious of the need for economy. On moving to Wapping in 1784, she wrote:

> I now begin to like living in Town which I cannot say I did at first – indeed what I disliked most was the extravagant prices of every thing, but when I consider that our gains from my being here will be more than could be saved by my living in the country, besides the happiness of our being together I think my removal was certainly for the best.[52]

They rented a house in Broad (now Reardon) Street, near St George-in-the-East. Wapping was not fashionable, though many of her neighbours were well-to-do. Next door lived Elijah Goff, coal merchant and supporter of several charities. His diary shows him travelling to the Exchange, dining in taverns, visiting dockyards and coal barges in the river and riding out to rural Plaistow. Betsy was more confined. She wrote to relatives, 'I wish I had any news to write you that could entertain you but I am so seldom abroad & the part of Town we live in is so much out of the world that I know little more than our domestic occurrences.'[53] She suffered low spirits during her pregnancies and felt tied to the nursery, describing herself as 'a mere nurse who passes the whole day with one child in her arms and another hanging upon her'.[54] It was in Wapping that she waited for Bligh to return from the *Bounty* voyage.

Bligh experienced successive mutinies in his career; Betsy was always his effective advocate. After long service in the navy, Bligh was appointed Governor of New South Wales in 1805 thanks to the support of Sir Joseph Banks and Duncan Campbell, who by now had experience of shipping convicts to Australia. Betsy nursed a horror of the sea and her health was no longer robust. Instead, her eldest daughter accompanied Bligh to run his household, half a world away. Her mother sent the latest fashions from England to help her fulfil the role. But Bligh's iron discipline caused the colonists to revolt and he was ousted. At once, Betsy lobbied Sir Joseph Banks, putting her husband's side of the case in a series of letters. She was not at all intimidated when writing to elite figures. She also had credentials as a collector, which raised her in Banks's estimation and made it easier to solicit his help. Partly to dispel her domestic trials, she had formed a shell collection. It included fine specimens from the South Seas, and she became one of the leading collectors in Britain. As a serious collector, she helped to integrate the Pacific world into existing knowledge, adding to the accounts of those who had gone there. The collection was dispersed at auction ten years after her death. Yet the naturalist William Swainson ensured that her reputation as a collector lived on. He compiled the auction catalogue and later illustrated his works with shells from her collection.

Would Bligh have recovered his career after each setback without his wife? Possibly not. He was a superb seaman and navigator. He also saved loyal crew members after the *Bounty* mutiny in a remarkable open boat voyage. But Betsy gave him a happy home life that helped to balance his traumas at sea. She was his confidante and champion. When he sent her news of the mutiny he knew that she would at once appreciate that the letter was a form of evidence. But this period in Wapping was a turning point: afterwards she not only had the usual anxieties of a naval wife but also feared for her husband's stability. His temper made him enemies and, tellingly, on return he moved his family to more rural Lambeth. The family still lived there in 1810 when he came back from his disastrous governorship in Australia. By this time, Betsy's health was broken. She died aged fifty-nine, barely two years later.

Widows and charity

The strange, exotic world of the South Seas entered polite London society through a network of contacts that included other women with maritime connections. James, the naval brother of diarist and novelist Fanny Burney, went on Cook's second and third voyages, and helped to edit Cook's journal of the third voyage for publication. Fanny's brother-in-law, another marine officer, witnessed Cook's death. Burney herself met Omai, who knew her brother, and listened as they conversed in Tahitian in her dining room. Clearly, too, the relaxed sexual behaviour of the islanders was discussed even in polite circles. A family friend twitted her about James wishing to return to Tahiti so that he could be reunited with his 'piece'.[55] Fanny's brother, Charles, who became a Greenwich schoolmaster then rector of St Paul's Deptford, would have seen the enthusiasm for exploration of a younger maritime generation at first hand. But if new maritime vistas opened for them, the widows of seamen faced ever-dwindling possibilities.

Society gave dependent widows little respect.[56] Naval widows from genteel backgrounds were considered vulnerable because unused to earning their keep. Officers' widows could therefore obtain pensions. Lower down the social scale, naval widows were reliant on poor relief and handouts; religious charity was vital to them.[57] Widows of seamen in the merchant service might be lucky enough to secure a place in the almshouses funded by Trinity House, intended for elderly pilots or masters of ships, or their widows. Candidates for admission had to be in reduced circumstances and unable to maintain themselves by working. After 1792 they also had to be at least sixty years old. The needy could petition for a place but only a recommendation secured one; the elder brethren of Trinity House usually took turns to make these representations. Couples were admitted and inmates might marry and move in together, which freed up rooms. Men had an allowance of twenty shillings each month and women sixteen shillings. Rarely did anyone leave before death unless they became chronically unwell or mentally unstable.

In Deptford's older almshouses, near the river, each unit comprised two rooms, the larger of which had a fireplace. They were refurbished in the 1780s and given smaller fireplaces to burn coal, not wood, and a drain each for waste water. (Fresh water was piped from the Lewisham Water Company.) There was an ablution block and brick-lined cesspits. Archaeological evidence shows that inhabitants enjoyed a variety of fish, including eel, ling, whiting, plaice, mackerel and herring, some of which could have been caught locally. Their meat was mostly sheep, chicken and rabbit, confirming their low status. But sometimes they enjoyed higher-quality meat: goose and duck. Rook bones show that they ate rook pie, a favourite eighteenth-century recipe. The buildings were maintained; from the 1790s into the early nineteenth century, Trinity House surveyed them annually and ordered repairs, but even so there was widespread rodent infestation.[58]

Occupants owned a range of pottery. It was largely utilitarian: storage jars, porringers and plates, ointment pots, and jars for dry medicines. But most vessels were good, indicating 'middling' status. Residents also had imported pottery, possibly because with seafaring backgrounds they had access to foreign wares rather than the wealth to purchase them in London, and they brought to the almshouses goods accumulated during their working lives. In contrast, the tobacco pipes purchased during their retirement were of a lower quality.

Crucially, residents were not necessarily local people, or even objects of local charity. Nor were almshouses necessarily run by locals. They stood at a remove from the parish, although reinforcing the importance of showing charity to poor mariners and their families. The few who ended their lives in this easy poverty were far outnumbered by those in desperate circumstances. Trinity House, being well funded, also made grants to seafaring people or their dependants, supplying printed forms to speed the process. In 1800, 3,682 people received Trinity House pensions. In 1815, the figure was 7,012.[59]

Residents of almshouses enjoyed a much better life than workhouse inmates. Husbands and wives might live together, move about freely, choose their own food and be surrounded by their own possessions. They kept cats and dogs as pets (their bones have been found, together with the gnawed bones of the food pets ate). Residents also kept songbirds. And finds of worked bone show how some old sailors continued to fill their leisure time.

Such links as existed between almshouses and workhouses were hierar-chical. Deranged inhabitants might be 'demoted' to a workhouse, and workhouse paupers might be apprenticed as servants in almshouses. On 7 March 1770, for example, the Greenwich workhouse sent Elizabeth

Prizeman upon liking to Mrs Ann Godby, a widow in the old Trinity House at Deptford. If both kinds of institutions were visible symbols of the importance of charity, at the same time, they allowed the better off to segregate those in need.

In London's maritime districts, the sea impacted on most aspects of life; women at all social levels were affected as well as men. The nation was often at war. Militarization, intermittent fears of invasion and the prospect of fighting at sea all put pressure on relations between the sexes. For the most part, gender divisions hardened. Yet being attached to a seaman was not like being married to an innkeeper or a blacksmith. Women could expect to be on their own (anxious, or even pleasantly free!) most of the time. Bligh's wife was worn down by the strain; Elizabeth Cook overcame tragedy to live a long life. In an age when such a high proportion of society was disadvantaged, the trials of women with absent menfolk were rarely singled out, and women's contribution to maritime London has tended to be neglected. The picture of their lives glimpsed here is sometimes grim but often inspiring. Without their input as wives, workers and business-women, the success of London's war effort and commercial activity would have been sorely compromised.

6

MONEY AND PLEASURE

The American War ended in humiliation. Who was to blame? There were several possible targets: the ministers who had judged the political situation so badly; the generals and admirals who had failed to obtain victories; the contractors who had made a packet out of supplying the armed forces. But ironically the long build-up to war had, in part, drawn the sting of political criticism. The arguments on both sides of the conflict had been rehearsed so often that the whole debate had become commonplace. Britain's military leaders had been a disappointment in America, but there was some pride in having held all the major European powers at bay while at the same time fighting colonial rebels. Now, conspicuously wealthy contractors were envied. Londoners hoped they would spread their money about. But, in the main, people set about trying to make the best of things. The well heeled sought to look out for themselves while doing what they could to stabilize their communities, aware that some thought the loss of the colonies was divine visitation on a society given over to luxury and private pleasure. They had no way of knowing but, for them, the 1780s were to be the good times.

The war had cost a phenomenal amount. By the end of it the National Debt had grown from £137 million to £232 million. Warfare had also dealt a heavy blow to commerce: trade declined by almost 20 per cent between 1772 and 1780. Exports to the North American mainland, Britain's largest market outside Europe, fell by almost a half. Gloomy merchants and statesmen feared economic decline and loss of status. When William Pitt the Younger became prime minister in 1783, his first challenge was the economy, and he at once set about reducing the government's debts. He cracked down on smuggling to increase the income from tax revenues. He also imposed more taxes – targeting luxury items such as hair powder, pleasure horses, gloves and female servants (male servants had been taxed since 1777). But whereas some male servants – footmen, butlers and the like – might have been kept for show, in London even the humblest of the middling sort employed one female domestic. The maidservant tax in 1785 coincided with a new tax on retail shops, based on the annual value of the premises. Both measures met with sharp protest as they were bound to hurt the hard-working middling sort, particularly in London where retailers and female domestics made up a significant proportion of the workforce.

The young Pitt was attacked for having no practical experience of trade. He was also accused of being unfair to women, given the limited number of jobs available to them and their lack of political voice. By implication, it was the debauched aristocracy who should have borne the weight of heavy taxation. Some of this criticism hit home. Pitt later abated the maidservant tax on families with numerous children who needed help with childcare. In this he was also responding to fears of a declining population at a time when Britain needed manpower to build up its military strength. The government was forced to cancel the tax on shops in 1789 and repeal the tax on maidservants altogether in 1792.

Yet Pitt soon demonstrated that he did understand how best to serve the British economy. He spent money on the navy (for commercial as well as defence reasons), increasing the naval establishment from 15,000 to 18,000 men. Between 1784 and 1790, fifteen new warships were built, bringing work to the dockyards and merchant shipyards along the Thames. In this arena, he relied heavily on Admiral Sir Charles Middleton.

Comptroller of the navy from 1778 to 1790, Middleton deserves most of the credit for reforming the naval dockyards and strengthening the fleet so that it was strong enough to face Napoleon. And trade picked up remarkably quickly. No other country at the time could match British manufactured goods for quality, variety or cost. Fortunately, the newly independent America still relied on Britain for these goods, so Anglo-American trade boomed. By 1800 the United States of America was taking more than a quarter of all British exports.[1]

London was now the greatest manufacturing city in the Western world. It did not have the large factories that were sprouting up in northern towns but it boasted huge numbers of workshops of every kind. These often experimented with new processes that were only later adopted in the provinces. Some commentators described London as a parasite, a centre of luxury and vice that sucked goods and people from other parts of the nation. But London drove the economy. Most imports of raw goods came into the Port of London. Most exports left it. Thousands were still employed in the textile and clothing trades, given that London's textile industries were only slowly losing out to cheaper producers in Nottingham, Leicester, Manchester and other towns. Crowded Clerkenwell was the centre for making watches and surgical, optical and nautical instruments, while mathematical instruments were also made in Wapping. The valuable leather and fur industry was still largely based in Southwark and Bermondsey, although shoemaking was beginning to be contracted out to workers in Northampton where wages were lower. Trades along the river were flourishing. Manufacturers there were leading national producers of a variety of goods including paint, varnish, printer's ink and glue, ships, sails, rope, barrels, ship's biscuit and beer.[2] In the maritime districts there were also many glasshouses, potteries, distilleries and sugar refineries.

In this bustling city, there were numerous connections between the serious business of making money and different forms of entertainment. Some business concerns – like the theatre – were obviously all about entertainment. But traders and manufacturers also had to advertise and market their goods and services, and many promotional activities involved entertainment and enjoyment. Shopping for luxury goods, for example, might be offered as a leisured and sociable experience. Women who ran businesses entertained at home in ways that assured friends and customers of their good standing in the community, although the role of women in generating wealth is easily overlooked. The pleasure that many people gained from doing good works or dispensing their wealth in charitable giving is also often disregarded, even though such activities might take up most of their leisure hours.

People enjoyed wide-ranging pastimes, from theatre-going to embroidery, from hunting and cockfighting to window shopping, and from gambling to debating societies and play-acting. But some public entertainments were more closely allied to business than others, and had greater impact on community culture. In this sense, they were more closely linked to London's commercial recovery after the American War. Already, its tradespeople had a finely gauged sense of their importance to the nation even as non-combatants. At the beginning of the American War, for instance, the Robin Hood Club, a debating society meeting regularly in Butchers Row, Wapping, discussed whether prudence in prosperity or fortitude in adversity had the greatest merit.[3] The vote went to fortitude, but that people should weigh up the merits of bravery and wealth accumulation at all is significant. The getting of wealth was even condoned by the Church. The Reverend Dr Colin Milne, a noted clergyman and lecturer at St Paul's Deptford, declared as a self-evident truth that 'the Christian Patriot will not only pray for the prosperity of his country, but, to the utmost of his power, contribute to it, by devoting himself and his labours to advantage'.[4] Good Christians saw to it that they made money.

Ship launches

One event that clearly united respectable profit and patriotic entertainment was a ship launch on the Thames. Part of the attraction of a launch was that things could go wrong. There was no means of accurately modelling the forces and weights that would come into play. Two or three hundred shipyard workers were needed to hammer away the stocks before a ship slid down the ways. The process could not be controlled and accidents were frequent. Yard workers might be crushed or drowned; spectators were also often injured. Earlier, the practice along the Thames had been to build larger ships in a dock and float them out when ready. But wartime pressures meant that docks were needed for ship repair. By the time of the Seven Years War, more and more ships were built on slipways. They were launched stern first, which offered a better chance of steering the ship as soon as it hit the water. In any case, the bow was better able to take the strain of the ropes.

A launch was fundamentally a display of power: of the nation, the navy and the shipbuilder who had completed the ship. It was a legitimate opportunity for him to promote his skill and competence.[5] The event could bring all classes together in one spot but class distinctions were still carefully maintained and many went to gawp at the dignitaries as much as to see the launch. In the 1770s, important guests were likely to be invited on board for the launch and dine afterwards in the ship's great cabin. By the 1780s, the focus of the ceremony had moved from ship to shore. A slipway launch was too dangerous for dignitaries to be gathered on the ship's quarterdeck – though a band or two might still be stationed there to play the national anthem or 'Britons, Strike Home!' as a warship entered the water. Tens of thousands could be expected at a launch, and in Deptford dockyard a temporary grandstand was often built for higher-class women to get a good view, away from the crush of people. Or ships might be anchored for them in the river. (To view from a small boat was much more dangerous as it could be overset by the swell.) Whenever there was a push to expand the navy, launches became frequent and the capacity of the Thames was tested to the limit. The construction of notable ships was talked up in the press for weeks beforehand, which ensured a good crowd. As excitement mounted, many would travel just to see the closing stages of a ship's progress, often from a boat in the river.

Royalty began to attend launches of important warships mid-century but were encouraged to participate regularly from the time of the American

War. Sometimes a member of the royal family named the ship, smashing a bottle of claret on the ship's side as it entered the water. Men and women could be given this honour; it was not until the nineteenth century that the person naming the ship had to be a woman. Clearly the event was an opportunity for people to show their patriotism but it also helped to make George III popular. He began bringing the royal children to such events.

When the king attended the launch of the *Grafton* at Deptford in 1771, he dressed in blue laced with gold, as a compliment to the navy. A magnificent pavilion was built for him to watch the spectacle and take refreshment, and he was given three cheers from crowds on land and on the river. On this occasion the crowd was carefully controlled by a detachment of foot guards. Before his arrival, there had been the added drama of fixing the royal standard flag to the warship's mainmast once more. It had not been properly secured and had dropped to the deck. No one was keen to scale the mast, swaying with the wind, but it had to be done and a ship's carpenter had eventually climbed to the top, some 70 feet (21 m) above the deck. After the launch, the king awarded a week's wages to each of the workers in the dockyard. It amounted to 10s. 11d. per man. Afterwards, he made regular, unannounced visits to the yard where he was always sure of a warm welcome.

The noise of the stocks being hammered away to release the ship, the cheers, gunfire, fanfares and drumming, the billowing flags, splendid Admiralty or livery barges in the river, and loud singing made a great ship launch one of the most exciting spectacles London had to offer. Roads would be thronging with carriages. Contemporary prints show crowds ecstatically waving their hats and cheering as a great vessel rushes into the water. Entertainments would be built around the ceremony: for the wealthy, dinners the evening before or after the event, with perhaps a ball at the local assembly rooms; for the rest, alehouses, street-food sellers and spontaneous dancing. Retailers, tradespeople and pickpockets all saw it as an opportunity to do good business. In certain circumstances, ship launches were also occasions for foreign diplomacy. In 1780, Russian, Swedish and Portuguese ambassadors were at the launch of a warship at Barnard's Deptford yard. In the evening, Lord Sandwich gave an 'elegant Entertainment' for dignitaries at his house on Blackheath.[6] But minor launches were also attractions, bringing people close to the actual production of complex vessels. In January 1793, the coal merchant Elijah Goff braved wind and rain to be present at the launch of the *Hindostan* at Barnard's yard, Deptford. Afterwards, he was one of the 180 or so who dined in the yard's mould loft, where months earlier the lines of the ship had been drawn out and full-size templates made. *Hindostan* was one of the largest East Indiamen of its time and Goff proudly marked the event in his diary.[7]

Theatres

The theatre was also enormously popular and a completely different experience to that enjoyed today. The Licensing Act of 1737 had tightened the censorship of drama. Only two theatres were licensed for spoken comedy and tragedy: Covent Garden and Drury Lane, which offered a 'mainpiece' and an 'afterpiece' each evening. From 1766, the smaller Theatre Royal in the Haymarket was also licensed during the summer season when the other two were closed. To avoid prosecution under the Act, every other theatre had to offer a mixed bill of pantomime, burletta (comic opera), ballet, rope dancing, tumbling, songs and glees – anything that avoided spoken dialogue. Sadler's Wells theatre also had great tanks that could be flooded from a nearby waterway so that naval battles could be staged. (Its model warships were carved at Woolwich dockyard.)

Lead actors became the pin-ups of the day. Their portraits were printed in magazines and people eagerly discussed their performances in different roles. Audiences were not the polite, deferential crowds that theatres attract now. People often ate and talked throughout the show. The most expensive seats were the boxes. These were at stage level, and at least two were at the sides of the stage, giving only a partial view. The next best seats were in the pit, or floor of the theatre. It was lower than the stage but people sat on raked benches and could stand at the very back. In the maritime parishes, most people who were in the professions or who had any social standing opted for the pit.[8] The cheapest seats were in the crowded galleries above where, farthest from the stage, it was hardest to hear and see. People in the upper gallery were accused of being noisy, drunk and rude. They interrupted the drama and sometimes threw bottles and other dangerous objects at those seated below them. But spectators in other parts of the house could be equally rowdy.[9]

The performance was candlelit, with overhead chandeliers and a row of footlights at the front of the stage – although side lighting was being introduced by placing candles on stands in the grooves that took scenery. The uncertain lighting added to the atmosphere but probably encouraged muttered conversation. Still, the live music from the orchestra was exhilarating and the whole experience – for an audience determined to enjoy itself – more than compensated for the smell of stale tobacco, guttering candles and sweat.

The two licensed theatres were steadily enlarged so that by 1790 they had more than doubled in size and each held about 2,300 people. Metal or ivory passes (rather than tickets) were issued to those who booked for a season. The showy passes were a means of audience engagement, not just a receipt for payment. Evidently, the potential audience for drama was larger still. The actor-manager John Palmer saw an opportunity to make money by opening premises in London's East End. He fixed on Well Close Square, Wapping, a district that had supported a theatre earlier in the century. His aim was to put on five-act plays, so he built at huge cost (£14,000), and signalled his ambition by naming his building the Royalty Theatre. The legal status of the district around the Tower was semi-autonomous; Palmer was counting on this to exempt him from the Licensing Act. He secured permission for his plan from the governor of the Tower and won support from the local magistrates, but neither assurance amounted to full legal authority.

Palmer opened the Royalty in 1787 with Shakespeare's *As You Like It* and gave the evening's profits to the London Hospital as a gesture of goodwill. All the same, his plans rattled the patent theatres, who at once set about trying to close him down. They accepted his argument that theatres could be schools for the poor, and that good acting might help to convey the principles of morality to untutored audiences, but declared that the licensed theatres already entertained thousands each night. There was no need for 'frequent and expensive diversions among the lower class of people'. They predicted that the Royalty would become 'a place of vicious amusement', attract 'bucks, bloods, and ladies of easy virtue', increase local crime, and encourage idle apprentices to leave work early.[10]

There was certainly an audience for drama in Wapping and its surrounds. The neighbourhood was large, and while most residents were lower class, many were respectable and affluent. Palmer, still trying to get a licence for the Royalty in the 1790s, argued that his theatre was miles away from Drury Lane and that he targeted audiences from Wapping, Limehouse, Shadwell, Poplar, Blackwell, Mile End, Stepney, Bow and Hackney.[11] It was expensive for those in the eastern parts of the city to get to a West End theatre if they did not own a carriage. The hackney fare at that distance added considerably to the cost of an evening. The alternative – a damp, cold boat on the river late at night – was not an attractive proposition. Despite his pleas, after the first night, Palmer never staged five-act plays at the Royalty. Crippled by debt, he went back to acting and was even imprisoned for fourteen days in 1789 as a rogue and a vagabond.

Under different management, the Royalty later offered a medley of permitted performances designed for local audiences. They responded enthusiastically. Happily, pantomime and music were well suited to mixed nationalities whose English was imperfect. The very absence of the spoken word even made it possible to treat sensitive issues like the slave trade and mixed-race relationships which touched local audiences. And whereas the Lord Chamberlain could censor drama likely to excite radical views, dumb shows had no text that he could run a red pencil through. Ironically, pantomime gave the Royalty opportunities to explore radical, and even subversive, political content.

This can be seen in a pantomime called *Harlequin Mungo; or, A Peep into the Tower*, which Palmer staged at the Royalty in 1787. In this show, Harlequin is a West Indian ex-slave called Mungo and

Columbine a plantation owner's daughter who has fallen in love with him. Conventionally, Harlequin always marries Columbine but this inter-racial match must have had distinct audience approval because the panto-mime was so popular it was played at least thirty-seven times.[12] The piece begins with a slave sale, which would have featured blacked-up actors – a counterfeit that drains power from the representation of Africans on stage and obscures the horror of the situation. Yet, once Mungo is trans-formed into Harlequin, he wears the traditional black mask of a much-loved character who is always accorded respect. The pantomime also includes a Chinaman – another popular touch as the East India Company had a refuge at Angel Gardens, Shadwell, for Chinese seamen awaiting passage home. In sum, it was just the kind of entertainment that appealed to a mixed, international audience of seamen and local residents.

In this period, drama was so popular that the acting of plays was used in the navy and in other military settings as a pastime to raise morale in the ranks.[13] Given the numbers of seamen in the Royalty's audience, the theatre staged pieces with a naval theme from the first. In 1787, it put on *The Recruiting Serjeant* and *True Blue; or, the Press Gang*. Such pieces helped to build the community's sense of its unique maritime identity. Yet the theatre took care to appeal to wealthier residents and to loyalist sentiment gener-ally. An evening performance in 1787 was staged for the benefit of the Marine Society. It included a '*back scene*' which revealed 'a view of the sea, a man of war with colours flying . . . Then a procession of the Marine boys, with officers and sailors.' The curtain dropped to 'Rule, Britannia!'[14]

The Royalty's distance from London's patent theatres and its obligation to avoid the spoken word meant that it funnelled talent and creativity into a different path. It not only presented topical material but also set out to engage specific audiences. One such attempt was *The Pirates; Or, the Calamities of Capt. Bligh*, first performed on 3 May 1789 and promising a full account of the *Bounty* mutiny. It can only have added to the notoriety of the Bligh household and made Betsy doubly anxious to vacate Wapping. The play included a dumb show with representations of familiar riverside locations as the *Bounty* was portrayed leaving London for the sea. The

166

piece had a dozen or so performances but was far from being a runaway success.[15] As details of the *Bounty* voyage seem to have been supplied by Bligh's own clerk, it may not have offered the gritty, lower-deck reasons for the mutiny that audiences sought.

Much of the non-dramatic material staged at the Royalty was also maritime in nature. Young women often performed 'Sea Songs', alluding to cases of cross-dressing women in warships and alleged displays of female valour. The varied fare in non-licensed theatres certainly offered more parts for women than the approved canon of drama in the patent theatres. It also gave opportunities for coarse adlibs that helped to justify the description of non-licensed theatres as places of 'vicious amusement'. 'The Merry Little Tar', performed at the Royalty in the 1790s by a 'Miss Gray', gives an indication of the fun to be had. It begins:

> I'm a merry little tar,
> And the ocean is my pot,
> And a pretty many brats has my dad;
> Yet each a fighting cock,
> A chip of the old block
> Like me, a wicked, saucy, dashing lad.
> For whether land or sea,
> It matter's not to me,
> 'Tis yeo, yeo, yeo! Kiss away the lasses.[16]

Predictably, in the 1790s, many of 'the most respectable and opulent Merchants, Shipbuilders, Ropemakers, and other Gentlemen' thereabouts complained that the Royalty would increase dissipation and criminal activity in the neighbourhood.[17]

Palmer, whose nickname was 'Plausible Jack', had a distinctive acting style. One contemporary admirer claimed, 'there was an air of swaggering gentility about Jack Palmer. He was a gentleman with a slight infusion of the footman.'[18] This may help to explain his ability to connect with lowly audiences. He led a rackety life and his career included several mishaps that caused him serious injury (he was stabbed when a spring dagger failed to close in a stage fight and fell through a stage trapdoor that opened too abruptly, needing months to recover). The untimely deaths of his wife and a young son exacerbated his failing health and he died in 1798 aged fifty-four. Though Palmer failed to get a licence for the Royalty, the playhouse had lasting impact. In 1813 it was seating 1,600. His struggle against its closure ignited a pamphlet war that continued after his death. The language of this debate reflected fiery arguments about rights and freedoms that were rife in the early 1790s after the French Revolution. His theatre proposals helped to prime a community to connect with these larger issues.

South of the river, people also enjoyed dramatic performances. Jonathan Oldfield, sometime dealer in tea and china, built a neat little theatre by converting the warehouse of a paper manufacturer next to the pub he ran on the Deptford Lower Road in Rotherhithe. Oldfield called his theatre the China Hall and he meant to run it as a summer venue, when light evenings would encourage attendance. It opened in 1776 and could hold 500 people. The prices for seats were three shillings for either a box or the pit, and one shilling for the gallery, which compared well with the more expensive West End theatres. The acting was also reputed to be better than in most theatres outside London. Performances were by and large musical comedies but drama was certainly attempted. In May 1776, both George Farquhar's *The Beaux' Stratagem* and Arthur Murphy's *The Citizen. A Farce* were staged – the proceeds going to the Rotherhithe poor. Growing bolder, that September Oldfield put on Shakespeare's *Cymbeline*, admittedly to mixed reviews.[19] Yet such was the local interest in drama, he was able to set up a 'theatrical academy' next door, where pupils rehearsed popular pieces. Their student performances were praised for being word-perfect, and costumes were said to be as good as in Drury Lane.[20]

By 1777, the China Hall was run by actor-manager Samuel Russell, who went on stage alongside his wife and son. On 23 July, he was giving a performance in Susannah Centlivre's play *A Bold Stroke for a Wife* when he was arrested and carried off to the house of correction. Local residents had informed against him. Either they objected to the content of the play, which satirized Quakers and capitalist greed, or they registered that Russell was breaking the licensing laws by staging spoken drama. On a more positive note, the 'spouting club' for young actors at the China Hall became a school of oratory, which held debates there from May 1780. These entertainments were part of the debating society movement, which raged from the late 1770s until 1795. At that date, the societies were repressed in the crackdown on free speech following the French Revolution.

The extraordinary thing is that women (who sometimes ran their own societies) attended mixed debates and dared to air their views in public, in spite of harsh criticism. Debating societies were well attended, so although admission cost less than a theatre ticket, events could still turn in a handsome profit. Attendees considered debates the kind of 'rational entertainment' a polite society ought to encourage. They questioned politics, morals and relations between the sexes. For example, a 1780 gathering at the China Hall considered, 'When the affections of the female sex are improperly attached, who is most blameable, the man or the woman?'[21] Later the China Hall seems to have degenerated somewhat. By 1783 cockfighting matches were held there for five guineas a battle. Specially bred birds were given long steel spurs and driven to fight to the death. Afternoon matches were well-advertised county-wide contests, aimed at gentlemen and preceded by a dinner.[22] By 1805 the venue was simply a public house.

The great English actor and singer of the 1780s and 1790s, Charles Bannister, grew up in Deptford where his father was an official in the navy's victualling yard. His career gives an insight into the local enthusiasm for drama. Bannister was besotted with the stage from his early years, thanks to the fame of David Garrick – even more so because his distance from Drury Lane Theatre and the difficulty of getting home at a late hour meant that he was rarely able to see Garrick perform. There were several local dramatic clubs, and as Charles had an exquisite voice, he was soon in great demand at musical and theatrical meetings. Being the son of an influential man, he took all the lead parts. In 1775–76 he was to be found acting Richard III, Romeo and other Shakespearean roles in a barn between Deptford and Greenwich. This came to the ears of his father who swiftly stopped his performances by taking his clothes away and locking him up. Left in this state of nakedness, Bannister was said to have filled his time rehearsing 'Poor Tom's a cold', the Fool's speech in *King Lear*, without even the prop of a blanket.

Punishment only made Bannister more determined. As soon as he got his clothes back, he returned to the drama of Deptford and afterwards succeeded as a professional actor.[23] He was a firm friend of Palmer, since they made their debut on the London stage together, and he took the lead in several musical entertainments at the Royalty Theatre. Famously, Bannister could not read a note of music but had a perfect ear and could sing any piece once he had learned it by heart. Whether theatres were a force for good or evil was a topic that debating societies took up. You can see what critics objected to from one of the songs Bannister sang at the Royalty:

If life is a bubble, and breaks with a blast,
You must toss off your wine, if you'd wish it to last;
For this bubble may well be destroy'd with a puff,
If it is not kept floating in liquor enough.[24]

Yet such material was all the rage. The songs performed in the Royalty and in other theatres were printed to meet popular demand, sometimes with the music.

Spouting clubs and debating societies across London promoted an articulate artisan class with its own heroes. In the maritime districts, theatre and musical performances helped to represent the aspirations of a community. Seating at these events may have been divided by class, but the subjects treated, the representations of familiar local sights and the experience of enjoying an event alongside hundreds of others all reinforced the identity of a local audience. The acting fever continued to build in Deptford. A new theatre opened there in 1786, giving performances that appealed directly to the culture, prosperity and maritime heritage of Kent.[25] Other entertainments included political meetings, dances and events held regularly at the assembly rooms at the Golden Eagle in Deptford Church Street, which had its own master of ceremonies. Clearly, local districts could make a variety of entertainments pay. Debate was curtailed in the 1790s, but the theatre's ability to reach so many people in a single interactive performance meant that it became a vital channel for wartime patriotism.

Shopping and other diversions

In the busy maritime districts, shopping was mostly a chore, not a pastime. Even so, the shopping experience of residents was changing and increasingly promised novelty and pleasure. Retail practices along the river were never going to be as crucial to sustaining polite culture as in the fashionable West End. Yet maritime Londoners were perhaps more conscious of the link between shopping and global trade, which they were helping to expand. This added a certain pride to their shopping experience. Households still sourced food and basic goods from markets, fairs and street-hawkers. Numerous local shops were simply the front street-level room of a tradesman's terraced house. Yet, however poor, every maritime parish had a few high-end shops.[26] Residents did not necessarily have to travel to the latest, upmarket premises in Oxford Street, or even to Cheapside, for choice goods. For example, J. Robinson had a carpet, bedding and furniture warehouse on Ratcliff Highway in the 1770s. In the 1780s, the local shoemaker in Wapping opened a boot and shoe warehouse near Hermitage Stairs.[27]

By the middle of the century, 'warehouse' was already coming into general use as a dignified term for 'shop'. The East India Company regularly auctioned the imports in its warehouses for retail sale. By association, 'warehouse' carried an exotic charge. China retailers were early adopters of the term, perhaps wishing to signal consumer choice. Early in the century, they would have bought most of the china in their shops at one of the East India Company's auctions. From 1753, the English china works at Bow called its retail and wholesale operation a 'warehouse'. It had modelled its factory in Stratford, Essex, on the East India Company's warehouses in Canton to signal its ambition to rival Chinese porcelain. Critics complained that soon there would be no such thing as a shop or tradesman in London because every 'little pimping shop' was termed a warehouse and every master of one dubbed himself a merchant.[28] China was a purchase that needed careful deliberation. Michael Henley's first wife found Wapping High Street, near the docks and its warehouses, well situated for shops. She shopped locally for basic goods and had family clothes made by a local seamstress. But in 1780, she travelled to Borough High Street to a 'glass, chinaman and potter' to choose a set of fashionable china figures.[29]

Shopping trends were linked to what was happening to local fairs, which had once been centres of trade and commerce. Fairs always included entertainments but that was not their prime purpose. In the late eighteenth century, this changed: booths offering amusements or shows began to outnumber those offering merchandise. As everyday goods were mostly bought in high streets and markets, fairs became unashamed opportunities for dissipation. Bartholomew Fair in Smithfield was by far the largest in London, held annually in September and attracting thousands. There were several others, including Southwark, Greenwich and Peckham fairs. All had the same ingredients: stalls selling food and beer, music and singing, quack doctors, puppet shows, wax or clockwork figures, conjurers, caged beasts, rope dancing, acrobats, fire eating and other performances. Crowds flocking to these events grew increasingly drunk and rowdy as the day wore on.

A great number of sailors went to Bartholomew Fair, which was within easy walking distance of Wapping. The crowds could be targeted by protestors. In 1783, after the Peace of Paris formally ended the American War, one wounded seaman distributed a tract there to get money. He complained that with the end of the war naval seamen were neglected:

> I'll tell you how we are rewarded for all our pains, to go in the streets and beg, thieve, or starve and be Hanged for what they care what become of us. We once fought like Men, the same as we go unregarded, and die like Dogs; we who was prized once, are now despised, and become the Objects of hatred.[30]

This was rousing stuff and very different from the usual begging on street corners. Such occurrences may have helped to prompt an uneasy sense that fairs could encourage civil unrest as well as general debauchery.

Fairs, and the disturbances they caused, attracted growing criticism. The closing scenes of Bartholomew Fair in 1784 were particularly sensational:

> On Tuesday night Bartholomew Fair closed with that kind of regularity which the public always expects in the fashionable circle of Smithfield bucks, Wapping beaux, and the black-eyed and bloody-nosed fair sex from Chick-Lane, saltpetre Bank, and Hedge and Petticoat Lanes. The music of the retreat was a discord; two penny drums, halfpenny trumpets, roaring boys, weeping children, hoarse sweeps as a thorough bass to the tender squalls of drunken doxies, and a general clash of mugs, jugs, and bottles as the Grand Finale.[31]

There had been a gathering of 20,000 people. The commentator continued, with some exaggeration, that it would have been hard to find one respectable tradesman or tradesman's servant in a hundred, most of the crowd being pickpockets. In short, the fair was a 'disgrace to decency' which should be stopped. The patronizing tone indicates that respectable Londoners were increasingly distancing themselves from such entertainments.

The worst excesses of the Horn Fair at Charlton were also tamed around this time. Traditionally, the crowd for this event met on 18 October, St Luke's Day, at Cuckold's Point on a sharp bend of the river at Rotherhithe. It then formed a procession through Deptford and Greenwich to Charlton, with participants wearing horns of different kinds. Most of the articles sold at the fair were goods made of horn. Licensed in 1204, the fair supposedly marked King John's seduction of a local villager's wife. It had always been very disorderly (horns were a symbol of a cuckolded husband). Women treated the day as an opportunity to disregard all normal social restrictions on their behaviour. Finally, in the 1780s, peace officers were ordered to attend the procession to Charlton.[32]

People of the time also laid wagers on feats of strength as a form of entertainment. Those desperate to earn money took advantage of the contemporary passion for gambling. For example, one noted swimmer, a Deptford waterman, bet ten guineas that he could swim from Greenwich to the opposite shore and back with a seven-pound weight tied to each foot and his son, a boy of ten years old, on his back. He made it without stopping, though perhaps his son helped with the leg strokes. At a Deptford pub, a man waged a guinea he could drink sixteen quarts of beer in sixteen draughts. He succeeded, without seeming unduly intoxicated. Unfortunately, a man who wagered he could drink a pint of gin standing expired soon afterwards.[33]

Other popular pastimes where money changed hands included bare-knuckle fighting. Prizefighting was outlawed in 1750 but illegal betting was rife. Blackheath was a notable venue for these bouts, although matches were sometimes held in central London. Several contests between so-called 'bruisers' would take place in one afternoon. Spectators formed a simple ring, though crowds could make the ring six-deep and the total number of spectators could reach thousands. Boxing matches were inevitably a target for pickpockets but they also attracted military men and enthusiasts who wished to try their strength. Sports journalism came into being during the closing decades of the century. A commentary on a twenty-minute contest between Doyle, a boxer who challenged all comers, and a Deptford sawyer named Edwards shows that spectators were beginning to expect some rules. Onlookers might intervene if they thought a blow was a foul:

> In the course of this by-battle, Doyle kicked his antagonist; and what added to the unfairness of the action was, that it was at a time when he lay on the ground. The spectators all joined in an universal hiss.[34]

Edwards afterwards went on to try his luck at other prizefights.

Maimed ex-seamen sometimes took to boxing as a means of making money. If one had lost a leg, both were tied to chairs and fought from a sitting position so that neither had an advantage. This was not as odd as it sounds. Before Daniel Mendoza became England's boxing champion in the 1790s there was little ducking and weaving in the sport. Boxers aimed to stand their ground and swap punches. By the 1780s, boxing was so fashionable that some well-heeled youths took lessons. The middling sort, being heavily engaged in good causes, took the opportunity to emphasize the corruption of the aristocracy. They pointed out that the rage for boxing was inconsistent with the contemporary passion for humanity, relieving the poor, abolishing the slave trade and setting up Sunday schools. Some even used this inconsistency to question commitment to humanitarian reform.[35]

Charitable giving

The middling sort drew satisfaction from a range of Christian good works. Successful businessmen, for example, demonstrated their status by taking leading roles in local charities. Much of this activity also offered opportunities for respectable amusements, in the form of annual sermons given by noted speakers, children's picnics, charity dinners and other social gatherings.

Increasing numbers of charity schools were established during the eighteenth century, following the foundation of the Society for Promoting Christian Knowledge in 1698. This was an Anglican movement set up to encourage Christian education and distribute Christian literature. It gave advice to charity schools and helped to coordinate them. The schools were landmark institutions in many London parishes including Poplar, Shadwell, Wapping and Greenwich. They taught reading, writing and basic arithmetic (girls were sometimes taught knitting and sewing instead of maths). Boys and girls were segregated, dressed in a sober uniform, and instructed in the need for humility and hard work. The curriculum was weighted towards the Bible and the Catechism, even after mid-century when more varied teaching materials were available. Yet parents were anxious to get their children into these schools, particularly because they helped to place pupils in apprenticeships. Even children who rebelled against the system, like Mary Lacey, derived some benefit from their charity school education.

The schools did not admit dregs from the gutter. Desperately poor and dysfunctional families could not give their children the time to learn their letters. Their children had to contribute to the family income. Nor could the indigent poor afford the basic items of uniform that schools sometimes asked parents to provide. As student places were limited, charity schools generally chose to admit children of the 'worthy poor'. These hard-working people might struggle to make ends meet but could be expected to support their children's education and uphold a school's religious framework.[36]

Charity schools were funded by subscription, endowment or individual sponsorship. Sound business sense was often linked to charitable motives; the middling sort avidly supported these schools as subscribers, managers and teachers.[37] After all, they stood to benefit from the resulting labour pool – maidservants who could count would not be cheated by lying tradesmen, and young labourers who were literate could more readily be trained up. The schools also offered wealthy women a rare opportunity to be active in the community. In 1791, Mary Slade was one of only two women in a list of seventy-five subscribers to Deptford's charity school.[38]

These parish schools always needed to fundraise and, at the very least, money was collected at an annual sermon to mark a school's foundation day. Charity sermons, delivered in the presence of the children, were eagerly anticipated events. Often a notable preacher like Dr Milne would be secured. A new hymn might be composed for the children to sing and afterwards printed with the names of the officiating clergy and the subscribers. This advertised their generosity and encouraged others to make donations. In St John's parish, Wapping, the boys and girls led a procession around the parish boundary after the church service, then everyone took refreshments in a garden near the river. The annual sermon was advertised in advance and well attended. One year, the guest preacher missed his way in Wapping and turned up at the wrong venue, to be faced by a disconcertingly empty church. A lowly official sheepishly explained to him that the congregation had mostly gone to a neighbouring church in order to hear the charity sermon. Realizing his mistake, the clergyman rushed off and got to his engagement with minutes to spare.[39]

Milne gained admiration and status through his passionate sermons on benevolence in the 1770s and 1780s. His oratory, especially on behalf of good causes like charity schools and lying-in hospitals, appealed directly to the emotions of his audience. It chimed well with society's increasing sympathy for the distressed and frequent calls for active philanthropy. His admirers – perhaps with some encouragement because he had a large family to provide for – praised him in the press and intimated that he was wasted on Deptford and should be preaching to fashionable audiences in St James's. When, in April 1786, the much-loved Rector of St Paul's, Richard Conyers, was seized with apoplexy in the pulpit and died shortly afterwards, an admirer of Milne wrote to a newspaper to lobby for Milne to take the vacancy. The clergyman, who by now had eleven children, some chronically ill, may have been prepared to do his utmost to get a good living, but the newspaper article smacked of indirect self-promotion. It irritated readers and Milne was passed over. He nevertheless obtained several preaching roles that kept him in the public eye. While he raised money for good causes, his son swiftly progressed up the naval ranks. The two developments were perhaps not unconnected.

Charity clearly functioned as a means of social control. The 'deserving poor' and those who seemed set on a path to reformation were favoured recipients. The element of display in charitable giving placed worthy causes above cases of mere desperation. It was this rational approach that helped to make sustained charitable work a highly esteemed interest, although impulsive generosity still won plaudits.

River pleasures and dangers

Britain's wealth was perhaps nowhere more visible than in the docks and wharves along the Thames, but the river was also a place of entertainment. Watermen held rowing races at Deptford on the anniversary of the King's coronation, which made a fine spectacle with music and flags, although regattas and races were mostly held upriver where there was less chance of conflict with commercial shipping. The 1775 regatta was particularly chaotic. It was reported in tones that reflected contemporary insecurities about the mixing of social ranks and government mishandling of the dispute with the North American colonies.[40] The message was that public events had to be well managed to convey social order. Fortunately, Deptford had its own annual ceremony in the Trinity House procession that was always under control. Each Trinity Monday the masters and elder brethren went downriver in the Admiralty barge from Trinity House on Tower Hill to their hall in Deptford where they elected the master and deputy master for the coming year. Wharves and ships on the river were decorated with bunting, passing vessels saluted them, and they were received at Deptford with cannon fire and other festivities. After visiting their almshouses and inspecting the poor, the brethren attended a sermon in St Nicholas's church before returning by water to Trinity Stairs. Then they went by carriage to Trinity House or to the London Tavern in Bishopsgate to dine with members of the nobility and other distinguished guests. The colourful spectacle was always reported in newspapers and the ritual served to reinforce the importance of the maritime parishes.

The river itself afforded opportunities for charitable work. In 1774, the Society for the Recovery of Persons Apparently Drowned, later called the Humane Society, was formed to help save people from drowning in the Thames. Few Londoners could swim, although many worked on the river. It was not the popular sport that it is today and children were not routinely taught to swim. The founders of this society – doctors William Hawes and Thomas Cogan – were worried that people dragged promptly from the Thames might be taken for dead and even buried alive. They promoted a technique likely to recover those who had inhaled water. The maritime parishes were active in this society, even though it operated from the London Coffee-House and other premises in the Strand.[41] Churches gave benefit sermons to raise money for it. The Society also harnessed the growing readership of newspapers to publicize its work, and its benevolence contributed to mounting awareness of the culture of 'politeness' in the maritime parishes. It gave a two-guinea reward to rescuers who pulled people from the river, and gave four guineas if they resuscitated someone.

A guinea went to those who allowed their premises to be used for treatment. The poor soon devised scams: one pretended to be a victim, another their rescuer, and they split the money afterwards. Financial rewards were later replaced with medals and certificates.

In 1783, Deptford residents set up a dispensary that gave medicines to the poor free of charge and paid for assistants to visit them in their own homes. There had been a smallpox outbreak two years earlier and local resistance to inoculation meant that ten to twenty a week died.[42] Many were still suspicious of inoculation while others had strong religious and ethical objections to it. This outbreak may have predisposed residents to look kindly on plans for a dispensary. Eight others had already been set up in London since 1770, including the Surrey Dispensary just south of London Bridge. Milne was considered 'the father of the Kent Dispensary', although it was the work of a local group. He promoted the idea in his sermons and his 'powerful appeal to the heart' encouraged Deptford's wealthier inhabitants, together with the nobility and gentry of western Kent, to give generously.[43] The MP Charles Marsham was elected its president in 1784. The dispensary boasted a medical committee (a physician and two surgeons who gave their services gratis) and it employed a resident apothecary, medical assistants and midwives. Mary Slade generously offered to build the dispensary if a suitable site could be found but the committee felt that her proposal could not be accepted.[44] Either the charity could not afford the land or its officials did not want a woman taking a key role. Instead, they took up the offer of space in a house on Deptford Broadway.

Given the number of local people in dangerous employment, accidents when people needed urgent medical attention were frequent. Benefactors realized that simply giving money to the injured poor did not ensure recovery since they were at the mercy of quack doctors. Many lost their lives taking spurious medicines.[45] Typically, the dispensary targeted the deserving poor: no lunatics, unmarried mothers or venereal cases were treated. The aim was to preserve 'the toiling hand of industry'.[46] The standard donation to the dispensary was one guinea, so William Barnard and John Dudman, both private shipbuilders, made a gesture when each gave ten guineas. Yet this was a charity they anticipated using to the full. Ten guineas entitled them to have ten patients treated at any one time.[47] Patients needed a recommendation from one of the charity's regular subscribers. Accident cases received urgent treatment but a recommendation had to be obtained for aftercare. The charity raised over £550 in the first four months. While the organizers received no salary, many were in trade and naturally they did good business in contracting with the dispensary, supplying wine, spirits, rhubarb, coal and stationery. The dispensary was extremely well run. Donations were carefully invested and the scale of its operation grew to cover an area from Rotherhithe to Woolwich. In the first two years, it treated nearly 4,000 patients. It also donated money to the Humane Society. William Barnard was one of the governors who oversaw investments and he signed off the accounts in the 1790s.

While this philanthropy was partly self-serving, since even those who did not benefit financially gained status from being involved in a prestigious venture, it does show growing sympathy for the distressed. One notorious case illustrates this. Early on, when the dispensary was a resource for victims of highway robbery, its staff were completely taken in by Bridget Bonner, found almost naked in a gravel pit on Blackheath in 1785. She claimed to have been dragged from her carriage and robbed of 500 guineas but it was an elaborate hoax. Either she and her accomplices hoped to benefit from a public collection, or they expected that the money she claimed to have lost would be reimbursed. Her story became ever more exaggerated until the charity distanced itself, claiming that 'her tale was too absurd to gain confidence with men of business'. The fact is, though, that spurred by humanity and fellow feeling, the dispensary had warmly taken up her case.[48]

London's colourful maritime districts offered a range of entertainments, outside the daily round of social visits, which contributed to a vibrant quality of life. The middling sort also encouraged cultural opportunities, including debate and drama, which in turn helped to advance and affirm their social position. Clearly, too, there was an increasing level of charitable activity which promoted local well-being. Growing philanthropy, which followed a national trend, underlines not just the needs of the poor but also the success of the middling ranks. In particular, charity provided opportunities for women to assert their presence in society. The middling sort in these hard-working districts had confidence in their ability and worth; they asserted this in the capable government of their own neighbourhoods. If they seized opportunities to display a feeling heart, as an aspect of polite behaviour, it was tempered by judgement. Conveniently, many businessmen and tradespeople who aspired to good breeding felt that they were bound to consider what they owed themselves, as well as others. Yet the best of them did not sacrifice character to wealth: Barnard was still dutifully overseeing the finances of the dispensary while ill and in the final year of his life.

It was just as well that London's maritime parishes were taking confident steps to educate the poor, address local health problems and create rational diversions. These energetic districts were crucial to the economy and to national defence. Systems that upheld stability were much needed: not least because there would soon be another war.

7

WAR WITH FRANCE

On 21 January 1793, Louis XVI of France went to the guillotine. When news reached England on the 23rd, George III cancelled his planned trip to the theatre. The following evening, the Haymarket closed its doors as a mark of respect to the dead monarch and out of loyalty to George. *The Times* reported:

> The REPUBLICAN TYRANTS OF FRANCE have now carried their bloody purposes to the uttermost diabolical stretch of savage cruelty. They have murdered their King without even the shadow of justice, and of course they cannot expect friendship nor intercourse with any civilized part of the world.[1]

There had been a remarkable change in British public opinion since the fall of the Bastille marked the beginning of the French Revolution in 1789. Then, many onlookers rejoiced that France seemed to be throwing off the yoke of tyrannical rule and pursuing the kind of constitutional government that England had enjoyed since its own struggles against absolute monarchy in the seventeenth century. Famously, William Wordsworth conveyed this enthusiasm when he wrote of his own youthful support for Revolutionary France, 'Bliss was it in that dawn to be alive'.[2] So when, in 1790, the politician Edmund Burke published his *Reflections on the Revolution in France*, warning of the dangers of the French people overthrowing their government and acting as a violent mob, many refuted him. They scorned his apparent fear of progress. And they mocked his defence of France's absolute monarchy, which most considered outmoded and despotic. Thomas Paine wrote the most effective rejoinder to Burke. His *Rights of Man* (1791–92) sold a million copies, so it is said. Paine strongly supported the revolution and set out the natural rights of the individual in such simple, compelling language that he helped to spark a popular movement in Britain. Yet Burke was soon proved right: revolution in France led to excess, anarchy and bloodshed.

The disappointment of British liberals at this turn of events is painfully evident in Charlotte Smith's *The Emigrants*, a poem in two books. In Book I, she strongly supports French demands for greater freedom. She imagines that liberty for all will lead to greater equality for women. (She herself was trapped in an unhappy marriage.) She turns her focus on British society, bravely denouncing 'oppression' and 'legal crimes' that made a 'mockery' of Britain's familiar boast that all were equal before the law. Book II is much darker. She wrote it after the Terror in the summer of 1792, when thousands of innocent citizens in Paris and other French cities went to the guillotine:

And see the Temple, which they fondly hop'd
Reason would raise to Liberty, destroy'd
By ruffian hands; while, on the ruin'd mass,
Flush'd with hot blood, the Fiend of Discord sits
In savage triumph; mocking every plea
Of policy and justice.[3]

Her lines convey the despair of those who had anticipated reform.

Britain, while remaining neutral after the French Revolution, had started to prepare for war with its old enemy in 1792. Towards the end of that year, French troops occupied Brussels and began to threaten British trade along the Scheldt into the Netherlands. After the execution of Louis XVI, the British government judged it timely to make a move. Although the British army was small, at 15,000 men, its navy was well prepared. Yet the government did not wish to seem the aggressor; there were many in Britain ready to oppose a costly war entailing higher taxes. It therefore manoeuvred France into declaring war on Britain and the Netherlands, which France did on 1 February 1793.

In the long wars that followed, lasting an entire generation, all Britons bore a heavy burden. Maritime London was particularly affected. While war raged, labour relations and working practices along the river, methods of cargo handling and even attitudes to seamen all underwent change. These developments emerged during bitter struggles that inevitably raised questions about who held power in society and who had responsibility for solving social problems.

Preparations for war

In 1792, the British government was confident that the Royal Navy would be effective against Revolutionary France. In 1790, the navy had easily seen off a Spanish threat to Britain's share of the fur trade at Nootka Sound, on the west coast of Canada's Vancouver Island. In that crisis, Britain mobilized a formidable battle fleet more quickly than any other western power could have done. Now these well-rehearsed procedures were again put into action. Private shipbuilders along the Thames were crucial to naval preparation, as in the American War: the government swiftly placed contracts with private yards for six new warships. Rendezvous houses were opened in the maritime districts so that seamen could enlist. Pressed men were held in an old frigate moored at the Tower before being taken downriver to the navy's anchorage at the Nore in the Thames Estuary. Victualling preparations in the Deptford yard were ramped up as provisions were sent to forces overseas. Cavalry troops were stationed at Deptford and Greenwich to protect military installations. Plans were even made to form veteran marines from Greenwich Hospital into companies to guard the royal dockyards, although each had its own battalion of volunteer employees for defence. In a new development, carpenters in Deptford dockyard were ordered to make prefabricated barracks, so that soldiers could be posted to key defensive points on the coast. People at all levels were caught up in the mobilization and for some the excitement was electric.

In these early months of war, the departure of three regiments of guards for the Continent was staged as a set piece. The ceremony – attended by the royal family – took place at the naval hospital in Greenwich and ran like clockwork. As each boat left the shore, the crowd gave three cheers, the King took off his hat, and the Queen and Princesses waved their handkerchiefs. Some shed a tear. This was the first of many embarkations of men and horses from the Thames. Most regiments marched to the river from central London, then found local quarters before boarding. Storage also had to be found for their provisions and animal fodder. All this caused disruption but also gave opportunities for moneymaking and displays of status. In June 1793, when eight troops of Dragoon Guards took ship from Mr Perry's Yard at Blackwall, he prepared an elegant pavilion for the King and the Prince of Wales. Perry impressed onlookers with an effective system for boarding startled horses and was later to negotiate part-use of his yard by the government in wartime.

In maritime London, military preparations were familiar. After all, in the eighteenth century the nation was often at war. But this time there was a real difference. The revolutionary principles that had ignited France had also found fertile ground in Britain, particularly in London, where pockets of radicalism flourished. The execution of the French royal family had done little to dampen the revolutionary enthusiasm of these groups. As the mobilization progressed, government supporters became uneasy. It was not simply that, as usual, war had its opponents: some had a nagging anxiety that the patriotism of key workers, on whom the nation depended for its defence, could not be trusted. Even Kent, which was not radical in the way that industrialized Middlesex or Southwark were, had groups actively pressing for parliamentary reform. These agitators had long aimed to reduce corrupt electioneering and to improve representation by increasing the number of MPs. Now they became linked to the revolution-aries across the Channel. Rising prices fuelled civil discontent. Local political debate, coloured by a strong undercurrent of sedition, contributed to the breathless trepidation with which some viewed the new conflict. Paine, fearing arrest, had gone to live in France. He was ostentatiously accused of betraying his country, while his wife was maliciously reported to be living in a Southwark workhouse.[4] Military preparations seemed poised to deal as much with the enemy within as the enemy without.

In anticipation of war, Pitt had already passed an Aliens Act in 1793, which banned French republicans from entering the country and stopped the exchange of visitors and public speakers. Officials were aware that French agents would be making assessments of Britain's wartime strength in just the same way that, up and down the river, sea captains were talking about enemy preparations. Those returning from the Continent with special knowledge about the French fleet, or about supply chains affecting key towns, hastily communicated it to ministers. There was nervousness about the infiltration of spies and radical ideas into the dockyards. At the end of 1792, a foreman was discharged at Plymouth dockyard for 'seditiously propagating Paine's works among the shipwrights' to subvert them from their duty to King and Country.[5] Already, other yards had tightened security. At Deptford, where there had been a case of arson in 1791, no strangers were admitted and known visitors with legitimate business had to be escorted. Even so, in July 1793 there was a mysterious fire in the sail loft which spread to the paint storerooms. No one could account for it as candles had not been in use.[6] But arson was a known resort of the power-less: it caused damage and delay, usually without loss of life.

The riverside parishes were bound to be conflicted about the onset of war. It directly impacted sailors, dockyard workers and those in numerous maritime-related trades. The navy alone expanded hugely, from 17,000 men in 1792 to over 130,000 by 1801.[7] Press gangs marching seamen away encountered derisive London crowds singing 'Britons never will be slaves'. Yet, as in other wars, sailors in the merchant service saw an opportunity to bargain for more pay. Shipwrights were glad of the extra work because Thameside shipyards had just gone through yet another slack period. William Barnard had written to newspapers in 1787 complaining that the Admiralty had placed no contracts for warships with private yards since 1782; the East India Company had placed no contracts since March 1785; 460 shipwrights and 170 sawyers had been laid off.[8] In the wake of the Nootka Sound crisis, shipwrights in Deptford dockyard had been relieved to be employed on a modest, 50-gun warship: to be discharged would have meant destitution. In a turn of events, by 1792 shipwrights were working double shifts and the dockyard had taken on more men.

Dockyard workers routinely became militant in wartime. The longer working hours were a strain and men seized chances to ask for higher wages while they were in a good negotiating position. In 1794, caulkers at Deptford demanded double pay to work on Sundays. This was granted at first but when the men queued for payment, the extra money was refused. Some went on strike but the dispute fizzled out. The determination of dockyard officials to stand firm may have discouraged immediate trouble at Deptford, though the following year, at Chatham, shipwrights went on strike for nearly a month. Naval shipwrights naturally compared their wages with the high salaries private yards offered due to labour shortages. In 1795, some private shipbuilders were paying shipwrights twenty shillings a day.[9] In January 1796, a serious dispute broke out at Deptford dockyard when shipwrights objected to house carpenters being employed to build ship cabins. Panelling a cabin was easier work than building a hull and shipwrights regarded it as a perk of their job. Six hundred shipwrights were promptly discharged. Loyalists commented that these disputes came at a time when 'people talk of their rights and forget their duties'.[10]

With the onset of war, 'democrat' had become a term of abuse, although even-handed observers recognized that the term 'aristocrat' implied faults as well. Some complained that until the elite set a better example, those who aimed to reform the lower orders by promoting schools of industry and Sunday schools were wasting their time.[11] As Pitt's government introduced increasingly repressive measures to deal with radicalism, ordinary people among the middling ranks were dismayed to find their own lives and interests constricted too. In the maritime parishes, a society set up in 1791 for the improvement of naval architecture soon faltered, although it experimented in the latest designs and was enthusiastically supported by local shipbuilders. Debating societies, which had been a mark of engagement in the civic realm, attracting all who could afford the price of admission, were now frowned upon.

The behaviour of women was a focus of attention. There had been growing anxieties about independently minded women since at least the mid-1780s. The French Revolution intensified these feelings. Commentators urged women to shun the harridan-like behaviour attributed to housewives in Revolutionary Paris. From the late 1790s, British publications aimed at female readers (mostly written by men) became more insistent that women should cultivate passive virtues: humble resignation and cheerful contentment. The *Ladies Magazine* featured hardly any political material. Amusingly, it portrayed a genteel metropolitan scene that was poles apart from the revolution raging 300 miles away in Paris. There was an assumed link between feminism and radicalism, so women were discouraged from meddling in politics. Those who did, like the writer and Dissenter Anna Laetitia Barbauld, were held up to ridicule and strongly criticized. Instead, the advice for respectable women was that they should restrict their activities to parenting and the 'social round': giving dinners, paying visits and gracing ceremonies such as funerals, where they were adept at sympathizing with the bereaved.

Images of Amazonian-type women were held up for ridicule and condemnation. Fashionable riding habits with a masculine cut, criticized during the American Revolutionary War, were now vehemently denounced as inappropriate wear for a woman: 'They wholly unsex her, and give her the unpleasing air of an Amazon, or a virago.'[12] Cross-dressing in plays became problematic.[13] Women's assumed fragility was reflected in the spate of advertisements for off-the-shelf remedies for female ailments. The 'scandalous immorality' of women from the lower orders, long frowned upon, attracted increasing disapproval. Admittedly, it was open knowledge that not even all tradesmen's daughters were chaste. Within their peer group, provided they behaved respectably in other matters, such women were still considered good marriage prospects.[14] Now the slipshod poor were more harshly caricatured as unreasonably envious and discontented with their God-given lot. The 'knowing coarseness' of the 'typical' Wapping landlady came in for sharper criticism.[15] The violent protest of some poor women may have hastened this reaction. In 1803, for example, when Admiralty officials inspected Deptford dockyard, they were 'pelted with mud by the women and boys' for the hardship their economies caused. The women could not be fired and acted to protect their men.[16]

Waving the flag

If some pursuits that the middling sort enjoyed were stifled, at least there was an acceptable outlet for social diversion in patriotic activity. The loyalist reaction to the growth of radicalism is usually dated to May 1792 when George III issued a royal proclamation against seditious publications, including Paine's answer to Burke. Loyalist organizations sprang up, encouraged by government, as fears of radical violence grew. The Association for Preserving Liberty and Property Against Republicans and Levellers was founded in November 1792 at the Crown and Anchor tavern in the Strand. It triggered offshoots in London's maritime parishes and across the country. In Deptford, William Barnard chaired the meeting. He was worried about the feeble powers of local magistrates to keep order and actively used the association to intimidate neighbours inclined to radical views. His was the only branch known to have investigated reports of seditious meetings in local pubs.[17] The Association was funded to print and distribute loyalist works, a major sponsor being the Corporation of Trinity House, keen to see this literature go to seamen and dockyard labourers.

In an age when newspapers were still relatively expensive, sermons and cheap tracts peddled on the streets remained the surest means of reaching a wide audience. Clergymen were expected to encourage and comfort their congregations amid disturbances and in wartime. In the run-up to the war, the national anthem was introduced at the end of church services, as it was in the theatre. *The Star*, London's first daily evening newspaper, expressed approval: 'The custom is surely better than that of semi-quavering a congregation out of their pews to the measure of a jig, or a quick march, which has lately been the practice.'[18]

Patriotic sermons responded directly to the war effort. The Reverend Dr Milne, for example, preaching a sermon before the Deptford Volunteers in 1798, argued passionately for the justice of a defensive war. Some who read the published version thought he spent too much time answering the 'frivolous' objections of 'enthusiasts' who queried whether the pursuit of war was consistent with Christianity. Milne, though, knew that many Dissenters in Deptford worried about national guilt and divine judgment, and tailored his sermon accordingly.[19] The presence of volunteer regiments in church made a colourful show while helping to underline their importance, though not all were gratified by the swagger of the middling sort in uniform. Several maritime parishes, including Ratcliff, Southwark and Deptford, published the sermons given before volunteers in a show of loyalty. Existing civic rituals were enhanced to demonstrate patriotism. In 1796, Prime Minister Pitt was master of Trinity House, so the annual water procession of the elder brethren to Deptford attracted more publicity than usual. Pitt chose Dr Thomas Rennell to preach on 'Great Britain's Insular Situation, Naval Strength, and Commercial Opulence, a source of gratitude to God, loyalty to the King, and concord among ourselves'. When published, sermons like this and related news items closely associated maritime London with the progress of the war.

The conflict re-energized the patriotic Anti-Gallican Society. Founded in the middle of the century, originally to promote British goods and discourage French imports, it depicted France as the natural enemy of Britain. It held an annual procession and feast on St George's Day. Its clubs combined convivial pleasure with a popular cause, and met regularly in coffee houses and taverns. The Society gradually went out of fashion after the defeat of Napoleon but Anti-Gallican taverns retained their name until recently in Southwark (155 Tooley Street) and in Greenwich (428 Woolwich

Road). While the Society was nationally based and organized meetings across the country, it had strong associations with Wapping, where freemasonry was also active. The United Mariner's Lodge for seafaring men met in Wapping, as did the masonic charity for clothing and educating the children of masons who had fallen on hard times. Anti-Gallicans set about collecting funds for the wounded, once war was declared, and wrote patriotic material designed to counter sedition. In 1793, its members published a songbook that clearly reveals anxiety about the disaffection of the lower classes. One composition warns that wicked men are seducing the populace with lies. It insists that the poor have no just cause to rebel:

> Our commerce is great, manufactors well paid,
> The world is our mart, so extensive our trade;
> All, all, have employment, the idle alone
> Have cause of complaint, but the fault is their own.[20]

The songs, mostly set to maritime tunes like 'Hearts of Oak', were also sung at masonic meetings in the riverside parishes. Yet membership of a lodge was chiefly attractive because masonic groups relieved soldiers and seamen who were sick or penniless.

Anti-Gallican publications throw light on the disloyal arguments that must have been current as the war dragged on. Some labouring people certainly thought they had nothing to lose if the French conquered Britain; they had no money or goods worth taking. Not so, Anti-Gallicans warned. French invaders would make them work like galley slaves, in gangs, with a guard to keep them at it. The weak and infirm would be goaded at bayonet point and whoever dared to look surly would be knocked down with the butt-end of a musket. In another reference to slavery, they warned that the French would deport Britons to work in French colonial possessions such as St Domingo, where they would most likely be killed by the climate.[21]

The official Anti-Gallican view that only the idle poor were suffering hardship was of course a gross misrepresentation. The radical breeches-maker, Francis Place, who grew up near the Strand, wrote in 1794 of the disillusionment of even the 'better sort' of labourer, who 'with no other means than those of his own hands to help himself' found his hopes of doing well in life slipping away as the number of his children increased:

> I have seen a vast many such, who . . . have kept on working steadily but hopelessly more like horses in a mill, or mere machines than human beings, their feelings blunted, poor stultified moving animals, working on yet unable to support their families in any thing like comfort, frequently wanting the common necessaries of life.[22]

Others, with no ambition to rise in the world but who had still expected to live in a decent way, despaired in inflationary times.

The price of many basic articles of life had doubled since mid-century.[23] Wages, meanwhile, had not risen at anything like that rate. In Deptford, where several leading families were Dissenters with a strong ethos of community service and self-help, a society promoting industry and economy was set up in 1793. It agreed to pay the rent of several residents, provided each could show that they would be able to clear their debts.[24] It was one way to promote social stability. Yet conditions got even worse. Grain, which had been plentiful for nearly two decades, causing memories of food riots to fade, was suddenly scarce. In 1794, the harvest failed at the same time as war disrupted grain imports. A harsh winter followed, which ruined the autumn-sown wheat, so in 1795 the poor again went hungry. Grain prices jumped from between 48 and 53 shillings a quarter in 1790, to 81 shillings a quarter in 1795.[25] The king's Privy Council sent out notices to parish clergymen advising them to save wheat by feeding the poor in their workhouses potatoes instead of bread.

In Greenwich, the workhouse committee noted that the bread its paupers ate was not of the finest sort. Still, it thought savings could be made and set about devising a new menu. It substituted potatoes for bread at every midday meal except on Saturdays, when rice and milk was served.[26] Savings were badly needed: the price of flour nearly doubled again between 1795 and 1800.[27] In 1795, Deptford residents stopped the carts carrying

flour from its corn mills to London and insisted that they should be fed
first. The story was twisted in newspaper reports so that it seemed that
beneficent millers only dispatched flour after 'their customers and friends
in the neighbourhood are first served'.[28] A week later, the Royal Scotch
Greys, crack troops mounted on grey horses, were ordered to move from
their camp in Kent to new locations in Deptford, Greenwich and Dartford
to keep order. So many horses quartered locally drove up the price of
fodder, adding yet another burden.

In the countryside, labourers became so distressed that rebellion was
feared. The relentless move, through Acts of Parliament, to enclose
common land deprived them of pastureland for cattle, firewood and the
small plots they had once cultivated to fend off starvation. The old social
ties between the classes seemed to have broken down; the hard-working
poor were getting no help from the gentry in time of need. In fact, the
traditional practices that had brought relief in previous crises now failed.
Justices of the Peace could no longer broker deals to make sure that
suppliers with food sold it at a price that the poor could afford. Farmers
and middlemen saw that they could keep prices high because soldiers
would be called in to enforce the peace. Those in power increasingly put
their faith in the free market, a key message taken from the economist
Adam Smith's *An Inquiry into the Nature and Causes of the Wealth of
Nations* (1776). They insisted that the market should be left to find its own
level and that meddling would only prolong distress.[29]

Yet there was obvious profiteering. Four gentlemen from Deptford
proved it by clubbing together to buy a bullock at Smithfield. They sold
the meat at four pence halfpenny a pound (the same price as the local
workhouse paid for meat), and although they could not have bought the
animal as cheaply as wholesale butchers who bought meat by the herd,
they still made five guineas profit.[30] In 1800, following another poor
harvest, there were more food shortages. Grain averaged nearly 114s. a
quarter. Bread riots broke out in London. (Before, the government had
made sure that at least the capital was fed.) Radical groups in London now
explicitly linked food shortages to their demands for reform.

The London Corresponding Society (LCS) was set up in 1792 to campaign for annual parliaments and universal male suffrage. A key aim was to educate people about their rights so it was soon suspected of inciting unrest among the lower orders and supporting those Irish who wanted an independent Ireland. Most members were shopkeepers, tradesmen and craftsmen. They sympathized with the poor, conscious of the short slide to poverty themselves; in 1794, their views even attracted waterside porters to the Society. LCS members criticized the war, claiming that it raised a few to fame and fortune but weakened multitudes of labourers. In their magazine, they denounced wartime taxes that raised prices and made the poor man suffer:

> [Taxes] go to gorge the throats, and swell the insolence of men who draw down poverty and disease upon him, and disdainfully shun the foulness and taint of his condition: they go to pay armies and fleets fighting, at one time on motives with which he has no concern; and at others, for objects destructive of his happiness . . . they give power to the arm that binds him on the wheel of his accursed fate.[31]

No wonder the government was worried and sent spies to infiltrate the Society's meetings. At its height, the LCS was never very large: it had around 3,000 active members, although thousands more went to meetings from time to time. But its importance exceeded mere numbers because from London it coordinated reform societies across Britain.

The LCS also had links with the anti-slavery movement. Olaudah Equiano, the most forceful spokesman of Britain's black community, was a member and on friendly terms with its founders. His life story, published in 1789, had fuelled demands for an end to slavery. In these years, there were still slave ships leaving the Thames for the coast of West Africa.[32] Radicals easily drew parallels between the struggle against slavery and the struggle against a corrupt ruling class. Poor people eagerly signed anti-slavery petitions, which worried the wealthy still more. In this context, it is easy to see why the efficient completion of Bligh's second breadfruit voyage (1791–94) was so crucial to the authorities after the disaster of the *Bounty* mutiny. The voyage was not simply economically important (breadfruit was needed as a cheap food for those enslaved on West Indian plantations, though it turned out they would not eat it);[33] the mere fact of its completion was also politically important, a reflection of the increasing power in British politics of wealthy merchants, who in this case had the backing of the Admiralty.

The LCS was active in the inner city but extended east to Wapping, Limehouse and Shadwell, and south to radical Southwark. In the summer of 1795, the residents of Greenwich contacted the organizers of the Society and asked to have a division established at the White Swan on the Greenwich Road.[34] Pitt was by now taking firm measures against sedition. As was usual in wartime, the Post Office had secretly begun to open mail from France and Ireland. In 1794, Pitt suspended the Habeas Corpus Act, meaning that people could be arrested and held 'on suspicion' without charges or a trial. In November 1795, government passed the Seditious Meetings Act, which restricted the size of public meetings to fifty people. In the same year, it agreed to the Treasonable and Seditious Practices Act. This was ostensibly to protect the King after a mob calling out 'No Pitt, No War, Bread, Peace, Peace!' stoned his carriage as he went to open Parliament. But it also criminalized those who stirred up opinion against the King and the laws of the realm. These two acts were known as the 'Gagging Acts'. So, when the LCS held its meeting at Greenwich, six constables burst in and threatened to have all present thrown on board a warship if they met again. Members secretly changed the location of their next meeting to a private house in New Cross. When the constables next turned up at the White Swan – twenty-four strong this time – they found just one member at the bar. Later, the Society met at a tobacconist's in Greenwich.

Foreign visitors to London registered the yawning gap between rich and poor. William Austin, an American recording his impressions for readers back home, wrote at the turn of the century: 'In New England you rarely see the emaciated, the deformed, the rickety, or the deficient: in England, you meet with them at every step. I have seen thousands of those miserable creatures.' He recorded his conversation with a merchant who insisted that there was more public spirit, patriotism and solid resistance against the French within the circumference of London than in all the rest of Europe. No other people on earth, the merchant claimed, had ever witnessed such luxury, liberty, commerce and strength of character. Austin interjected that the poor of Wapping must have found their situation ironic: 'The luxuries of the South and the elegancies of the East' were brought upriver to their doors but never for them to enjoy. The merchant complacently replied that in every city prosperous districts were balanced by areas of poverty. Commerce was vital if a small country like Britain was to preserve its independence; in a market, some sectors of society would always lose out. Austin concluded that England was a land of the oppressed.[35]

Doubtless Austin flattered his American readers. Yet he did point out that in London, if not in America, Africans had their freedom. He also admitted that poverty in London was alleviated by the generosity of thousands. Merchants were celebrated for their charity – though he compared it to the grand gestures of highwaymen who might return a part of their booty. Why did the poor tolerate such inequality? Austin could only put it down to their stupidity and torpor. Labourers became resigned to their fate, aspired only to earn enough to get drunk, and assumed that the parish would save them. Austin condemned 'the futility of a government, which affects liberty on the hereditary principle, which reduces the people to beggary, and, like the crocodile, devours its own offspring'.[36] Austin was a biased witness but the suffering of the poor was real enough.

Francis Place, looking back on the achievement of the LCS, credited it with opening the minds of the lowest class. In debate, members learned the importance of being able to give reasons for their opinions, to listen to others, and to evaluate the explanations offered in support of views contrary to their own. Some were elected to positions of responsibility. The LCS offered a disenfranchised class immediate participation in political life, as well as hope for the future. And Pitt's Gagging Acts did stir up wider opposition. For instance, members of the Friendly Association of

Merchant Shipwrights, which numbered almost a thousand, met in November 1795 with shipwrights of Deptford and Woolwich dockyards at the St Helena Tavern in Rotherhithe. They agreed to petition against the two Acts then going through Parliament. Shipwrights were worried that the new laws would make it treasonable to strike in wartime. Their action shows that private and naval yards could cooperate when mutual interests were at stake; it also indicates the strength of local opposition to Pitt's repressive legislation. Nevertheless, there remained plenty of loyalist organizations working against so-called republicanism.

Militia and volunteers

Government, worried by the level of civil unrest, had ordered the militia to assemble at the end of 1792. This part-time force, made up of civilians, was used for national defence and to keep public order. County and parish regiments were raised by ballot but individuals could avoid service by paying for a substitute. Some, like seamen and apprentices, were exempt from service but not dockyard labourers. Early in 1794, invasion fears coupled with worries about violent disorder prompted government to call upon communities to set up self-funded, part-time defence forces to support the militia. These were organized on a volunteer basis and so were less likely to inflame British prejudices against a large professional army that could be used against the people. Radical politicians like Sir Joseph Mawbey in Southwark spoke out against subscriptions to raise volunteer forces; he hinted that aristocrats, subscribing large sums, hoped to gain financially by the movement. An opposition newspaper reported Mawbey's objections to the war. Fears of invasion had been fired up, he said. Politicians who had once opposed war now secretly welcomed the chance France gave them of dropping inconvenient principles that had gained them no advancement. Instead, war brought the elite the promise of titles, pensions, medals and places. Mawbey was shouted down and the subscription went ahead.[37] After the attempt on the King's life in 1795, it was harder than ever to oppose the volunteer movement.

While part-time forces could strengthen community spirit, many thought it was foolhardy to arm the man in the street, given the growth of radical societies.[38] The LCS was accused of firing on loyalists in London and other cities. But the LCS, playing on words, denied that government had armed the people – though suggesting government liked to claim it had – since volunteers in dashing military uniform were by no means 'the people'. Volunteer officers had money.[39] Most were from the middle classes, armed and equipped at their own expense; they used the movement to help establish their position in society. Yet volunteering could benefit the lower classes, too. There was pay just for turning up to train, a clothing allowance, and the opportunity to avoid serving in the regular militia or army – which some regarded as a form of slavery. But volunteer groups soon became involved in peacekeeping. In the summer of 1795 the magistrates of Tower Hamlets were grateful when the Light Horse Regiment of London and Westminster, 300 strong, turned out to quell a riot. By 1800 it was second nature for the magistrates of Shadwell to call out the volunteers of Wapping, Limehouse and Ratcliff, merely at the sight of an angry crowd at a baker's shop in the Highway.[40] Armed forces were now routinely used to quell protest.

There were drills and parades of volunteers all over the country, usually after divine service on Sunday. In maritime London, regiments of volunteers were formed in Tower Hamlets, Wapping, Poplar and Blackwell, Southwark, Deptford and Greenwich. Their commanders had medals made for the best shot and to reward other military feats. Commissions were reported in newspapers, bolstering the status of regiments. Barnard's son, William, for example, was commissioned a cornet in the Deptford cavalry in 1798.

Faced with repeated threats of invasion, the public responded to these calls for volunteers in great numbers. Many in the LCS reckoned that Pitt exaggerated invasion threats to turn people against radicalism. During the 1797–98 invasion scare, Pitt passed an Act inviting parishes to form themselves into new associations of infantry and cavalry for local defence. The rank and file of these Armed Associations only received pay if they extended their service from the merely local to the military district in which they were based. Even so, the response was enthusiastic. In maritime parishes, even surly watermen volunteered their services. Armed Associations provided training in the use of arms to keep the peace and briefly helped to give different social classes a common cause.

In contrast, militia service remained unpopular because it could take men from home. Many paid for substitutes. In every parish, the cost of equipping the militia fell on the middling sort and became burdensome. No wonder that, in 1796, Tower Hamlets opposed an Act to improve the raising of its militia and increase the regiment to 1,120 men. Locals complained that many residents were ineligible for service, being seafarers, watermen, labourers with infirmities, undersized (particularly weavers) or foreigners, which at least gives an insight into the make-up of the district. The plea was unsuccessful. A larger regiment was formed. When it needed to build morale, William Liquorish, a shoemaker by trade but musical, composed a regimental march and quickstep, which in 1796 was sold as sheet music for the piano. As elsewhere during the 1797–98 invasion scare, Armed Associations were more popular and Tower Hamlets created six. But in 1809, government removed this option altogether, absorbing volunteers into the local militia on economic grounds.

Ironically, the presence of recruiting officers on the streets added to the violence of the times. Recruiting laws were often violated, prompting bitterness between soldiers and civilians. In 1794, for instance, two privates from the Inniskilling Regiment of Light Dragoons, recruiting at New Cross on a Sunday evening, forced the king's shilling on a man and declared that he had enlisted. A scuffle ensued. The soldiers, who had been drinking, drew their swords and cut the man across the belly. Afterwards, they made him walk to the recruiting office in town so that they could collect the usual reward. The officer in charge of the recruiting office in Charing Cross was privately alarmed by the man's wound. He ordered the soldiers to bring him to St Martin's watch-house but, once there, got the drunken soldiers secured and sent for a surgeon. The victim was cured at the parish expense but then allegedly did a deal with the soldiers, demanding half the two guineas bounty that they got for recruiting him.

In this environment, the Royalty Theatre in Wapping, which, as we saw in Chapter Six, was still pushing to get its licence, was never going to succeed. Residents might deserve the amusements available to those in the West End but traders and merchants in prosperous Well Close Square successfully petitioned that to distract workers with a theatre at this juncture would be as absurd as to introduce 'idleness and dissipation into a bee-hive'.[41]

Crisis and mutiny

The early years of the war were marked by one domestic problem after another. A tremendous fire devastated Wapping in July 1794 – the worst in London since the Great Fire of 1666. In a barge-builder's yard at Cock Hill near Ratcliff, a cauldron of pitch left unattended boiled over. It was low water and the flames spread to a barge on the foreshore. The vessel was laden with saltpetre, a key ingredient in gunpowder; it blew up, throwing large flakes of fire on East India Company warehouses nearby. This depot held more saltpetre from Bengal, though luckily twenty tons had been removed to the Tower just a day earlier. Now there was a huge explosion. Onlookers compared it to the eruption of a volcano. Flames were thrown high into the air and the shower of fiery particles nearly suffocated firefighters below. Because it was low tide, no engines could deliver water from the Thames and a strong south wind blew the flames towards Brook Street. Ratcliff's roads were so narrow that both sides caught fire at once. Frightened horses refused to approach the flames; no fire engines could be brought to bear. Almost all houses were destroyed eastwards as far as Ratcliff Cross, leaving about 1,400 people homeless. The blaze spread to nearby timber and rope warehouses; several ships in the river were burned. The damage totalled millions of pounds. One sugar warehouse alone had contained more than £40,000 worth of goods, and the East India Company was reckoned to have lost £200,000. It was a huge blow to the war effort.

The years from 1796 to 1798 were a time of crisis. Pawnbrokers in Deptford were so inundated with unredeemed pledges (mostly clothes and household goods) that they auctioned the lot. Then, in 1797, although invasion was feared, the British fleet that was anchored at Spithead near Portsmouth suddenly mutinied, leaving a huge hole in the nation's defence. Seamen demanded higher wages and better conditions. They had a good case: their pay had not risen since the seventeenth century. To counter potential unrest in the wake of the mutiny, loyal addresses were sent to the King. These were placarded in public places and circulated as handbills to influence public opinion. Trinity House promptly sent a loyal address and published Rennell's Deptford sermon of the year before. The situation was saved by the personal intervention of Admiral Lord Howe, whom sailors trusted. His negotiated agreement incorporated most of their demands. But no sooner had this dispute been settled than the fleet at the Nore, in the Thames Estuary, mutinied. This rupture was more violent and won less sympathy. Seamen raided nearby villages and boarded merchant ships for supplies; they blockaded the Thames, preventing trade. It seemed they might hold London to ransom. The mutineers were suspected of being linked to revolutionary groups, and their demands did extend to a call for immediate peace with France. This infuriated the Admiralty, which refused more concessions.

London shipowners, merchants and insurers met at the Marine Society office in the City and pledged to counter the mutiny. They raised funds, offering two guineas to any officer in the merchant service and one guinea to any seaman willing to join the navy. The group was careful to promise that seamen would be released once the emergency was over, since one of the mutineers' complaints was that they were rarely given shore leave to see their families. It hired a room at the Dundee Arms in Wapping to raise men and got a boat ready to take volunteers out to the nearest warship. Meanwhile, the Admiralty prepared to starve the rebels of food and water. By mid-June the mutiny was over, its ringleaders hanged. The guard ship on which the mutiny began, the *Sandwich*, was broken up in a Thameside yard rather than repaired. The fact was reported at the same time as a notice that vegetables were being shipped from Deptford to the North Sea fleet, an obvious attempt to combine resolution with a show of better treatment for seamen.[42] The Nore Mutiny did much to shatter the comfortable image of the obedient, loyal Jack Tar on whose courage the defence of the nation largely rested.[43] It also lessened tolerance of wayward communities in maritime London.

Government spies reported at the beginning of 1798 that the LCS had contacted mutineers at both Spithead and the Nore. The society had continued to meet secretly, at Wapping and other places.[44] In contrast, the middling sort in maritime districts now redoubled efforts to demonstrate loyalty. During the invasion crisis, government called for voluntary contributions to aid the war effort, and church committees were set up to receive funds. In February 1798, churchwardens and other officials of St Paul's Deptford set up just such a subscription. Over £236 was raised at its first meeting. Unusually, the churchwardens printed a notice about this patriotic measure, explaining that the collection would be extended on a house-to-house basis as all parishioners had a duty to help defeat the enemy. Whether the less well off appreciated the gesture is doubtful but many dockyard employees, including Benjamin Slade, paid up, raising over £800.

Other parishes caused concern. In 1798, Wapping became especially volatile. From late summer, there had been a wave of migration from Ireland after a failed rebellion of United Irishmen. Migrants circulated tales of the brutal reprisals that had taken place. Irish coal heavers in Wapping were all the more ready to fight the new marine police who tried to stop them taking their customary share of coal as they unloaded ships, long regarded a perk of the job. On the evening of 16 October, an angry mob gathered outside the Marine Police Office in Wapping High Street. Constables had arrested Charles Eyres, together with another coal heaver and a watchman's boy, for 'stealing coal'. The two Justices of the Peace on duty, John Harriott and Patrick Colquhoun, found the men guilty and fined them forty shillings each. The penalty was part of a police crackdown on traditional practices in dockside work but coal heavers burned with a deep sense of wrong. That August, during one of many struggles between press gangs and river workers, an Irishman, Joseph Leahey, had been stabbed to death. Members of the press gang pleaded that they had been intimidated and feared for their lives. They were found guilty of manslaughter, fined one shilling each and released. Compared with this sentence, a forty-shilling fine for taking a customary allowance of coal seemed an injustice.

As Charles Eyres was leaving the police office that evening, his brother James came up to him. Charles explained that two friends had paid the fine. James ordered his brother to go and ask for the money back. A crowd gathered, bent on trouble. One leader was a man nicknamed Attey, whose behaviour had never been stable after a hole had been drilled in his skull to relieve concussion. The crowd began chanting 'We will have the money back!' and threatened to pull the office down. Inside, the police grew nervous. The entrance to their premises led onto a dark, narrow alley, not directly into the street; the mob would be able to block their exit and pick them off, one by one. Soon the crowd outside began throwing paving stones at the shutters of the police office. One of the first targets was the candle lantern above the office door. Harriott, who had served during the Seven Years War, opted for decisive action and ordered up firearms. By rights, he should have read the Riot Act and only ordered the police to fire on the crowd if it failed to disperse. Harriott later claimed that the sight of guns being primed and loaded took him back to earlier days and made him feel young again. He instructed officers to shoot from the upper windows. One of the rioters, James Hanks, was killed outright and dragged away.

In the lull that followed, Colquhoun went out with Harriott and some other officers into the alley. Standing on a stone block used for mounting horses, facing more missiles and curses, he hurriedly read the Riot Act. The mob was mostly a few yards to the west at Dung Wharf, where London's excrement was loaded onto boats and taken to manure outlying fields and gardens. Officers could barely see the rioters in the dark, smelly street but their shouts were terrifying enough. Gabriel Franks, a foreman 'lumper' or cargo handler, and one of the casual staff attached to the police office, came from a nearby pub to see if he could identify any of the rioters. Somehow, he managed to get a cutlass from the police office and, although outnumbered, advanced on the mob. He had no sooner turned around to warn a colleague, 'For God's sake, Perry, take care', when he was shot in the back.[45] The rioters slowly melted away. The Wapping and Union Volunteer Corps turned out afterwards and patrolled the streets long into the night.

Franks lingered in hospital for about a week before dying on 21 October. He was never able to identify his killer but said without hesitation that the man was a coal heaver. The King offered a pardon and a £100 reward to anyone giving information leading to an arrest but it was always going to be difficult to determine who had fired the fatal shot. In the days after the riot, James Eyres gave himself up to the authorities as one of those involved. He could be easily identified and probably hoped for lenient treatment if he came forward. He certainly had no intention of admitting responsibility for shooting Franks. Yet, when the new year came and the authorities still had not found the killer, they decided to put Eyres on trial not just for his part in the riot but also for murder.

The evidence against Eyres was full of discrepancies but these were anxious times; the authorities needed a scapegoat. They also wanted to make an example to discourage others from rioting. Eyres was defended at the Old Bailey by John Gurney, a Dissenter and sometime supporter of the French Revolution, but not even the ingenuity of that able barrister could get Eyres off. Witnesses gave conflicting evidence about where the shot was fired from. There was more than one ball in Franks's body but, oddly, nothing was made of the fact. A part-time coal heaver and soldier swore that there were no firearms among the rioters and he only saw shots fired from the police office. One witness, Elizabeth Forrester from Gravel Lane and the wife of a police officer, testified that she heard Eyre shout to someone in the mob, 'Fire, you bugger, fire!'[46] But her evidence was muddled and neighbours gave her a very bad character. One of them said he would never believe her testimony if she were to swear a hundred oaths. The judge properly discounted her evidence in his summing up but her words affected the jury. The court could not pin the murder on Eyres but in law all those involved in a riot were answerable for its outcome, and there was no doubt that Eyres had been a ringleader. After thirty minutes, the jury found him guilty and he was sentenced to execution and dissection. He received his sentence with composure.

One point that the authorities would have taken from the riot, which perhaps made them all the keener to convict, was that several of the men involved had military experience and possibly access to arms. A key witness in the trial was a soldier; Eyres himself was a former soldier and his brother, Charles, had served part-time in the Guards. The landlord of the nearby Rose and Crown pub testified that he heard the rioters say that they would go home, fetch arms and blow up the police office.

A petition on Eyres's behalf, signed by fifty people in Shadwell, had little hope of success. The police office expected strong official support in its attempt to reduce crime on the river. Meanwhile, the death of the rioter Franks was recorded as 'justifiable homicide', since the police had been defending themselves and their building against determined assailants. A turning point came on 21 January when a new witness, Edward Thompson, wrote to the Home Secretary to say that Eyres ought to be pardoned. Thompson explained that he had been in the police office the whole time and that when the riot was over, the talk was that Franks had been shot from the windows by the officers themselves: 'I don't Mean to say willfully shot but By Chance where at [*sic*] my dying words I would say that I firmly believed that the Rioters had no fire arms.'[47] This finally convinced the authorities; Eyres's sentence was reduced to transportation for life.

All this time, there were other, less obvious indications of wartime stress within maritime London. Numerous amputees displayed the effects of war. William Blizard, surgeon at the London Hospital and formerly a supporter of John Wilkes, set up a society at the hospital in 1791 for men needing lengthy treatment and artificial limbs. He gave lectures and wrote pamphlets in plain language chiefly for sailors about first aid and the use of tourniquets. Thomas Mann of Bradford began to experiment with lighter artificial wooden limbs and trialled them on wounded seamen in London from the mid-1790s. As well as the physically damaged, the mentally disturbed returned from battle. Understanding of mental illness was in its infancy, although the King's own bouts of insanity were beginning to give it a higher profile. When James Carse, a seaman who served under Nelson, returned in 1787 and slit a prostitute's throat, he was described as suffering from 'sunstroke'.[48] The stress that many seamen endured, particularly landsmen unused to the hardships and seemingly tyrannical nature of shipboard life, is evident in some of their letters home. James Whitworth wrote to his wife in Deptford, 'Fortune has done her worst to me and life is no longer worth [living] . . . I think I cannot long bear this life I feel myself weaker every day and my spirits drooping continually.'[49] In 1802, two seamen were brought before the Lord Mayor, each accusing the other of having information about a recent murder. One had run down a dark alley near Wapping shouting, 'There he is!' 'That's him!' and claimed to have seen a dead man.[50] No body was found: the sailor was delusional.

Mental patients of the time might be confined in Bedlam, straitjacketed in a local workhouse or sent to commercially run, private madhouses. The navy kept some insane patients at Haslar, its purpose-built hospital in Portsmouth. It also sent them to a private madhouse in Hoxton. Between 1792 and 1814, the number of sailors sent to Hoxton House from Haslar and from the *Batavia* hospital ship moored in the Thames off Woolwich increased by 733 per cent, although the numbers were still comparatively small, rising to 150 in 1814.[51] Common seamen, rather than officers, accounted for over 90 per cent of these cases. Given that the population was rising and there was growing awareness of mental illness, it is impossible to ascribe the increase in numbers to a single cause. It does suggest, though, that the strain of war for seamen by no means decreased after the victory at Trafalgar in 1805. The public at large was affected too: the number of madhouses in London also grew rapidly, from sixteen in 1774 to twenty-four in 1815.

Labour issues

With so many men serving in the military, and for such a long period, London's maritime districts suffered a shortage of key workers to meet the demands of wartime production. The Baptist shipbuilder, Henry Fletcher of Shadwell Dock, wrote to his timber supplier in 1800, 'We are exceeding busy & hurried preparing a number of ships for Government service & have scarcely time to get our meals or to lose one hours Daylight.'[52]

Women played a large part in the war effort, despite the repressive, anti-feminist climate. Wives and girlfriends did much to recruit men for the army, and supported men in both the army and navy.[53] As we have seen, women ran their own businesses and widows might continue their husbands' trade. When ship chandler Michael Browne died at his Wapping home in 1777, his wife immediately signalled her intention to manage the business herself. She advertised in newspapers asking for 'the continuence and favors of all the friends and customers of her late husband'.[54] Such practices explain how, in 1779, the Greenwich workhouse came to be supplied by a female blacksmith while much of the ironmongery for the naval dockyards in the 1780s came from Mrs Crowley and Co., a firm in the Northeast.[55] If dependent widows got scant respect, it was different for those who meant to pay their way. Widows in maritime-related trades got a sympathetic hearing when they asked the Navy Board to continue existing contracts. Economically active, they made a substantial contribution to commercial London, as they did in maritime communities throughout Britain.[56]

Frances Barnard, who took over the Deptford shipyard on her husband's death in 1795, had a complex business to run. William Barnard had been ailing since 1793, so there had been time to consider how things would work, although he made his will only a week before his death and may have worsened suddenly. After her husband was buried in Butt Lane's Dissenting burial ground, Frances had her eldest son William, just nineteen, write to the Navy Board to explain where things stood:

Honourable Sirs

While I inform Your Honours of an unfortunate event; the Death of a Father, permit me to solicit a continuance of your favours on behalf of my Mother who will carry on the Business for the benefit of herself and family (with the assistance of a very able foreman who served his time to my father and who has acted as foreman under him upward of twenty years, and who since his long and unfortunate illness of more than twelve months has conducted the whole of the Business) until myself and Brother shall have served the remainder of our apprenticeship and shall be in a situation to join her.

That no opportunity will be omitted on her part to render herself worthy of your Honor's patronage I can take it upon myself to assure your Honors, and that it will be her constant study to shew her Gratitude by a diligent, punctual and Conscientious performance of any Contract with which your Honors may favour her.[57]

The Navy Board annotated the letter 'No answer' but continued to contract with Barnard's yard. Businesses up and down the river were linked by bonds of trust and worked to accepted procedures that, in turn, were backed up by the enforcement of property law. Frances had more limited access to this network than her husband but did not have to rely solely on her experienced foreman. Others were willing to do business with her. After all, shipowners and other maritime concerns were used to making financial arrangements with seamen's wives. Traders' correspondence reveals that an easy means to establish good relations with business contacts was to enquire after the health of family members and, in the case of seagoing men, try to support wives in their absence. Frances seems to have been on terms of trust with local shipbuilders. In September 1795, she had to write to the Navy Board to explain that the contract they had just agreed for a 64-gun warship, the *York*, had been copied from an earlier document without considering the increased price of materials. It would leave the firm £5,240 out of pocket. She asked for an additional £3,000 so that her price would at least match the price that Rotherhithe shipbuilder Randall, Brent & Sons charged for a same-sized warship. She enclosed a comparison of her costs and Randall's, in a detailed breakdown that can only have been made with the help of Randall's themselves.[58]

Frances also had to cope with higher wage demands in wartime. In 1795, sawyers wanted more money; their demands were judged exorbitant. Private shipyards united to break their strike in October, advertising for sawyers from all over the country. Men were offered a five-guinea bounty, employment guaranteed for three years and payment by the day at generous rates until they had learnt task work. That December, when the Navy Board asked why the *York* was behind schedule, Frances gave this strike as her main excuse. She assured officials that no exertions would be spared to finish the warship and that she hoped to launch it the following March; she made the launch date with a week to spare. After this shaky start, her business seems to have settled down. In May 1796, Barnard's launched the *Walmer Castle*, said to be the largest ship serving the East India Company, and even secured the Lord Chancellor to name the ship.[59] By 1797 Frances was writing routinely to the Board for permission to launch the latest naval vessel built in her yard, and was rewarded with contracts for larger, 74-gun warships.

In 1799, Frances saw her son William marry Harriet, daughter of the wealthy brewer Henry Goodwyn junior, who lived in Blackheath. William now took on his full share of managing the business and did the honours at launches. Frances had kept up these great social events, which were useful opportunities to advertise the family's patriotism. In 1806, Barnard's also gave £50, one of the largest contributions, to Lloyd's Patriotic Fund. This charity, founded in 1803, supported the wounded and families of those killed in battle. At the outset, it had also rewarded acts of bravery but found that, in straitened times, all its funds were needed for those in distress.

There were bound to be pay disputes in inflationary times. Between 1790 and 1810 there were as many as 1,000 riots across the country, sparked by the cost of food, political discontent or clashes with the military. The years 1795 and 1800–1 were particularly fractious because of the shortage of provisions.[60] In July 1801, London officials received information that over 20,000 men – mostly tradesmen suffering from high food prices – were assembling in small groups against the government. They were said to be particularly numerous around Wapping and Ratcliff Highway. Protesters expected a military response (by now routine), and had collected weapons and caltrops made of twisted, spiked nails to slow down the advance of cavalry.[61] At this point, dockyard workers continued to be unruly. In 1801 the bakers in charge of ovens making ship's biscuit in Deptford and Rotherhithe went on strike for more pay. Without supplies, ships could not sail. All strikers were discharged. The Navy Board replaced them with 100 or so men brought from Edinburgh and Newcastle.[62]

When the Peace of Amiens came at the end of March 1802, there was yet more trouble. Shipyards along the Thames tried to reduce wages to a peacetime rate. On 10 May, the sawyers in yards along the river struck, demanding wages so high that not only shipbuilders but most tradesmen using sawyers now felt obliged to resist them. Work along the river was badly affected. Henry Fletcher wrote crossly to one of his timber suppliers in Germany on 29 June explaining that 'All the Workmen at the principal ship yards in the River Thames have struck from their work on acct of wages.' Employers could no longer afford to pay the wartime rate since shipping freights had dropped and there were few orders for new merchant ships. He told this to the captain of his timber supplier's ship when he docked for repairs, and asked him to wait while he found men willing to work. Impatient, the captain went to a rogue yard in Limehouse still paying men the wartime rate. The cost of repairs would be greater, Fletcher warned. He was all the more annoyed because he had lost the chance to use the cargo of timber secretly and evade customs duty. Partly in retaliation, he warned his supplier that the sudden peace had made business on the river very slack and he would only be buying as much timber as he had immediate use for.[63]

The sawyers returned to work on 29 July, starved into submission. But a more serious dispute was underway: both shipwrights and caulkers went on strike. In wartime, shipwrights' wages in the private yards had increased from 3s. 6d. to 5s. 3d. a day. With piecework, some earned even more. Now employers wanted to pay a daily rate of 4s. 4½d. The men insisted on 5s. with overtime extra. They had accumulated a large fund to support their campaign, each man contributing 3s. 6d. from every pound earned, and the shipbuilders could not break the strike. Builders stood to incur severe financial penalties if they did not fulfil their contracts on time.

And if East Indiamen on the stocks were not completed, they could not sail that season. Desperate builders asked the East India Company to intervene with the Admiralty and request workers from naval dockyards to help protect Britain's trading interests. The Admiralty obligingly sent up 100 caulkers from Chatham. On 26 July, Deptford men stopped these caulkers on the road. Threatening murder if they broke the strike, they forced them back to their homes. Frances Barnard wrote that day to the Navy Board:

> We have to beg your Honor's advice how to act in the present conjuncture as from the threats and abuse made use of by the men who oppose us we neither consider the people free from danger nor our property from depredation.[64]

Her yard was given police protection. The Admiralty was also prepared to use military force and took its caulkers and shipwrights by warship upriver to Deptford. The dispute grew uglier.

John Randall, head of Randall, Brent & Sons, the East India Company's main supplier of ships, also got scab labour from the naval dockyards. The Admiralty threatened to sack any of its men who refused to work for him. When Randall's striking shipwrights heard the noise of shipbuilding in his yard, they knew that their cause was lost unless the work could be stopped. On 21 August, they sent word to Greenwich and Woolwich, gathering together about 300 shipwrights. These men assembled in the fields west of Deptford, then marched towards the yard. Randall's failed to lock their gates quickly enough; the men charged in and threatened to drown the naval shipwrights if they did not lay down their tools. Strikers paid them for their day's work and sent them home. Then they threatened to pull down Randall's quarters in the yard. He came out and tried to reason with them to no effect; that afternoon, the Coldstream Guards and Light Dragoons arrived to keep the peace. The event led directly to Randall's death, two days later. He was only forty-seven. Some said that a blow from one of the shipwrights had brought on a fever. More probably, the strain of the strike had been too much for him. It came after a period of great stress: one of the warships built in his yard, the 74-gun *Ajax*, had been found defective, and that year it had docked for a second round of expensive repairs.

Both sides in the dispute manipulated the media. The radical shipwright, John Gast, egged on by fellow workers, wrote a pamphlet vindicating the strike. Gast was self-educated, a remarkable public speaker, and a fluent writer who could quote Virgil as readily as the Bible. His vindication was published by a printer on Deptford Broadway and Gast sold copies for sixpence each at his house in Butt Lane, opposite St Paul's church. He presented a more reasonable picture of the strikers' action than that reported in newspapers and denied any physical violence against Randall himself. Gast, an early trade unionist, argued that shipwrights would never be aggressors 'if their masters would let them live by their labor'. He claimed that 'nothing but the severe oppression of the masters' could make men unite in resistance or form 'an illegal combination' under the law.[65] He insisted that the shipwrights had petitioned for five shillings a day even before the 1802 peace, because food and tools cost more than ever before. He also identified the source of an artisan's pride and self-worth, arguing that as far as a skilled worker is concerned, the produce of his labour is as much an inheritance as the right of ownership over tracts of land. In fact, a man's right to a fair wage for his labour stands on a firmer basis than the legal right to landed property because land ownership depends upon custom, though sanctioned by law. Gast deftly turned the tables, claiming that it was the builders who had formed an 'illegal combination': they had worked in unison to ignore the shipwrights' petition, reduce their daily pay and fix it at a lower rate. Masters and workers, he argued, should be subject to the same laws regarding united action.

As scab labour completed ships in the Thameside yards, most workers, seeing their livelihoods threatened, gave up the strike. They remained disruptive: in Rotherhithe, when shipbuilder Peter Maestiers used his shipwrights to caulk as well as build, he received death threats.[66] Private yards retained some naval workers until November; a naval sloop, *Diligence*, anchored in the river until February 1803 to enforce obedience on a discontented workforce.[67] Some disputes were not settled until 21 September 1803. It was the major labour crisis of the age. Caulkers and sawyers failed in their bids but shipwrights gained five shillings a day and overtime at the same rate. However, their victory was obscured: war resumed and yards once more became frenetically busy.

The fortunes of war

War was a driving force for change and social mobility. Between 1783 and 1802, Britain's economy grew at nearly 6 per cent a year. London continued to be a magnet for workers; in 1801, it contained 12 per cent of the population of England and Wales.[68] If the poor suffered intermittently during the long French Wars, others made a great deal of money.

From the early 1790s it was obvious that wealthy merchants and financiers had increasing political power; collectively, they were termed the 'monied interest'.[69] But lesser tradesmen also profited from war. Wapping's canny slopsellers are a case in point. They sold ready-made clothes, 'slops', to seafarers and shipowners, taking advantage of less-skilled tailors (often women) doing piecework. John Ponsford, a slopseller who died in 1795, left his wife household furniture, plate, linen, china, watches, rings, books, pictures, prints and all his stock in trade as well as money invested in government funds. Isaac Hill, another slopseller, left a similar assortment of goods and investments, and made enough money to retire to Essex before his death in 1808. Mary Maccartney, a widowed slopseller who died in 1809, left plate, a freehold house with land, and her share of a small tenement to her son. To others, she left bequests totalling £50 and gifts of wearing apparel. The fittings of her shop in Wapping went to the wife of a local mariner.[70]

The war years saw increasing mechanization of industry as well as a hardening of attitudes in labour relations. Strikes and naval demands accelerated this transformation. Hand-sawing, for example, had persisted in the face of wind- and water-powered mills, because it needed no capital investment and was flexible (a saw pit could be dug anywhere). Now timber merchants were more inclined to set up sawmills to avoid wage disputes. The cumulative effect of the 1802 strikes and the alleged scandalous waste of public money on the *Ajax* temporarily heightened distrust between the Navy Board and private shipyards. The Board was unimpressed when shipbuilders hastily tightened up contracts so that they would not be held responsible if the navy accepted warships that proved faulty. Meanwhile, shipwrights in the yards had registered that the united action of workers against masters could affect wages. Shipwrights would become key players in the early trades union movement that gained ground across the country after the Napoleonic Wars.

If naval dockyards and maritime parishes were centres of fierce patriotism during this turbulent period, they were also places that helped to foster radicalism and industrial action. The forces of commerce and industry were accelerating as never before along the riverside, generating excitement but also creating anxiety. The far-sighted could see already that steam power would bring a lasting revolution. In this climate, workers would increasingly struggle to make their voices heard.

8

GRAND DESIGNS

In the 1790s, trade in the Port of London reached extreme heights. Exports exceeded imports as never before. This was due to Britain's manufacturing growth and a huge increase in the volume of foreign goods being re-shipped and exported. At the same time, the coastal trade nearly doubled. The Thames, already busy, became even more crowded. War with France added to the problem: once the convoy system got under way to protect foreign trade, merchant ships entered the river all at once, in a fleet. The situation became chaotic. Vessels got in each other's way. Smaller ships seized any empty berth, though the depth of water might be greater than they needed. Larger ships, forced into shallow water, might be beached at low tide with heavy cargoes, then damaged as they 'sat on their anchors' or 'broke their backs'. And when ships unloaded, tons of imports sat on the quays for weeks, exposed to the weather and theft, while tardy revenue officers completed their records.

West India merchants, importing mostly sugar, rum and dyewoods, were especially affected by the congestion. The East India Company used even larger ships, which could not get so far upriver. They lightened their freight at Gravesend, then unloaded at Blackwall. West India vessels carried heavy cargos and, due to prevailing winds, were only in the river from the end of May to October. Both factors added to bottlenecks. A cargo of sugar averaged 284 hogsheads, and each cask could weigh over a ton (1,016 kg). London's quays could be crammed with sugar-hogsheads piled six and eight high, together with bales, barrels, boxes and bags heaped together in confusion. The West India trade was a valuable one; its merchants were powerful. Although their ships were restricted to a season, they carried one-third by value of all London's import trade: £7 million out of a total £23 million in 1798.[1] From the early 1790s, as the Port of London became choked, merchants gathered in truculent meetings to complain about overcrowding, delay and theft. They determined that things would have to change.

What merchants had in mind were enclosed docks for the import of goods. They had before them the examples of Greenland Dock at Rotherhithe, mainly used for the whaling trade, and the Brunswick Dock that John Perry had just built at his yard in Blackwall. Both were mostly used for ship repair and refitting, rather than for loading and unloading goods. Strictly speaking, London had no dockland or dockside areas, although Liverpool and Hull already benefited from wet docks. So West India merchants looked for a site where they could build docks in the capital. A prime mover in this task was the merchant and naval architect William Vaughan. From as early as 1793, he held meetings, canvassed opinion and published tracts calling for the construction of docks in London. He identified four sites: Wapping, the Isle of Dogs, St Katharine's and Rotherhithe. He favoured Wapping and declared that there was never a better moment to push for government support, presumably because ministers would be anxious to maximize customs revenues to help pay for the war with France.[2] Newspapers, which catered mostly for the upper and middling ranks, talked up Vaughan's plans, stoking rivalry between London and Liverpool, and assuring wealthy Londoners that docks would be a profitable investment.[3] Towards the end of 1795, merchants formally approved of the Wapping site and, in just a few hours, subscribed £800,000 to fund the works. The creation of new docks would have a huge impact on local communities and change maritime London for ever.

The MP William Manning, from a West India planter family and linked by marriage to Vaughan, presented the merchants' petition for docks in Wapping to Parliament on 3 February 1796. He encountered strong opposition from the Corporation of London. The City controlled the Port of London and saw that any movement of trade from that port would diminish the City's wealth and influence. Manning, by nature a peacemaker, won approval from MPs to bring in a bill for the Wapping scheme. Cynics were already joking that West India merchants should wait to see whether or not Britain lost its sugar islands to France before building increased capacity for their trade.[4] In this context, the government may have wished to send out a signal that it was confident about its conduct of the war. Obviously, it was vital to prevent France from seizing Britain's lucrative West Indian colonies if the nation was to have the economic strength to prevail. As West India merchants built up their case for wet docks, circulating pamphlets and posters that argued the economic advantages in the face of high port charges at existing wharves, the Corporation of London was stung into action. To counter the Wapping plan, the City was forced to present an alternative. George Dance, its clerk of works, set up a team that hurriedly came up with cheaper proposals in the Isle of Dogs.

A bitter power struggle ensued between the West India Merchants and the City. In March 1796, the bill to create new docks at Wapping was discussed again in Parliament. By this time, there were also proposals for a canal across the Isle of Dogs so that ships could avoid the troublesome route around it. Discussion in the House was animated; the merchant interest and the City interest traded insults. Such was the complexity of the issue and the strength of feeling on both sides that Prime Minister Pitt referred all proposals to a committee of enquiry. This gave the City a chance to work up its rival scheme.

In May 1796, the findings of the committee of enquiry were presented to Parliament. Its members had dealt with numerous plans and considered rival interests. For instance, the residents of Wapping, after the great fire of 1779, had repeatedly proposed widening their streets even if it meant encroaching on the river.[5] Others insisted that the Thames was so obstructed by shoals, caused by grounded vessels, offal and other detritus, that it had to be dredged. Civil engineers gave this view some support at the beginning of 1796 when they surveyed the Thames from Blackfriars Bridge to Deptford. They concluded that the narrowing of the river in London caused floods in distant Maidenhead and Putney. One option would be to return the river to its former width.[6]

Faced with conflicting proposals, the committee had turned to customs records for a factual picture. The trade figures alone were impressive. Not only had the number of ships using the Port of London doubled within the century, the size of the vessels in the foreign trade had also doubled. Much of this expansion had taken place in the last fifty years. In 1750, the number of ships entering London's port had been 6,396 whereas in 1795 it was 11,964. Imports had increased by 168 per cent since 1750 and exports by 96 per cent. The trend showed no signs of halting despite war with France. There had been a 29 per cent increase in shipping since 1790 alone when 9,278 ships used the port.[7] In the Pool of London, there were sometimes as many as 775 vessels, moored in tiers five or six deep, although pilots from Trinity House advised that ships were too closely packed for safety and that only 545 should be accommodated. Each ship needed several lighters to get the cargo ashore. A West India ship needed seven, doubling the space it took up on the river.

The committee carefully documented the capacity of the Port of London. By tradition, all goods incurring customs duties had to be unloaded at the Legal Quays, on the north bank of the Thames between London Bridge and the Tower. The Quays had been established in the reign of Elizabeth I and were only 1,464 feet (446 m) long. Goods unloaded here were moved to nearby warehouses or stored on the quayside itself. A fifth of the frontage was taken up with landing stairs and the coasting traffic alone. To cope with the increase in trade, Suffrance Wharves had been built on the south bank opposite, and more on the north. Here dutiable goods were allowed or 'suffered' to be unloaded, but the distance of these wharves from the City caused further delays and inefficiencies. Heavy carts clogged up Lower Thames Street and caused accidents. Sometimes, goods were even left for a period in lighters themselves, which became floating warehouses.

Most proposals to improve London's port featured enclosed docks. Only one scheme offered an alternative. It came from Edward Ogle, a leading wharfinger (wharf owner or keeper). Ogle said it would be best to enlarge the Legal Quays and divide ships in the Thames by trade and need for depth of water. Using complex, multi-coloured plans, he triumphantly demonstrated that it was possible to get 1,199 ships in the river between London Bridge and Deptford (450 more than at any time since 1795). Ogle's own business comprised nearly one-quarter of the warehouse room on the Legal Quays. He stood to lose money if valuable West Indian goods were stored in enclosed docks. This helps to explain the expense he suffered to push forward his alternative scheme. It was dismissed because he presupposed that the Thames could be deepened, improved and maintained in that condition at low cost. Defeated in this, Ogle sought a new challenge. He went on to buy an estate in Worthing and developed that village into a resort to rival nearby Brighton. This scheme at least had lasting impact. Jane Austen met him when she stayed in Worthing with her sister Cassandra in 1805. His seaside project was an inspiration for *Sanditon*, the novel unfinished at her death.

The House of Commons committee took care to question surveyors and engineers about each scheme. It also interviewed merchants, wharfingers and river workers. Conflicting interests meant that testimony was often biased but slowly a picture emerged of outdated practices, exploitation and peculation. The Port of London seemed to work in spite of these annoyances rather than as efficiently as it could. Overcrowding and outdated systems encouraged pilfering on a large scale. For instance, captains who arrived with cargoes of rum had thirty days to unload once they had reported to customs. Revenue officers came aboard to sample the casks and judge the strength of the spirit to assess the level of customs duty: a percentage of the cargo disappeared in the process. Similarly, each hogshead was sampled at least twice and several pounds of sugar removed each time. Sugar losses were hard to estimate because liquid from the moist sugar was expected to drain from the barrels homeward bound, leaving them lighter.

One problem was that a merchant ship was not unloaded by its crew. In peacetime, it was difficult to keep seamen on the ship after a long voyage. In wartime, most were pressed in the Downs before the ship even entered port. Lumpers (cargo handlers) were hired instead, who worked without proper supervision and smuggled goods ashore. It was the fashion, in the 1790s, for women to wear padding under their muslin dresses so that they looked pregnant. Commentators joked that these accessories were hardly an invention: women in Wapping had worn them for years to carry about goods stolen from the river.[8] West India merchants estimated that the annual cost of all this theft was £200,000 to £300,000. It was a loss to them and a loss to the Revenue.[9] Another worry was that if the Port of London got a bad reputation, it might lose trade to other British ports or even to foreign ones.

When the committee presented its findings, they carried weight. Despite the negative discoveries about theft and fraud, ministers were gratified to find that, although war had closed some commercial opportunities, trade was flourishing. Britain had largely taken over the trade of France and Holland, which had been damaged by war.[10] Thousands worked on the river and thousands more were indirectly dependent on river work. There were an estimated 120,000 workers and, if their families were included, the number supported reached 500,000.[11] Coal merchants were relieved to find that wet docks would not affect them. Colliers accounted for much of the river traffic, making 3,897 entries a year. As many as ninety colliers could be unloading at the same time, each using twelve to sixteen lighters. But the committee accepted that, with this many voyages, coal merchants could not afford dock dues.[12] Colliers had to moor in the centre of London anyway to be able to deliver coal in all directions. Crucially, the parliamentary committee accepted that improvements to the port were essential. Yet it did not back any one plan; most proposals were at an early stage.

In a related development, Patrick Colquhoun, former Glasgow tobacco merchant, took it upon himself to produce a detailed study of crime in London. Since 1792, he had been a paid magistrate at Shoreditch police office. In the mid-1790s, he proposed setting up a system of policing that would help to prevent crime, regulate the lower orders and also raise revenue. He was eager to advance his career and to prove his worth. Not all his ideas were new but his study made striking use of statistics. In his tiny, neat handwriting he filled page upon page, enumerating significant public losses wholly due to the criminality of the delinquent poor. He got nowhere with Home Secretary Henry Dundas, who had been advised that the scheme was badly drafted, threatened civil liberties and would be difficult to get through Parliament. Dundas refused even to spare the time to see him.

Frustrated but not deterred, Colquhoun worked up his proposals and published them in 1796 as *A Treatise on the Police of the Metropolis*. While his volume was in the press, he sent the manuscript to Charles Jenkinson (Baron Hawkesbury, soon to be Lord Liverpool, and President of the Board of Trade). Colquhoun warned of the dangers posed by the criminal classes unless they were kept in check. Playing on fears of the French Revolution crossing the Channel to Britain, he pointed out that in Paris, just prior to the Revolution, there was 'never less than 20,000 of this depraved class', and that when stable government broke down this rabble fell under the influence of revolutionaries and perpetrated horrible crimes.[13] In London, he thought there was nearly half that number, ready to engage in 'every species of mischief'. With no trace of embarrassment, Colquhoun finished his letter by asking Hawkesbury if he thought his work was worthy of being presented to the King. Hawkesbury, unimaginative and hard-working, was said to have the confidence of George III. Colquhoun soon gained the recognition he craved. His novel and persuasive use of statistics in the *Treatise* immediately caught the public eye and brought him to wider notice.

Colquhoun's publication was timely. While trade on the river was increasing, so was crime. A range of predators, including the bum boat men who supplied ships, stood ready to loot valuable cargoes. Already, in the mid-1780s, these 'fresh-water pirates' had proved so active that captains and shipowners set up a fund to pay for armed men to patrol the river in boats at night. Thieves who were caught and found guilty were hanged at Execution Dock in Wapping, as occasionally pirates of the high seas still were. Piracy was much rarer than in the days of Captain Kidd a hundred years earlier, but rotting corpses still swung from gibbets on the Thames.[14] On land, despite a harsh penal system, parts of Wapping were so lawless that shipowners lobbied for a local magistrates' court, but chiefly they wanted constables to monitor the riverside and arrest thieves.[15]

The merchants' dock proposals in Wapping and Colquhoun's plan for better metropolitan policing had features in common. Both proposed authoritarian systems that threatened traditional rights, if not civil liberties; both made use of statistics in ways that were superficially impressive. It was no surprise that in 1798 the West India merchants approached Colquhoun and asked him to set up a Thames police force to protect their shipping. Colquhoun later allowed the public to think that the innovation had been all his own. In fact, he merely put into operation an idea that had come from John Harriott, his fellow magistrate. Harriott had failed to win support for a marine police force, which he put down to his inability to be obsequious. The point irked him. In his autobiography, he pointedly claimed ownership of the idea while acknowledging that Colquhoun had made it happen. He described Colquhoun as 'not only one of the most punctual men living, but . . . the most indefatigable persevering man I ever knew in whatever he undertakes'.[16]

Approval for the dockyards

From 1796, the rival schemes to improve the Port of London were refined and expensively illustrated to win support. They were reported at length in newspapers as the different factions competed for public approval. Vaughan was a visionary who had his sights set on the national interest. His early proposal for docks at Wapping had ended with a call to action. He wrote, 'We need only to open our eyes, sacrifice our prejudices, and grasp at the substance instead of the shadow, and we shall then find the surest means of encouraging our industry, and extending our commerce to bounds yet unknown.'[17] Vaughan corresponded with Thomas Jefferson, later President of the United States; they shared an interest in naval architecture and mathematics. Vaughan was active in public life: he supported the programme of canal-building in Britain, raised money for the war effort, and later served as a committee member of the Society for Bettering the Condition of the Poor. As far as the docks were concerned, he focused on the big picture, not the puny details. He favoured a Wapping site because it was close to the City. He downplayed the fact that it was densely populated and that many businesses, including the Shadwell Water Works, which supplied over 8,000 houses and public buildings, would be ruined if the scheme went ahead.

Many opposed the Wapping docks, although from 1796 merchants tactically renamed their project 'The London Dock Company'. The *Morning Chronicle*, an opposition newspaper, was a forceful critic. The Company of Lightermen warned that 5,000 of their members would be put out of work. Wharfingers, carmen and porters all signed a petition against the idea. The City of London licensed these workers and drew a sizeable income from their fees.[18] Inflammatory handbills were pasted in every street. One called upon the people of Southwark to resist the 'monstrous scheme' which would monopolize business, bring ruin to hard-working people and push up the price of basic goods.[19] The Borough of Southwark did formally object to docks in Wapping, arguing that a great proportion of its business came from trade in the Pool of London. There were also fears that London's financial centre would follow the new docks and shift east, damaging the economy.[20] (Earnings from the City of London were crucial even in this period.)

Because the West India merchants were powerful and because no one wished to appear complacent about river crime, criticism of their plans, which targeted them as a group, was often satirical. One critic, writing under the pseudonym Quoz, published a series of letters implying that the merchants' scheme was a bold-faced power-grab and an attack on property. The letters were so popular that he collected them in a publication called *Eastward Ho!!!* which went through several editions. Self-interested merchants, he suggested, had seized an opportunity to subdue the pride of City magnates by drawing a large part of their business farther east:

> We shall soon see the pride of the Citizens lowered! – House-rent will become cheaper, the streets will be less encumbered with carts and waggons, and less annoyed with noise and confusion. Some may object that the value of estates in and about the City will be depreciated – What then, have they not had their turn?[21]

Quoz pretended to encourage a subscription to fund the new docks, because clearly they would be costlier than anticipated. He made light of proposed charges on ships using the docks: the money would be needed to pay investors their promised dividend. How could anyone suppose that enough profits would be made just by taking all existing business from wharfingers, lightermen and quay-holders? He also touched on the destruction facing many Wapping residents:

> Some people affect a great deal of concern for the inhabitants of about 1800 houses, which are doomed to destruction, to make room for these Docks, and talk of the hardship of turning twelve thousand persons into the streets, or driving them to find new establishments at increased rents in places where they have no connection. – But what then? – if they cannot maintain themselves, we all know the parish must support them. Men of large minds, in the prosecution of great and splendid schemes, know how to overlook such petty considerations.[22]

Quoz mischievously questioned the merchants' selective use of facts – the great emphasis placed on the 1,464 feet of the Legal Quays, unchanged in extent since they had been rebuilt after the Great Fire of London, and the failure to mention the Suffrance Wharves, which could deal with the increase in trade. These had more than four times the capacity of the Legal Quays, were substantially built and shipowners would use them by preference if antiquated City regulations were swept aside.

Given this swell of opposition to docks at Wapping, the City's rival plan on the Isle of Dogs began to seem a better option. Robert Milligan, who had grown up on his family's sugar plantations in Jamaica and was now a merchant in London, had long favoured the Isle of Dogs alternative. In a crucial meeting, just a few days after most of his associates had opted for Wapping in 1795, he convinced leading West India merchant and wharfinger George Hibbert that the relatively remote Isle of Dogs was a better location. Milligan had logic on his side. Docks there could be made more secure and built more cheaply. Most West Indiamen were too large to make it easily up to the Pool of London. Their cargo was looted chiefly in the upper reaches of the Thames. It was here that an enclosed, secure dock needed to be built. By 1798, Hibbert was also a City alderman. His conversion was crucial, though he later gave Milligan full credit for planning the docks on the Isle of Dogs. Several West India merchants who had subscribed to the Wapping fund switched their support in 1797–98, backing proposals on the Isle of Dogs. These two schemes were now clear front-runners, and the choice between them was as bitterly fought as rival plans for a new runway at Heathrow or Gatwick today.

The committee stage of the bill to make wet docks for the Port of London uncovered a mass of uncomfortable detail. In his 1793 treatise, Vaughan claimed that Wapping had:

> Already, a *vacant space unoccupied* by any buildings, large enough for an extensive dock and warehouses of large dimensions, upon pulling down a few straggling houses: and if there was due encouragement, by the removal of a few inferior streets that are intersected with gardens and with rope-walks.[23]

This statement had been refuted by a pamphleteer who pointed out that new houses and streets were under construction on this supposed wasteland.[24] After all, the population of east London was increasing. Quoz, too, had questioned whether there was vacant space at Wapping. But Quoz had been slapped down by another pamphleteer who insisted that the houses on the proposed site were 'but few, and generally old, a few excepted, in bad repair, of little or no value, and in many parts a recepticle [*sic*] of vice, poverty and distress'.[25] This writer argued that most residents would be happy to leave the area: they were on short-term leases, their houses on the verge of falling in. He implied that slum clearance would be a benefit. But evidence at the bill's committee stage spelled out the extent of the demolition needed. The docks would extend over 80 acres: between Nightingale Lane in the west, Ratcliff Highway to the north, New Gravel Lane to the east and Wapping Street to the south. Daniel Alexander, the scheme's surveyor, testified that 2,200 houses would need to be destroyed. He did argue that 1,483 were old houses and tenements, but admitted that the area was extremely populous. His estimate of the cost of buying out all these inhabitants seemed unrealistically low.[26]

In opposition to Alexander's view, a petition from the parish of St George-in-the-East in 1797 insisted that some very fine houses would be taken down. The parish wanted compensation for loss of poor relief when wealthy residents left.[27] Insurance records of the time support the parish view. John Philipps of the Star Brewhouse in Wapping insured his house, business premises and goods for £31,700. If he was exceptional, there were many more Wapping tradesmen who were comfortably off. They included Charles Edwards, a ship chandler who insured his house, warehouse and goods for £800, and Mary Clark and John Milner, mastmakers who insured their premises for £1,300.[28] The manager of the Shadwell Water Works told the Committee that not only would his own business be ruined but the destruction would drive all wealthy businessmen from that quarter: wharfingers, distillers and brewers. Residents of Wapping presented a petition to the House of Commons in February 1799 explaining that many depended on their businesses or on the rents of properties that were earmarked for demolition. If the scheme went ahead, they and their families would be brought to poverty and ruin.

Some critics maintained that the Port of London could cope with increased trade if efficient systems were introduced. The committee stage of the dock bill revealed instances of malpractice and rivalry between the

Legal Quays and Suffrance Wharves (which mostly handled domestic trade – lesser value goods). Seemingly, wharfingers on the Legal Quays often told merchants that they had room for their sugar to prevent them using Suffrance Wharves (which merchants were entitled to do if the Legal Quays were full). In fact, they had no warehouse room. Cargos might then be piled on the Legal Quays and kept from market for a fortnight, though all duties had been paid.[29] The Legal Quays also thought coffee, another valuable commodity, was theirs by right and opposed it being stored elsewhere. If restrictions were lifted on Suffrance Wharves, unloading could be shortened. As it was, a West Indiaman might spend a month unloading in the river, even in peacetime. Captains could be forced to supervise the unloading of their vessel so that theft was prevented. Crews instead of lumpers could be tasked with unloading their ships. But restrictive practices were legion; wholesale reform would be difficult.

In scandalous detail, the committee revealed how ships were plundered. Coopers came on board to repair the enormous hogsheads of sugar before unloading and helped themselves to the contents. Then lumpers came, dressed to steal:

> Lumpers are clothed in a common Jacket and long Trowsers, with an Apron on, in the Inside of which is a large Pocket or Bag; over the Jacket is hung various empty Bags, tied to their Shoulders, hanging down their Backs, and also in Front, exclusive of the secondary Mode of Hats, Shoes, etc; over the Jacket is wore a large stiff Canvas Frock, which entirely conceals the Bags and Dress underneath.[30]

Workers helped each other to load up with stolen cargo before calling a boat to go ashore on the pretence of getting food or drink. If challenged, they dropped their bags straight into the water because they could only be prosecuted if stolen goods were found on them.

Ships' crews were often complicit in the theft of sugar or rum when it was sampled on board. Theft could bring them more money than their wages for the whole voyage. Lower ranks of revenue officers might be party to the racket. They were paid the same as common labourers but expected to dress more respectably and struggled to feed families on their wages alone.

Once goods were warehoused, there were more 'losses'. Not all were due to theft. A system of perquisites operated because wages were inadequate. The amount that merchants paid coopers to repair barrels did not cover materials and labour. Merchants therefore allowed coopers to keep a proportion of the 'samples' of sugar taken from each hogshead: once at point of sale and again on delivery. The sample drawn each time was 3 lb or 4 lb but the amount given to the buyer for examination was just 4 oz or 5 oz. The cooper kept the rest. And sometimes he sampled each hogshead three times. Merchants who had condoned the practice began to think of this as 'plunder' and tried to curb excess.[31] Coopers and warehouse workers were also entitled to the 'sweepings' of sugar from the warehouse floor. The disposal of waste benefited employers since it kept the premises clean and preserved the purity of the goods. Casual labourers in the warehouses, taken on during busy periods, might be offered sugar or coffee as payment. There was a shortage of small coin in the country and payment in kind suited everyone. But the system was open to abuse and the actions of labourers working on the margins of legality could be challenged. Constables might arrest them for theft if they were found carrying off sugar. In court, workers claimed that the goods were theirs by custom, or that the sugar was dirty, not fit for sale, and given to them in payment. Their fate might depend on the quantity and quality of the goods seized. To add to the confusion, different warehouses had different customs. No wonder plans to ease congestion in the port were viewed as an opportunity to reform labour practices.[32]

When port improvements were again discussed in Parliament in 1799, Pitt referred both schemes to a House of Commons Select Committee for decision. It was obvious by now that only enclosed docks would allow merchants to crack down on theft. Docks would also stop the annoying practice lawyers had of stirring up grievances by dispatching clerks to merchant ships on arrival to ask seamen if they had complaints about wages.[33] The Select Committee recommended that both schemes should go ahead. Something had to be done without delay, so it prioritized docks on the Isle of Dogs as less expensive and more easily completed. The new docks were to have a monopoly on the West India Trade (except tobacco) for twenty-one years. Though the London Docks Company fiercely contested this point, supporters of the West India Docks insisted that unless the whole trade was compelled to use them, they could not make the docks pay. The monopoly meant that subscribers to the dock scheme could not fail to make money.

Funding the marine police

Colquhoun's marine police force, although deeply unpopular with river workers, reduced theft after 1798. Colquhoun lost no opportunity for self-promotion. When claiming expenses for his force from the Home Office, he boasted that two police boats constantly patrolled the river at night but warned that the least relaxation would bring back the worst offenders.[34] His next object was to get permanent government funding for the police. He resorted to his usual method of producing a statistical study to influence opinion, expanding a chapter on river crime in his earlier work on policing London. In his *Treatise on the Commerce and Police of the River Thames*, he naturally painted the blackest view of lawlessness along the river to boost his case. Criminality on the Thames, he claimed, was 'unparalleled in any district of the same extent in the known World'.[35] In detailing how this had come about and how it might be remedied, he described a system of theft and corruption that seemed to have spread like a contagion through the lower social ranks. It demanded a strong remedy.

Deliberately stoking fears of a threatening underclass, Colquhoun listed the various types of robbery on the Thames, apparently using thieves' own cant, although he may well have invented the descriptive terms himself. These included 'River Piracy', when freebooters reconnoitred the river by day and looted chosen vessels at night, taking goods to receivers who kept iron and junk shops along the river. Then there were 'Night Plunderers' or gangs of dissolute watermen in league with watchmen who guarded lighters full of goods. 'Light-Horsemen' stole valuable items like sugar and coffee by night, goaded by receivers and in league with ships' mates and revenue officers who usually went to bed while the robbery was underway so that they might not see it. These gangs used sacks dyed black, called 'Black Strap', which would not be seen when stowed in the bottom of a rowing boat at night. 'Heavy Horsemen' were the lumpers who filled secret pockets with goods by day. Colquhoun noted that ship masters, too mean to feed these labourers on board, gave them an excuse to go ashore for meals, sometimes three times daily. The contracting lumper who hired them might even make a deal so that they worked without pay and trusted to plunder. Then there were 'Mud-larks' who loitered in the mud about a ship or dock gates, pretending to grub for useful debris but really waiting for lumpers to throw them bags of sugar or for dockworkers to toss them sheets of copper and nails. A 'mud-lark' was the slang term for a hog, which indicates the status of such people. The lowest class of thieves, whom Colquhoun called the scum of society, were the 'Scuffle-hunters' or casual quayside labourers who came prepared with long aprons in which to conceal whatever they could pilfer before quickly disappearing.[36]

Colquhoun noted that seamen were implicated in this network of corruption, and so further lessened the public image of the British sailor, already damaged by the 1797 mutinies. He explained that they were generally 'under the influence of the lowest and most profligate class of females, who often plunder them of their fair earnings, and then seduce them into acts of pillage and thieving'.[37] He called British seamen a 'brave, but a thoughtless and dissipated race of men' whose way of life erased barriers to certain types of theft. Though sailors might be repelled by the idea of committing a robbery on shore, they reconciled their minds to stealing imported goods from their ship. A police force, he said, would restrain this useful class of men from delinquency just when the nation needed them most.

Colquhoun got some of his information from informers who probably soon learnt what he most wanted to hear. In his *Treatise on the Police* he had uncovered huge losses, so he claimed, owing to the depravity of individuals whom the public might not even recognize as thieves. For instance, 'a considerable dealer in Rags and Old Iron, and other Metals' had revealed to him the existence of a network of receivers of stolen goods.[38] Now Colquhoun asserted that commercial property in the Port of London was 'prey to regular and systematic Depredation'.[39] While Ogle said coopers might take as much as 4 lb (1.8 kg) when sampling casks, Colquhoun put the estimate higher and claimed that in the warehouse each hogshead was plundered by 16 lb (7.3 kg) on average, amounting to a loss of about £70,000 a year in sampling alone.[40] Whereas West India merchants estimated their annual losses to be in the region of £200,000 to £300,000, Colquhoun preferred to emphasize the £500,000 that the port as a whole lost each year. He surveyed a 'Pandemonium *of Iniquity*' that, appropriately enough for a militarized nation after years of warfare, seemed to demand a military response. He thought of himself as a general, engaged in 'a warfare upon hosts of Criminal Delinquents', thwarting their 'hostile plans', protecting the innocent community with the aim of 'eradicating the mischief by an *ultimate conquest*'.[41]

Colquhoun's system of policing appealed to merchants because it not only promised to reduce pilfering, but also seemed likely to reduce their labour costs. For example, he claimed that under the 'Police System', where three or four coopers had repaired barrels before, in most cases only one was needed and then only for half a day.[42] The new Marine Police Office operated as a centre where lumpers could be hired: vetted men sworn to honesty and paid by the office. Customary perks or privileges were now criminalized. Colquhoun's zealous, moral approach was perhaps well intentioned but ultimately chilling: it justified reducing swathes of river workers to honest misery.

Colquhoun, a twin, had been dispatched from Glasgow to Virginia at fifteen to learn the tobacco trade. He returned after ten years to become a leading tobacco merchant and held several advisory offices at a young age, although ironically his Glasgow business failed and he had to relocate to London. The story that he once confided to business colleagues that 'Even I myself have made a mistake' is probably apocryphal, but it circulated in

Scotland long after his departure as an indication of his character.[43] Insecure and praise-seeking, Colquhoun always had one eye on posterity. He compiled manuscript notes on his long service to the country for his biographer, who happened to be his son-in-law, David Yates Grant. The biography was published in 1818, after Colquhoun's retirement but before his death, and is hugely complimentary. Grant claims that in twenty-five years of public service, Colquhoun never cost the state one farthing since his suggestions netted such large savings.

Colquhoun was quick to take offence if his writings were criticized, but there were some dissenting voices. One critic who pointedly titled himself 'a Citizen of London' took exception to Colquhoun's *Treatise on the Police*. He accused him of alarming the timid, of making people unfairly suspicious of others, and of casting aspersions on a range of useful trades that had many honest workers. He said Colquhoun's calculations were 'exaggerated', pointing out that many of his statistics came from criminal and semi-criminal sources that were not to be trusted. He implied that Colquhoun lacked candour and liberality. And he claimed that when the magistrate described London's workshop labourers as '*the most disorderly, profligate debauched set of human beings perhaps on the whole earth*', he gave a wholly false impression of Londoners to foreigners.[44] Colquhoun said that these men earned large sums by working hard but always spent their cash on drink. Idle while the money lasted, their whole life was spent between labour and debauchery. But Colquhoun's critic refuted this. On the contrary, he said, the nation depended on the work of this industrious multitude. Those who worked for their sustenance were the only truly independent people in the world, as opposed to those who lived upon the work of others. If the poor were drawn to pubs, it was because they could not afford to cook or heat their own homes, and it was wholly wrong to accuse the lower orders of 'universal profligacy'.[45] Yet even he had to admit that Colquhoun's work was widely read. As Colquhoun had hoped, before long George III was to thank him for his *Treatise*.[46]

Colquhoun's lobbying skills impressed readers. Gouverneur Morris, who met Colquhoun when working for the American government, thought him 'a very positive and opinionated Man'. But he noted that his great facility with numbers could bamboozle most. Colquhoun's knowledge of business and accounting techniques helped him to produce cogent reports for those in power.[47] His *Treatise on the Commerce and Police of the River Thames* was summarized in highly favourable reviews that credited him with popularizing commercial information that had not been widely available before.[48] He also knew how to appeal to prejudice. In his *Treatise* he depicted the poor as insects feeding on the blood of others, stealing exotic items that the middling sort paid a hefty price for, due to tax. His descriptions of audacious robberies on the river, such as boatmen cutting away a ship's anchors in broad daylight and, when officers rushed on deck, civilly bidding their victims 'Good day' as the ship floated away, became the stuff of legend. This story was repeated in popular magazines into the Victorian period.[49]

Building the docks

The bill to create enclosed docks in the Isle of Dogs became law in July 1799. The West India Dock Company started work at once to make its vision a reality. Its board of directors met weekly, chaired by George Hibbert. (The choice of chair shows that already, in this partnership, merchants had the upper hand over the City.) The project, given that wartime usually stultifies construction, was a mammoth undertaking. Investors subscribed £500,000 and government agreed to loan money to pay for the canal across the island and to compensate those whose interests were damaged. Finding enough labourers to dig out the docks was hard at times: up to 20 per cent of the male population was in some form of military service.[50] The company had engineers and surveyors but needed brickmakers, carpenters, masons, plumbers, slaters, ironmongers, painters and glaziers. Excavation began in February 1800. It was subcontracted to four different firms but only Holmes and Bough of Poplar could maintain the gruelling pace. It charged 11d. a cubic yard (0.76 m³) once its workers reached a depth of 6 feet (1.8 m). The firm Boulton and Watt near Birmingham supplied steam engines for pumping water from the excavation and, later, for pile-driving iron-tipped timbers to dam the dock entrances. Pipes, laid below the level of the low water mark, drained water into the Thames.[51] Much of the Isle of Dogs was then pasture for cattle. The fields not covered with spoil from the excavation continued to be rented to families with milk cows.

The West India Company's committee drove the work ahead while pressing down on costs. It was backbreaking labour, the men using picks, shovels and wheelbarrows. They were paid by the hour, so whenever the excavation flooded, or bad weather prevented work, they received no pay. Contractors also lost money when flooding hampered the dig. In the winter months when roads were bad, Holmes and Bough threatened to lay men off and re-hire in the spring when there was less mud and work could proceed more quickly. The number of labourers on site in any one week therefore fluctuated from about 450 to over 1,500. Facilities for them were basic and their suffering evident. In April 1800, Colquhoun recommended that the men be supplied with soup from a Quaker charity nearby. He was a supporter of soup kitchens in Wapping and other eastern parishes because he reasoned that free soup helped to prevent food riots. The price of provisions was so high by 1801 that one contractor insisted he would not be able to complete his share of the digging unless food for the men was provided.

As the excavation progressed, committee members themselves were amazed at the scale of the works. Millions of bricks were ordered to line the docks. Millions more were needed to build the warehouses. It was hard to get this quantity made and delivered, so the company ordered trials to see if bricks could be made from the excavated clay. They could, but the bricks were inferior and only good for use in the security wall around the docks. The war meant shortages of other materials, and John Perry offered timber, ropes and tar. In February 1799, he had petitioned for compensation along with John Wells and William Wells the younger, since the new scheme would impinge on his own wet dock. All the same, he was content to supply the project with materials: his contract was worth hundreds of pounds.

There was enormous pressure to complete in 1802: company investors wished to reap their profits and West India merchants were pushing to use the docks. The steam engine working at the dock entrance at Limehouse Hole was kept working night and day. In July that year, there was a serious accident when a cofferdam gave way at high tide. Labourers were excavating a basin between two cofferdams at a depth of 30 feet when a supervisor saw a timber pile in one of the dams start to give way. 'For God's sake, come up; the coffer-dams blown' he yelled, and the workmen rushed in all directions.[52] Five men and a boy were drowned as the basin filled with water in a minute. All the dead men were married; their wives were pregnant and most also had young children. An inquest recorded a verdict of accidental death, although engineers had inspected the dams just beforehand and declared them safe. Faced with lurid publicity and pressure to offer generous compensation, the company paid each widow a lump sum, roughly equivalent to their husband's annual wage adjusted to the size of each family.

As the warehouses went up, committee members began to worry about sabotage and pilfering. They knew that there were many groups, including lightermen and watermen, who wished the project ill. Inflation and high taxes were making life hard for the poor and even the middling sort. Men who feared that the new docks would rob them of their livelihood might be tempted to flood the works or set fire to buildings. In March 1802, the company applied to government for a military patrol at night. The government agreed, provided the company built barracks on site for an officer and thirty men. Sentry boxes were constructed at strategic points around the dock wall. The contractor building the warehouses was also told to hire watchmen and arm them with muskets and bayonets.

The opening ceremony had to be deferred twice but at last the West India Docks were ready. On 27 August 1802, a crowd of thousands watched as two ships entered the import dock. Security was tight and the military guard was on duty day and night before the event. Onlookers were stupefied by the scale of the achievement and the opening was regarded as a national event. The export dock, to the south, and the massive warehouse complex were not completed until 1806 but the import dock alone extended over 28 acres. The site was heavily protected: enclosed by a wall that was 30 feet (9 m) high at least 300 feet (90 m) from the nearest building, surrounded by a moat 12 feet (3.7 m) wide and 6 feet (1.8 m) deep. The docks were run on military lines. No person was admitted without a ticket, which had to be shown to the armed guard at the entrance. A ship's crew, except for one responsible officer, had to leave the docks once their vessel was moored. The company used its own labourers to unload cargoes. These men were given a uniform of jacket and trousers, and not allowed their own clothes until they left work. They were paid 3s. 6d. a day. If they were found taking goods, they were prosecuted and lost their job; a head constable was always on hand to take men who were caught before a magistrate. Because of the value of the goods handled and the threats the West India Docks received, the military guard remained a permanent feature.

Meanwhile, in May 1801, the London Docks at Wapping won government approval. These docks would enjoy a twenty-one-year monopoly on wine, rice, brandy and other imports not covered by the West India Dock agreement. Work began promptly but, as predicted, land purchase proved tortuous. Daniel Alexander, the London Dock Company's surveyor, contacted property owners in the area targeted for demolition and asked them for a valuation of what their property was worth. Before compensation was paid, this valuation was challenged by the company's own surveyors. Initial estimates may well have been inflated, but typically owners got only two-thirds of their asking price. Some took their case to court but this was a high-risk option: in one notable dispute the owner got only half what he said his property was worth.[53] The process of buying up properties reveals the development of modern accounting techniques: the company's valuations include an early application of the concept of depreciation, typically used to reduce the purchase price.[54]

The scheme intimidated local institutions but some refused to be cowed. When Alexander wrote to the London Hospital asking to purchase the land at the back of the building, its House Committee immediately checked the legal position, discovered that the dock bill did not entitle the company to issue what would today be termed a compulsory purchase order, and rejected its claims. The hospital had good relations with the City, which had already removed an offensive horse slaughterhouse and a cart-grease works to a distance, and could have enlisted its support against the merchants. The hospital planned to build houses on the land at the back and rent them out for income. It needed the money: there were always twice as many sick people pleading for admission than it could admit. Many of the sick were Irish and foreign labourers, entirely dependent on their physical strength, and the hospital knew that when these men could not work their families starved. Because of its location, fronting a busy road and near the river, the hospital admitted more accident patients than any other in London. Accident cases were never turned away.[55] Having ruffled the hospital committee's feathers, the London Dock Company prudently donated £100 for the admission of patients, anticipating injuries during the building works. Several of the merchants on its board of directors were already regular subscribers to the hospital, and routinely sent sick seamen there.

The onset of construction in Wapping brought massive disruption. Gangs of labourers, renting or squatting locally, increased tensions. The Society for the Suppression of Vice wrote to the company complaining that its labourers were working on Sundays and that the evil effects of this practice would corrupt the neighbourhood. Company directors replied haughtily that Sunday working was unavoidable in projects of great magnitude, whereupon the Society enlisted the help of the Bishop of London. The Bishop insisted on a personal reply from the dock company but backed down once he had secured a face-saving letter saying that work on the Lord's Day would take place only under 'circumstances of the most urgent necessity'.[56] Lighters carrying spoil downriver to Greenwich collided repeatedly with the Marine Society vessel moored off Deptford Creek, which lightermen hit deliberately to help them navigate the bend in the river. The master of the Society eventually asked the company to forbid a practice that endangered lives.[57] The company found it as hard to obtain building materials as the West India Dock Company did. From time to time they competed for the same products. Periodically, swathes of its workforce were pressed into military service, as in 1803 and 1804. On the plus side, it saw a rapid take-up of steam power. The docks were excavated with the help of steam engines to drain water and haul dirt wagons. Engines also ground mortar for the brickwork.

As work progressed, Wapping became strange to its own residents: the parish changed before their eyes. Workhouses and charity schools were knocked down. Businesses that had stood over sixty years were swept away, along with more recent ones such as the soup kitchen, which had to be relocated. The familiar street pattern was obliterated. Finally, at the end of January 1805, the company advertised that the London Docks were ready for business; vessels using them would be subject to agreed fees. On 1 February, a ship made its way into the dock for the formal opening, its progress hindered by thick ice. Spectators took shelter from the biting cold under sheds opposite the warehouses. Few of the nobility bothered to turn up. 'God Save the King' was played as loudly as ever, but the ceremony, held in sub-zero conditions, was an inauspicious beginning.

London and the slave trade

London was a slaving port until 1807, when Parliament outlawed the British slave trade. In the first few years of the nineteenth century, London's involvement actually intensified. Between 1802, when the West India Docks opened, and 1807, when the slave trade was abolished, an esti-mated 74 vessels made 127 voyages to West Africa. Official records show that in this period London slave captains purchased 38,001 Africans destined for the Americas; 4,280 died at sea.[58] The massive investment in docks for West Indian produce shows how much confidence merchants had in a system that depended on slavery. The wet docks had been insti-gated by West India merchants who, if they were not actually transporting enslaved Africans to the Caribbean, owned plantations that depended on slave labour, or else dealt in the produce of those plantations. William Vaughan, the project's prime mover, was heir to estates in the West Indies. The politicians who helped to get the bills for the new docks through

238

Parliament in 1799 and 1800 had financial interests in the West Indies. William Manning, the MP who lobbied hard for docks at Wapping, was a leading West India merchant and plantation owner. Sir William Young, his key supporter in Parliament, was also a West India planter and owned 1,300 slaves. He was a strong opponent of the campaign to abolish the slave trade.

The 'West India Interest' took a lead in managing the dock projects. Sir Richard Neave, chair of the London Dock Company, and George Hibbert, chair of the West India Dock Company, were both prominent West India merchants. Thomas King, a former slave-ship captain and owner of estates in British Guiana, living in Blackheath, was an early subscriber to the Wapping scheme and served as a director of the London Docks Company. He was a partner in Camden, Calvert and King, one of the largest ship-owning firms in London, with business interests extending across the globe.[59] The firm was involved in the slave trade, as well as being contracted to ship convicts on the Second and Third Fleets to Sydney's penal settlement, during the years 1789 to 1791. William Camden, a Wapping biscuit manufacturer, had retired from the business in 1783. Anthony Calvert, the managing partner, was hard-edged and much criticized for the death rate on the convict voyages to Botany Bay. A tough negotiator, he was able to influence the enquiry into wet docks for the Port of London as an elder brother of Trinity House.

The two dock schemes were financed by London's merchants and businessmen. Merchants trading overseas counted for a third of subscribers in both schemes, and in the case of the West India Docks contributed 40 per cent of the money needed. Most of the other businessmen who invested ran shipping-related industries along the river: ropemakers, anchorsmiths, sailmakers and shipbuilders (the Perrys invested in the Wapping scheme). Some investors were in domestic trades with no relation to the port, attracted simply by the chance to make money.[60] Obviously, the West India Dock project was an opportunity to invest in the West Indian trade. Absentee plantation owners living in London invested heavily. But both dock projects had investors with ties to the slave economy – about a third of the total number – hardly surprising given that West India merchants had first supported docks in Wapping and only a proportion switched funds to the Isle of Dogs scheme. Those with close ties included: slave traders; slave factors, who bought cargoes of enslaved Africans and re-sold them to plantation owners; absentee slave-owners, who might never have visited their plantations; and 'West India Merchants' who traded with plantation owners, selling their sugar and supplying them with provisions, finance and slaves. Other investors, such as wholesale grocers, were only incidentally involved. Patrick Colquhoun, who did so much to support the West India merchants, was also linked to the slave trade. He was the London agent for the planters of the Virgin Islands, finding buyers for their produce.

A striking finding is that the dock schemes also attracted fervent abolitionists, including Quaker bankers. The wet dock subscription lists, which included both supporters of the slave trade and abolitionists, show how the two groups were intertwined. They moved in the same circles and were sometimes members of the same family. The Atlantic slave economy was pervasive, affecting almost every aspect of commercial life and contributing much to the capital's wealth. And the West India docks enticed new investors into that slave economy. The corrupt power wielded by the West Indian merchants tainted society. The African Ottobah Cugoano saw this clearly. Cugoano, born in modern-day Ghana, was sold into slavery and worked on a plantation in Grenada before being purchased by a merchant and taken to England. Once in London, he was given his freedom. He became a member of the Sons of Africa, an abolitionist group that included Olaudah Equiano and other leading members of the black community who campaigned against the evil of slavery. When Cugoano tried to understand how a Christian country like Britain could tolerate a trade that ignored 'the natural rights of mankind', he inadvertently described the corrupt influence of the West Indian merchants:

Men of activity and affluence, by whatever way they are possessed of riches, or have acquired a greatness of such property, they are always

240

preferred to take the lead in matters of government, so that the greatest depredators, warriors, contracting companies of merchants, and rich slave-holders, always endeavour to push themselves on to get power and interest in their favour; that whatever crimes any of them commit they are seldom brought to a just punishment.[61]

The 'West Indian Interest' came to power because its merchants were rich. Social inequalities deepened as they used power to gain more wealth: in times of war, for example, these men were best placed to profit while the rest of the population had to work harder to clear a rising national debt. Cugoano's criticism of the slave trade extended to criticism of an unfair society in which *'the rich grind the face of the poor'*.[62]

Rebellion thwarted

The new docks were firmly associated in the minds of the lower classes with state oppression and social inequality. The Despard Plot shows this clearly. At the turn of the century, Pitt's network of spies continued to track radical groups. In 1802, agents fixed on Colonel Edward Despard. He had been recalled in 1790 from his post as superintendent of the Bay of Honduras (present-day Belize) and was living in London with his African-Caribbean wife and son. Despard, from an Anglo-Irish military family, was a brave officer who had fought alongside Nelson in the West Indies during the American Revolutionary War. He was less successful as a civilian governor: he lost the support of British settlers in Honduras and the government thought it best to recall him. It was years before he was exonerated. Meanwhile he lived on half-pay, his official expenses unpaid.

Despard became increasingly disillusioned and made contact with the London Corresponding Society and revolutionary United Irishmen. In 1798, he was a key figure in a plot to incite simultaneous uprisings in England and Ireland, timed to coincide with a French invasion. When the plot was discovered, he was imprisoned in the House of Correction in Cold Bath Fields. The prison was known as 'The English Bastille' and

Despard received the harshest treatment of all political prisoners there. Catherine, his wife, lobbied tirelessly on his behalf but, as habeas corpus was suspended a few months later, the government could lock him up indefinitely. Conditions in the prison were brought to the attention of the House of Commons in 1799, when Sir William Young was one of the politicians who claimed that it would be folly to transfer these state prisoners to the Tower of London. There was a band of United Irishmen in Wapping, he argued, which had threatened to take the Tower. If ever such a plot succeeded, political prisoners in the Tower would be put at the head of a daring gang. Despard was not released until 1801 when the suspension of habeas corpus lapsed. He retired to the family estate in Ireland but enjoyed only a few months of rest.

In 1802, revolutionaries in Ireland persuaded Despard to return to London. His task was to coordinate Irish labourers and disaffected guards in London and Windsor, and persuade them to hold off any action until it would coincide with another revolt in Ireland and support from France. As an officer, he could sway rank and file soldiers. The plotters, who included shoemakers and carpenters, met in pubs across London but it was in the eastern parishes that rebels were expected to rise in force. Thousands recently discharged from building the wet docks were thought to be ready to join the cause, along with the homeless poor resulting from neighbourhood clearances in Wapping. Action was planned for the opening of Parliament on 23 November, when allegedly the conspirators planned to assassinate the king. Thanks to government spies, Despard was arrested at the Oakley Arms in Lambeth, together with forty labouring men, a week beforehand.

Despard's trial attracted enormous publicity. Nelson gave him a glowing character reference – 'no man could have shewn more zealous attachment to his Sovereign and his Country' – but could only speak for his earlier career.[63] The case against Despard lacked important detail: government was wary of setting out the full extent of the plot (which extended to other English cities) in case it alarmed the public. Nor did government wish to reveal its intelligence sources. Despard's defence was equally restrained, perhaps because he guessed the difficulties the government was under and did not mean to implicate himself further by giving away information. Still, one key piece of intelligence at his trial was that, when arrested, he had been discussing the military defence of the docks in the Isle of Dogs. The docks had opened that August but work was ongoing. They were an irritant to London's river workers who felt that their livelihoods were threatened, that their voices had not been heard, and that action was needed to recover lost liberties.

The jury found Despard guilty of treason but recommended mercy because of his military service. The government still pressed ahead with the death sentence; as a traitor, Despard would be hanged, drawn and quartered. His wife's desperate lobbying and other appeals got the sentence commuted. He was hanged in February 1803 and his corpse merely decapitated. Ironically, Despard was entitled as a resident in the parish to be buried in cemetery of St Faith, which had long ago been incorporated into the grounds of St Paul's Cathedral. His widow ensured that his body was interred near the cathedral's north door. With this failed conspiracy died all immediate hopes of London's radical poor securing a fairer society.

The effect of the docks

The enormous new docks had a deep and lasting impact on maritime London. Parishes east of the Tower – Wapping, Shadwell and, to a lesser extent, Ratcliff – became less prosperous as the London Dock Company bought up businesses and forced them to close or relocate. (The displaced poor were more easily sacrificed to a development that was perceived to be in the nation's interest.) Remaining firms may have gained something by being close to the London Docks. Newspaper advertisements of nearby buildings for sale show that their owners claimed an economic benefit. The company itself bought more land than it needed and later sold it at a profit. But Wapping's old commercial heartland had been ripped out. The high dock wall was a visible reminder of monopoly, corporate power and segregation.

The dock schemes contributed to the establishment of a waged society. Colquhoun's marine police force helped merchants replace a system based on perquisites with wage payments. The hardships caused by his policy were already apparent by 1799. To win support for his river police that year, Colquhoun used profits from confiscated goods to buy 1,500 loaves of bread for distribution to Wapping's poor. The relief was temporary but paved the way for claims that the neighbourhood's 'industrious poor' saw that the police acted in their interest.[64] In the short term, a river worker's customary 'perk' of sugar or coffee was replaced by soup at a charity kitchen. Colquhoun's vivid description of a riverside network of receivers (grocers, publicans, spirit dealers and junk shops), all dealing in loot from merchant ships, helped to reconcile wealthier observers to the wholesale destruction of a community.

In both docks, amenities for workers were minimal. Safety and hygiene were largely ignored. The West India Docks were more strictly run, but though it employed its own labour force and had a military guard it never completely stopped petty theft. The London Docks soon attracted incomers from many nations looking for work. Dockers were poorly paid at 5d. an hour (the work was irregular and about £40 a year was needed to keep a family). They were also badly housed. Areas around the docks became desperately crowded and blighted by poor sanitation, inadequate lighting and disease. The poor rate in nearby parishes now fell on people who could barely afford to pay. Affluent tradesmen, who had bolstered the poor rate and contributed to philanthropic causes, had been driven out, leaving only the needy. The docks had not really affected the Henleys' coal business but the Henleys still joined the exodus of wealthy people from Wapping. Joseph moved to Putney in 1800; Michael retired to Derby in 1805.

Colquhoun, writing about poverty in Spitalfields in 1806, lamented that the assessed taxes in this poor district could never raise enough to provide for the numbers who were destitute:

The opulent manufacturers and others, for whom the poor exhaust their strength by laborious occupations, reside within the limits of the city of London, where the labouring people do not dwell, because they can find no cheap habitations.[65]

The wealthiest manufacturers and merchants, who ultimately reaped the benefit of the silk weavers' labour, could not be compelled to contribute to their relief: the well-to-do congregated where the poor could not afford to live. So in rich parishes, the burden of the poor rate actually lessened. Did Colquhoun make the connection with similar developments in the parish of St George-in-the-East, Wapping? Lesser craftsmen who had lost their employment because of the docks were left to petition their freemason lodges for funds. Colquhoun's stance was ambivalent: determined to keep poor workers in their place, he nevertheless supported charitable works to help them improve their lives, as long they did not get ideas above their station. A sense of London divided into West End and East End was becoming entrenched.

The West India Dock Company was consistently profitable. Its shares soon doubled in value.[66] It paid out to investors the maximum possible dividend of 10 per cent from 1806 until 1823, when its monopoly expired – an example of how London benefited from the slave economy. Investors in the company were assured of a good income because West India vessels were compelled to use the docks. Even Edward Ogle, who had fought against enclosed docks, shrewdly invested in the West India scheme: it could not fail to make money. The prospect of handsome profits may have encouraged merchants to opt for a visionary dock scheme in the first place rather than adopt short-term improvements by reforming corrupt practices. But the London Docks, although profitable, never made the same high dividends. With hindsight, it was perverse of the merchants who backed this scheme to choose a site that involved so much expense on land purchase, legal fees and demolition.

Even West India merchants who had not invested directly in the two dock companies benefited. Yes, their profits were hit by wartime disruption, fluctuating sugar prices, higher import duties on sugar as government increased wartime taxes, and the abolition of the slave trade in 1807. But the docks reduced their shipping costs by 40 per cent. (Hibbert estimated the financial saving in handling and warehousing alone to be 18 per cent, without even thinking about the cash value of the time saved.)[67] Merchants also saved an estimated £300,000 annually, thanks to the reduction in pilferage.

Government inquiries into how best to improve the Port of London, and the well-reported progress of the dock bills through Parliament, resulted in more people having a better understanding of the geography of the river and the commercial activity it supported. New methods of handling goods clearly impacted on wharfingers and lightermen but extended wider still, bringing changes almost as dramatic as the container revolution 170 years later. Government now had a sharper appreciation of the relationship of political power and trade. If Britain had profited from protectionism, the new docks gave London the facilities it needed to thrive in the era of free trade that many predicted would come with peace. Among conservatives, too, patriotic descriptions of the new Port of London served to underline an increasingly nationalistic view of Britain's political and moral pre-eminence. The port was to endure until the early 1980s, when containerization led to larger ships that could not get upriver. But the great docks are still a major influence on the shape of modern London. Regenerated as 'Docklands', with a financial centre at Canary Wharf, they are still famous worldwide.

CONCLUSION
London Against Napoleon

The creation of the docks turned a spotlight on London's maritime districts. The military and commercial importance of maritime London meant that any signs of unrest or degeneration there caused sharp concern, especially among wealthier classes who had little or no knowledge of the communities themselves, and who merely associated them with high crime rates. Given the amount of unrecorded crime in this period, it is impossible to determine statistically whether crime was higher in the maritime districts than in other parts of London. But certainly, Colquhoun's books helped to create this perception, and the record of trials held at the Old Bailey confirms that after 1805 crime in these parishes was on the rise.

This fact helps to explain the enormous public interest shown in the murder of Isaac Blight, a Rotherhithe ship-breaker shot in his own parlour in 1805. Not only was it one of the earliest cases in which forensic evidence was used to secure a conviction, but also it acted as a barometer by which to measure public confidence in the power of the law to uphold a stable society. The case gained in significance because of its riverside location. Blight was a prominent citizen, a former merchant and sometime investor in the West India Dock Company. Yet his affairs had taken a turn for the worse. He was on the verge of bankruptcy. To protect his property from his creditors, he nominally made it over to Richard Patch, whom he had taken in penniless in 1803 but who had since worked his way up to become a trusted foreman. It was fraud but a common ploy. On 23 September 1805, for no obvious reason, Blight was shot in the abdomen and died the following day. It made headline news. The nation was tense anyway due to recent developments in the war. Nelson had sailed to take command of the British forces off Cadiz, with the aim of drawing the Franco-Spanish fleet into a decisive engagement. People went about their normal business but at the back of everyone's mind was anxiety about the imminent battle at sea. Blight's murder offered a displacement for that unease.

It was a classic murder mystery. There were no eyewitnesses and, if Blight's maid was telling the truth, no way that anyone could have gained access to the room where he had been sitting. His home and wharf were on the river at Greenland Dock, close by the Dog and Duck Stairs in Rotherhithe. No one could have escaped by river as it was low tide. The route to the house by land was temporarily limited by dock excavations on the Surrey side of the river. There was a narrow path, then a gate. A couple happened to be there and had seen no one pass. In court, the prosecution relied on floor plans and a model of Blight's premises to convince the jury that Patch was the murderer. Patch had gone to the outside privy, pleading bowel troubles. The maid had heard the privy door slam, then immediately afterwards was deafened by the gunshot. The victim had seen only an arm and the weapon, pointing at him around the parlour door. But Patch's alibi did not protect him for long, especially once the pistol's ramrod was found in the privy. He had slipped off his shoes and sneaked silently back into the house to murder Blight and secure his property for good.

What made the crime worse was that it featured an ungrateful domestic. It took on symbolic proportions. The trial gripped public interest for months, was reported in unprecedented detail and was even attended by royalty. The assassination of Prime Minister Spencer Perceval in 1812 is said to have been the key event that alerted the elite to the danger of an assassin's gun. But Blight's murder was an earlier wake-up call. The injustice of it, given that Blight had shown charity to Patch, and the fear of lower orders rising against masters, added to the scandal. It was crucial for public confidence to demonstrate that law officers had the tools and intelligence to catch the criminal and that wrongdoing would be punished in full. The significance of the case justified a tomb in Blight's memory in St Paul's churchyard, Deptford. Artists depicted the tomb and for many years it featured in local guidebooks.

The Ratcliff Highway murders in December 1811 were another profound shock to public trust. People worried that men brutalized by war and inured to extreme violence were at large in the community. This was a credible fear, especially as there was little expectation that the lower orders would cultivate the humanitarian spirit that officers had to demonstrate in wartime. During the space of twelve days, in two separate attacks, seven people were bludgeoned to death or had their throats cut. The first victims were a linen draper and his family at 29 Ratcliff Highway. The maid, who had been sent out on errands, gave the alarm. Neighbours entered the house to find a bloodbath. 'The body of Mr. Marr and his shop boy, the latter of whom appeared, from evident marks, to have struggled for life with the assassins, near each other; that of Mrs. Marr in the passage; and the infant in its cradle, all dead, but yet warm and weltering in their blood.'[1] A murder weapon, a shipwright's hammer or maul, was later identified but did not lead to the killer.

The second attack occurred in the King's Arms at 81 New Gravel Lane (now Garnet Street). The elderly tavern keeper, his wife and female servant were battered and had their throats slit. In neither case did theft appear to be the motive. By now there was public panic; people were not safe in their homes. The Prince Regent was so alarmed that he gave his servants instructions not to admit anyone to Carlton House after 8 p.m.[2] In a subtle indictment of 'progress', waste ground belonging to the London Dock Company was singled out as the murderer's escape route on both occasions.[3]

Eventually a seaman named John Williams was arrested. Before he could be brought to trial, he hanged himself in prison, or else was murdered. The investigation had been led by the same magistrate who had been so successful in the Blight case, but this time the outcome was less convincing.

The legal process was closed hurriedly to calm the public. Williams's body was paraded on a barrow around Wapping so that the populace could see the danger was over. The grisly procession stopped for ten minutes at the location of each murder. Thousands lined the route. Afterwards, the corpse was buried at the crossroads of Cable Street and Cannon Street with a stake driven through the heart. If the wrong man had paid the penalty, the chilling ritual still acted as both warning and release.

War and society

The impact of revolutionary war on maritime London was dramatic and helped to aggravate social divisions. At the same time, the contribution the maritime parishes made to the war effort, and to the economy more widely, was increasingly apparent. In the struggle against Napoleon, much depended on ordinary working people, far from the conflict zone. The ruling class was anxious to keep the poor in their place, by force if necessary, while making sure that workers remained productive. By the late 1790s, Pitt had created an extremely repressive state. Employees were forbidden by law to act collectively for better conditions. The nation was highly militarized. At the height of the struggle against France, from 1804 to 1807, between 11 and 14 per cent of the adult male population was in the military.[4] Then again, militia and volunteer forces did bring different classes together in some measure as they trained alongside each other in a common cause.

People in maritime districts nurtured their distinct cultures as one way of offsetting the pressures of seafaring and war. Sales catalogues suggest that wealthy residents actively collected prints that celebrated naval dockyards, naval victories, maritime-related charities like the Humane Society, and sentimental and patriotic works like *The Sailor Boy's Return*. Such prints, alongside iconic images of patriotic sacrifice like *The Death of General Wolfe*, reinforced pride in the local maritime tradition.[5] Riverside parishes housed both deep-rooted and mobile communities. Each, in turn, had local and global ties. The same was true of other parts of the metropolis but in maritime London these circumstances were pronounced. The cultivation of a maritime identity that had strong emotional appeal helped to glue the different communities together. Charitable initiatives and peer-group application of standards of respectability went some way towards dealing with social problems. New restrictions on the labour force, enclosed docks and stricter law enforcement aimed to contain radical and criminal elements. Bow Street constables, for instance, cracked down on organized fights between mobile groups of Irish workers along the river, sending troublemakers into the navy.[6]

In a parallel development, the Admiralty again targeted corruption in the naval dockyards. In the early years of the nineteenth century, procedures were tightened up. Older officials were encouraged to retire and much younger men took their place. Greater professionalization replaced a system heavily dependent on 'fees'. After the 1802 disturbances, improved efficiency and prompt payment of wages brought a highly unusual strike-free period, which lasted until the end of the war in 1815.[7] Dockyard reform directly affected Benjamin Slade's long career. Slade was in the firing line after an awkward episode involving a loss to Deptford dockyard of over £11,500.[8] The case was heard at the Old Bailey in 1800. John Collinridge, employed to obtain timber and advanced public funds for that purpose, had died insolvent in 1798 apparently owing the dockyard money. George Thomas, the attorney hired to sort out the dead man's affairs, wrote to the yard asking for help with the box of papers he had found. He wrote personally to Benjamin Slade twice, supposing him to know more about it than any other person. Slade discussed these letters with the Navy Board's legal advisor who advised Thomas to make up his accounts from the paperwork he had, counting only receipts for goods delivered. The yard could then calculate what Collinridge owed the government from its record of the funds advanced to him.

Events did not turn out as expected. Thomas obtained confirmation of Collinridge's last accounts, settled in 1791, and asked Slade to tell him how much timber Collinridge had supplied since that date. Oddly, Thomas then turned up numerous receipts for goods and services that Collinridge had seemingly delivered. These showed that the dead man was not in debt to the yard at all but was owed £1,200. The Navy Board finally looked into the matter. The bills Thomas now submitted were so numerous and for such small amounts that, although it was obvious that some were forged, the Board was inclined to draw a line under the affair. After all, the country was at war and there were better things to do. Then someone noticed that several forgeries were in the attorney's own hand. It was soon evident that Thomas had produced the bulk of the receipts himself – to what end, it was hard to guess. Either he intended to pocket the money, or he pitied the dead man's debtors – poor cartmen and the like – desperate to be paid what was owed them. He was sentenced to death, although recommended for mercy because of his former good character.

In wartime, there were thousands of pounds' worth of goods coming into the dockyard weekly, so officials could be forgiven if not every item of paperwork was properly processed. All the same, when Collinridge died he owed the Navy Board a mammoth sum. His accounts had not been formally made up for seven years. There is no evidence that Slade was openly criticized; he was not called to testify at the trial. But he had placed contracts with an unreliable supplier, however well known to the yard (Collinridge was a former shipwright). Slade had been unable to provide Thomas with clear records of how much timber Collinridge had delivered. A system of rigid pricing and traditional practice had fallen short.[9] The attorney had taken advantage of this chaos to attempt to defraud the Board of another large sum. In July 1801, the reforming Earl of St Vincent became First Lord of the Admiralty, determined to root out dockyard malpractice. Slade was vulnerable, like many elderly officials who were no longer on top of the job. He left his post of purveyor at once but he was not quite of an age to retire. After the Peace of Amiens was negotiated, he was made master boatbuilder at the dockyard.

The post was a sinecure: Slade's reckonable service was calculated from the date he stopped being purveyor.[10] In 1805, after nearly fifty-six years in public employment, he was granted a pension of £150 a year. Although now due to retire, there is a still suggestion that he was 'pensioned off'. A newspaper commented on the naval pension list:

Every man who has any regard for the public welfare, must object to pensions being granted to persons like these, merely for the sake of making their offices empty for the purpose of putting others, and generally worse qualified persons, into them.[11]

The criticism is a little unfair. Britain won the war against Napoleon thanks to its naval and economic power; the superiority of the British navy compared to that of France and Spain has long been acknowledged. But the dockyards also made a vital contribution, and the logistical feats performed by officials have received less recognition.

Slade retired to Egham in Surrey, dying in 1809. His will illustrates the impact of wartime taxation on the middling sort. He left £2,200 in shares, together with books and pictures to his four children. He left £1,666 in shares to his second wife (probably a tax evasion since Pitt's 1796 tax did not apply to personal legacies left to a surviving partner). His executors made a careful note on his will that his personal estate did not exceed £3,000, which suggests that estate duty was paid to avoid death duties on his possessions. He left the house in Deptford's Butt Lane, inherited from his aunt, Mary Slade, to his eldest son, Benjamin. The property Mary Slade had left his two younger sons had already been sold, possibly to avoid the higher taxes that Pitt had imposed on inhabited houses in 1797. So, the property base of the Slades in Deptford evaporated. Yet if the local presence of the Slades was but a shadow of what it once had been, Benjamin senior still asked for his body to be returned and buried in one or other of the family vaults at St Nicholas's or St Paul's, Deptford. It would have made the journey by river.

The longer-term impact of war

War slowly changed the experience of living along the river. At the beginning of the century, the scurrilous Ned Ward, an early commentator on London, joked that in Deptford women far outnumbered men. The sea took husbands away, he wrote, leaving women desperate for male company and making a sore trial of their virtue:

Here a pretty Woman or two at a Door, there another or two at a
Window, all looking as melancholy as old Maids and Widows, for want
of Male Conversation; gazing upon each Man that pass'd 'em, with as
much Earnestness and Desire, as ever our Great Grand-Mother did
upon the forbidden Fruit.[12]

A hundred years later, the 1811 census showed that Deptford had almost
the same number of men as women, even discounting the hundreds of
soldiers and sailors who might be temporarily lodged there. War and the
expansion of job opportunities in maritime trades brought population
growth, house building and a boost to the local economy.

At the same time, the development of an intensely regulated, waged
workforce in Britain is illustrated by changes in labour relations along the
Thames: the coal heavers and cargo handlers denied the custom of taking
goods in lieu of wages or as supplements to income; the Marine Police,
made directly responsible for setting piecework rates in the West India
Docks; the shipwrights put on task work and urged to become more efficient.[13] Sometimes depicted entirely as a class struggle, this development
was also a response to prolonged warfare, reflecting Britain's need to maximize its naval strength and its income from international trade. The crisis
of war added urgency to labour reforms, which, in London's maritime
districts, must have seemed wholly in the national interest to the ruling
classes.

The Port of London was at the centre of Britain's wealth and Britain
now saw the greatest expansion of trade of any nation. Imports from all
over the world flowed into the Thames. The wartime building of the wet
docks brought huge advantages: if some branches of commerce were badly
affected by war, others flourished, and the West India Docks gave facilities
for more trade with all parts of the world. Contemporaries soon noted that
with the construction of the docks and various favourable warehousing
acts, Britain had become a free port into which foreign goods of every
description could be imported and re-exported without payment of duties.
Merchants of other countries, whether neutrals, enemies or allies, rushed

to send their goods to London for safety and sale. This opened up new markets for Britain, as did its wartime conquests.[14] In November 1806, Napoleon placed an embargo on British trade with all European countries allied to France or under French control, hoping to bring Britain to its knees. The blockade lasted until April 1814 and periodically it did have some effect but nothing could stop Britain's extensive trade with the rest of the world. The fundamental wealth of the country continued to grow.

London's enclosed docks remained controversial, despite the enormous economic contribution they made to Britain's wartime coffers in increased tax revenues, and the visible inadequacies of the old port they had helped to address. The West India Dock Committee, at its 1809 meeting, admitted that the docks had met with hostility almost in proportion to their enormous success. The situation was inevitable, merchants stated, since the docks had largely removed theft and depredation from trade.[15] They also claimed that many of the inconveniences attributed to the dock system were actually the result of wartime disruption, tax regulations and the vagaries of trade, none of which they could control. The self-protective tone of their report shows that the company was conscious that its monopoly elicited both envy and accusations of profiteering. Yet, in the final analysis, no matter how self-serving merchants were, their ambitious efforts ensured that London remained the trading metropolis of the world despite the turbulence of war years.

Thames shipyards fared less well. As the long war came to an end, there was a severe recession. The ending of the East India Company's monopoly on trade with India in 1813 meant that afterwards the Company ordered fewer ships. It had already been making its ships sail more voyages before replacing them. It was also building them in Bombay, using teak, which lasted longer than oak. The Navy Board, too, was placing fewer contracts for warships: the navy had captured a great many enemy vessels, and the slow release of transports at the end of hostilities also meant that more ships were available. The slipways and repair yards along the river fell silent. In 1813, twelve ships had been launched, only one of them an East Indiaman. In comparison, in 1802, forty-eight ships had been launched, including sixteen East Indiamen. In 1813, the average number of ship-wrights employed in the Thames shipyards was 1,474. A year later the figure had dropped to 657.[16] Just one ship was being built and twenty-six receiving repairs. In a dramatic reversal of fortune, families were on the verge of starvation and workhouses full.

Barnard's weathered the shipbuilding slump better than other ship-yards, although it only survived until 1819 and did not make the transi-tion into building steamships.[17] Frances Barnard had retired at sixty-seven to Mitcham, Surrey, in 1803. There she surrounded herself with memen-toes of her shipbuilding days. She died in 1825 a rich woman, leaving her surviving son, Edward George, 'all pictures, models, draughts of ships drawings, instruments, moulds, cabinets of woods and such printed books as are anyway related to the art of shipbuilding'.[18] Her promising elder son, William, had died at twenty-nine in 1805. Edward George took over the business but extricated himself as soon as he could.

As most of the private shipyards on the Thames went to the wall, the ambitions of the Deptford shipwright John Gast were crushed. He had confidently expected to become foreman at Dudman's Yard, but Dudman virtually ceased business at the end of 1812 and sold up in the autumn of 1813. Gast went broke and even had to give up his public house, the King of Prussia, in Union Street.[19] More ignominy followed. In December 1814, he was imprisoned for fortune telling. The Thames shipbuilding industry was dependent on government policy. The workforce had met wartime demands only to find that government callously neglected the yards when they were no longer so important. Gast's experience of the post-war depression drove him to radical movements. In the struggle that followed between employers and employees, he proved a hard-working activist for workers' rights and better working conditions.

The importance of Deptford dockyard also declined. As road transport improved, its proximity to London mattered less. Naval experiments were increasingly carried out at Portsmouth dockyard, which was larger and better located for sea trials. In 1750 it had taken more than a day to get to Portsmouth. By 1811, with turnpike roads and fast mail coaches, the journey could be made overnight in a little over ten hours. Still, Deptford remained vital to maritime London's operation. It was a component in a unique riverside formation that saw the different trades, manufactures, shipowners and merchants working together to maximize wealth and efficiency. Local suppliers still anxiously competed for naval contracts.

The experience to be gained in maritime London meant that it produced notable politicians. The sons and grandsons of its foremost businessmen often aspired to secure an estate large enough for them to be considered gentry. Younger generations did not always take to the family business. Yet a background that involved management, administrative detail and forging social networks equipped some for politics. Inherited values of hard work and community responsibility may even have inclined them to political office. William Wells's son, John, became a Justice of the Peace and Tory MP for Maidstone in 1820. Joseph Henley's son, Joseph Warner, was educated at Oxford then spent two years in his father's London office before becoming a country gentleman, chairman of the quarter sessions and MP for Oxfordshire in 1841. Nominally Tory, he increasingly took an independent line. His sound business insights eventually secured him the presidency of the Board of Trade. William Barnard's younger son, Edward George, became MP for Greenwich when it became a constituency in 1832; he was regarded as ultra-radical. London's maritime parishes witnessed conditions that made them a furnace of political activism and debate. The next generation profited from experiences that not only crossed the social divide at home but which were also informed by a broad, international outlook.

The period 1750 to 1815 is crucial to the history of Britain and of the world. In peace and war, the importance of maritime London was clear to people of the time. Rarely acknowledged today, the efforts of ordinary people made sure that London remained a global trading metropolis while playing a vital role in successive conflicts. London's riverside districts doubtless changed spatially over time. Yet to see the history of London in terms of an affluent West End and poverty-stricken East End is just wrong. The distinction was not accepted until the mid-nineteenth century anyway.

There is a different perspective, that of maritime London, which takes in both sides of the river. Traces of it survive. After the Napoleonic Wars, maritime London could even stand for the entire city. Lord Byron described the view from Shooter's Hill in *Don Juan*:

> A mighty mass of brick, and smoke, and shipping,
> Dirty and dusky, but as wide as eye
> Could reach, with here and there a sail just skipping
> In sight, then lost amidst the forestry
> Of masts; a wilderness of steeples peeping
> On tiptoe through their sea-coal canopy;
> A huge, dun cupola, like a foolscap crown
> On a fool's head – and there is London Town![20]

This being a satire, Don Juan's paean to British liberty is cut short by highway robbers. But the effect of the lines depends on their having some truth. There were other Londons – the West End, Westminster and Parliament – but all were touched by the significance of a port vital to the nation, backed by maritime institutions in the City, and the seething riverside parishes which provided the labour to keep it working. No narrative history of Britain in this half-century is complete without considering the history of maritime London.

NOTES

Introduction

1. *Elements of Geography for the Use of Mr Alexander's Academy, Hampstead* (London: printed for the author, 1785), 35. The Port of London Authority states today that the tidal range of the Thames varies between five and seven metres.
2. *The Craftsman; or Say's Weekly Journal*, 19 Aug. 1775, 3; Janet Macdonald, *The British Navy's Victualling Board, 1793–1815: Management Competence and Incompetence* (Woodbridge: Boydell Press, 2010), 63.
3. *Gazetteer and New Daily Advertiser*, 22 Jul. 1783, 3.
4. *St James's Chronicle or the British Evening Post*, 16–18 Jun. 1768, 4.

1 London's Riverside

1. E.g. *OBP*, Jul. 1783, trial of Emanuel Pinto, Antonio Da Costa (t17830723-1).
2. John Stow, *A Survey of London* (London: John Wolfe, 1598), 347; Watts Phillips, *The Wild Tribes of London* (London: Ward and Lock, 1855), 19.
3. Derek Morris and Kenneth Cozens, 'The Shadwell Waterfront in the Eighteenth Century', *The Mariner's Mirror* 99, no. 1 (2013): 86–91 (pp. 89–90).
4. Ibid., 87.
5. Sophie Ploeg, *Staged Experiences: Architecture and Rhetoric in the Work of Sir Henry Wotton, Nicholas Hawksmoor and Sir John Vanbrugh* (Groningen, Netherlands: Rijksuniversiteit Groningen, 2006), 198.
6. Derek Morris and Ken Cozens, *London's Sailortown 1600–1800* (London: The East London History Society, 2014), 46–7.
7. *The Monthly Register and Encyclopedian Magazine* 2, no. 8, Dec. 1802, 150–6.v.
8. *The Gentleman's Magazine* (*GM*), 37 (1767), 141.
9. See surviving plaques at the ends of the U-shaped almshouses.
10. *Gazetteer and New Daily Advertiser*, 14 Jun. 1770, 2.

11. L. D. Schwarz, *London in the Age of Industrialization: Entrepreneurs, Labour Force and Living Conditions, 1700–1850* (1993), 53.

12. Derek Morris and Ken Cozens, *Wapping 1600–1800* (London: The East London History Society, 2009), 5–6.

13. Derek Morris, *Mile End Old Town, 1740–1780: A Social History of an Early Modern London Suburb* (London: The East London History Society, 2002), 92.

14. *OBP*, April 1762, trial of John Clark (t17620421-4).

15. The others being the Black Lion, the King of Prussia and the King's Arms.

16. *Daily Advertiser*, 10 Mar. 1796, 4; *Public Ledger*, 21 Mar. 1796, 3.

17. BL 004977492.

18. Shipwrights were paid 2s. 1d. a day, although there was overtime in war years; labourers about 1s. 6d. a day.

19. Peter Guillery, *The Small House in Eighteenth-Century London: A Social and Architectural History* (New Haven & London: Yale University Press, 2004), 35 and 52.

20. *The Times*, 21 Apr. 1800, 4.

21. *St. James's Chronicle or the British Evening Post*, 9–12 Jan. 1762, 5.

22. *Morning Chronicle and London Advertiser*, 6 Jun. 1788, 4.

23. *The Times*, 23 Feb. 1797, 4. A pub of the same name remained on the site until 2004.

24. GHC G ID/12.2, 16 Mar. 1771. Having a wooden leg was apparently no handicap.

25. *Gazetteer and New Daily Advertiser*, 14 Jun. 1770, 2.

26. Daniel Defoe, *A Tour Thro' the Whole Island of Great Britain* (London: Penguin, 1971; 1st published 1724–26), 316.

27. John Barrow, bart., *Travels in China: containing descriptions, observations and comparisons made and collected in the course of a short residence at the Imperial Palace of Yuen-min-yuen, and on a subsequent journey from Pekin to Canton* (London: T. Cadell & W. Davies, 1804), 71.

2 Opportunities and Pressures of a World City

1. Anne Currie, *Henleys of Wapping: A London Shipowning Family, 1770–1830* (London: National Maritime Museum, 1988).

2. Ibid., 10.

3. Geo. III Cap. 36, 1781 for Relief of the Poor.

4. See NMM HNL/6/28.

5. George F. D. Rudé, *Hanoverian London, 1714–1808* (Berkeley and Los Angeles: University of California Press, 1971), 197.

6. *Lloyd's Evening Post*, 29 Jul.–1 Aug. 1768, 110.

7. *GM* (1768), 242; *St. James's Chronicle*, 7–10 May, 1768, 3; *Lloyd's Evening Post*, 6–9 May, 1768, 5; *St. James's Chronicle or the British Evening Post*, 19–21 May, 1768, 1.

8. *Lloyd's Evening Post*, 6–9 May, 1768, 5.

9. *St. James's Chronicle or the British Evening Post*, 18–21 May 1768, 4.

10. *GM*, 39 (1769), 183.

11. Mark Knights, 'The 1780 Protestant petitions and the culture of petitioning', in Ian Haywood and John Seed, eds, *The Gordon Riots: Politics, Culture and Insurrection in Late Eighteenth-Century Britain* (Cambridge: Cambridge University Press, 2012), 54; *Morning Post and Daily Advertiser*, 27 Jan. 1780, 2.

12. Adrian Randall, *Riotous Assemblies: Popular Protest in Hanoverian England* (Oxford: Oxford University Press, 2007), 203.

13. Peter Fryer, *Staying Power: The History of Black People in Britain* (London: Pluto Press, 1984), 81.

14. *OBP*, May 1798, trial of Mary Mason Ann Davies (t17980523-11).

15. *Whitehall Evening Post*, 5–8 Feb. 1780, 3.

16. *Journals of the House of Commons from November the 20th 1798 to August the 27th 1799*, vol. 54 (London: HM Stationery Office, 1803), 192.

17. BL Add MS 78624; 78616.
18. *Proceedings Relative to Ships Tendered for the Service of the United East-India Company, from the First of January, 1780, to the Thirty-First of March, 1791; with an Appendix*, vol. 530 (London: E. Cox, 1802), 133–4, [Sept.], 1782. W. Wells to R. Neave.
19. Ibid., 305–6, 349.
20. John E. Barnard, *Building Britain's Wooden Walls: The Barnard Dynasty c. 1697–1851* (Oswestry: Antony Nelson, 1997), 51.
21. Edward Hasted, *The History and Topographical Survey of the County of Kent*, 12 vols, 2nd edn (Canterbury: W. Bristow, 1797–1801), I, 368–9.
22. James Thomas, *The Poll for the Knights of the Shire for the County of Surrey. Taken at Guildford in the said County, the 20th and 21st days of October, 1774* (Guildford: J. Russell, 1774).
23. Sir Lewis Namier and John Brooke, *The House of Commons 1754–1790*, The History of Parliament (London: HMSO, 1964), III, 112.
24. Daniel Defoe, *A Tour Thro' the Whole Island of Great Britain* (London: Penguin, 1971; first published 1724–26), 128.
25. *Morning Herald and Daily Advertiser*, 26 Apr. 1784, 2.
26. W. Cobbett, *Parliamentary History of England, from the Earliest Period to the Year 1803*, XXXVI, 1801–3, (London: T. C. Hansard, 1820), 462.
27. Randolph Cock, ' "The Finest Invention in the World": The Royal Navy's Early Trials of Copper Sheathing, 1708–1770', *Mariner's Mirror* 87, no. 4 (2001): 446–59.
28. *St. James's Chronicle, or the British Evening Post*, 8–10 Aug. 1769, 1.
29. Ibid., 13–15 Nov. 1781, 3.
30. *General Evening Post*, 18–21 Jan. 1772, 3; *Gazetteer and New Daily Advertiser*, 17 Jun. 1785, 2.
31. *Lloyd's Evening Post*, 17–20 Dec. 1773, 5; *General Evening Post*, 21–24 Aug. 1773, 4.
32. *Middlesex Journal and Evening Advertiser*, 24–27 Feb. 1776, 4; *St. James's Chronicle or the British Evening Post*, 22–25 Aug. 1778, 4; *St. James's Chronicle or the British Evening Post*, 9–12 Oct. 1779, 4; *Public Advertiser*, 4 Aug. 1780, 2; *St. James's Chronicle or the British Evening Post*, 18 Nov. 1784, 4.
33. *Middlesex Journal or Chronicle of Liberty*, 21–23 Jan. 1772, 3.
34. *Diary or Woodfall's Register*, 31 Oct. 1789, 2.
35. *Lloyd's Evening Post*, 15–17 Aug. 1770, 9.
36. *Public Advertiser*, 12 Oct. 1779, 3; *London Chronicle*, 13 Dec. 1781, 8.
37. James Sumner, *Brewing Science, Technology and Print, 1700–1880* (London: Pickering & Chatto, 2013), 40 and fn 30.
38. *General Evening Post*, 12 Dec. 1789, 3.
39. Dulcie Powell, 'The Voyage of the Plant Nursery H.M.S. Providence, 1791–1793', *Economic Botany* 31, no. 4 (1977): 387–431, p. 405.
40. *Gardeners' Chronicle & New Horticulturist*, 165 (1969): 12.
41. Norma Landau, *The Justices of the Peace 1679–1760* (Berkeley and Los Angeles: University of California Press, 1984), 52–5.
42. William Mainwaring, *An Address to the Grand Jury of the County of Middlesex* (London: H. Reynell, 1785), 3, 5.
43. MLD, Thames Navigation Company Minutes, C (Apr. 1782 to Jul. 1787), 104, 8 Oct. 1783.
44. J. Ross Dancy, *The Myth of the Press Gang. Volunteers, Impressment and the Naval Manpower Problem in the Eighteenth Century* (Woodbridge: Boydell Press, 2015), 112.
45. *St. James's Chronicle*, 28–30 Nov. 1769, 4.
46. *General Evening Post*, 7–9 Jan. 1783, 1; 29–31 May 1783, 1.
47. Simon Schaffer, ' "The Charter'd Thames": naval architecture and experimental spaces in Georgian Britain', in *The Mindful Hand: Inquiry and Invention from the Late Renaissance to Early Industrialisation*, ed. Lissa Roberts, Simon Schaffer and Peter Dear (Amsterdam: Royal Netherlands Academy of Arts and Sciences, 2007), 291.

3 War with America

1. R. J. B. Knight, 'The Royal Dockyards in England at the Time of the American War of Independence' (PhD thesis, University of London, 1972), 211.
2. TNA ADM 106/1205/9.
3. TNA ADM 106 1205/118.
4. TNA ADM 106/1193/148.
5. TNA ADM 106/1177/87, ADM 106/1193/89. 1 load = 50 cubic feet.
6. LMA X092/183 (9 May 1774).
7. TNA ADM 106/1193/175.
8. Knight, 'The, Royal Dockyards', 399
9. Robert D. Hume, 'The Value of Money in Eighteenth-Century England: Incomes, Prices, Buying Power – and some Problems in Cultural Economics', *Huntington Library Quarterly* 77, no. 4 (2015): 373–416.
10. GHC G ID/12.2 (5 Jan. 1771, 29 Aug. 1772); G ID/12/4 (26 Jun. 1779, 4 Mar. 1780); G ID/12/5 (30 Jun. 1781).
11. GHC G ID/12.5 (10 Mar. 1781, 7 Sept. 1782); G ID/12/4 (12 Apr. 1777); G ID/12/3 (26 Jun. 1773).
12. GHC G ID/12.4 (27 Sept. 1777).
13. GHC G ID/12.2 (1 Jun. 1771); G ID/12/2 (2 May 1772).
14. GHC G ID/12.2 (8 Aug. 1778, 16 Oct. 1779, 16 Jan. 1779); G ID/12/4 (7 & 14 Nov. 1778).
15. *Independent Chronicle* 25–27 Oct. 1769, 4.
16. *Public Advertiser*, 1 Sept. 1768, 2; *General Evening Post*, 10–12 May 1770, 4; *London Evening Post*, 29–31 May 1770, 1.
17. *London Evening Post* 25–27 Sept. 1770, 1; *Lloyd's Evening Post* 26–28 Sept. 1770, 307.
18. TNA ADM 106/1204/72; ADM 106/1204/116; *Morning Chronicle and London Advertiser* 27 May. 1773, 3.
19. *St. James's Chronicle or the British Evening Post*, 5–8 Aug. 1775, 1.
20. Ibid., 29 Jul.–1 Aug. 1775, 4.
21. Ibid., 23–25 Jan. 1776, 2.
22. *General Evening Post*, 9–11 Jul. 1776, 4.
23. *Morning Chronicle and London Advertiser*, 19 Aug. 1772, 2.
24. R. J. B. Knight. 'Pilfering and Theft from the Dockyards at the Time of the American War of Independence', *Mariner's Mirror*, 61, no. 3 (1975): 215–25.
25. *Middlesex Journal and Evening Advertiser*, 1–4 Jun. 1776, 3.
26. *London Evening Post*, 5–8 Feb. 1779, 5; 6–9 Feb. 1779, 1.
27. David Syrett, *Shipping and the American War, 1775–83: A Study of British Transport Organization* (London: Athlone Press, 1970), 222–3.
28. *St. James's Chronicle or the British Evening Post*, 26–29 Oct. 1776, 2.
29. Nicholas Rogers, *The Press Gang: Naval Impressment and its Opponents in Georgian Britain* (London: Continuum, 2007), 40–1.
30. *Morning Chronicle and London Advertiser*, 30 Dec. 1776, 2.
31. *General Advertiser and Morning Intelligencer*, 29 Jan. 1778, 4; *St. James's Chronicle or the British Evening Post*, 18–20 May, 1779, 5.
32. *General Advertiser and Morning Intelligencer*, 28 Mar. 1778, 2.
33. NMM POR/A/29.
34. *Morning Chronicle and London Advertiser*, 1 Sept. 1775, 4; *St. James's Chronicle or the British Evening Post*, 20–23 Jul. 1776, 4.
35. *London Chronicle*, 16–18 Mar. 1780, 270.
36. *Lloyd's Evening Post*, 21–23 Mar. 1781, 287.
37. Ibid., 3–6 Aug. 1782, 5.

38. A. B. and A. M. G. McLeod, 'John Cleveley the Elder's "The Floating Out of the Cambridge": Problems and Patrons', *The Mariner's Mirror* 100, no. 4 (2014): 449–54. In 1745 he was living in a smaller house in Back Lane.

39. I owe this point to Brian Lavery.

40. *The British landing at Kip's Bay, New York Island. 15 September 1776*, NMMPAH9491.

41. *Public Advertiser*, 14 Jul. 1784, 1.

42. *Gazetteer and New Daily Advertiser*, 25 Feb. 1785, 2; *General Evening Post*, 7–9 Jun. 1785, 1.

43. Roger Knight, *Britain Against Napoleon: The Organization of Victory 1793–1815* (London: Allen Lane, 2013), 27–8.

44. Peter Guillery, *The Small House in Eighteenth-Century London: A Social and Architectural History* (New Haven & London: Yale University Press, 2004), 206.

4 Crime and Punishment

1. Details of this episode are taken from *OBP*, Sept. 1776, trial of Robert Harley, Edward George (t17760911-42), *London Evening Post*, 23–25 May, 1776, p. 4. *Morning Chronicle and London Advertiser*, 27 May 1776, p. 4. 16 Sept. 1776, p. 4.

2. Tide surveyors boarded and searched East Indiamen for contraband.

3. *Morning Chronicle and London Advertiser*, 16 Sept. 1776, 4.

4. *OBP*, Sept. 1776, trial of Robert Harley, Edward George (t17760911-42).

5. *A Declaration of the Rights of Englishmen. Declaration of those Rights of the Commonalty of Great-Britain without which they cannot be Free* (London: [n.p.] *c.* 1795). Quoted in John Phillip Reid, *The Concept of Liberty in the Age of the American Revolution* (Chicago and London: University of Chicago Press, 1988), 43.

6. TNA HO 42/15/81 (14 Oct. 1789). Cf. (for Surrey) HO 47/7/96 (31 Mar. 1788).

7. Reid, *The Concept of Liberty*, 63.

8. See Adam Smith, *An Inquiry into the Nature and Causes of The Wealth of Nations*, ed. Edwin Cannan, 2 vols (London: Methuen, 1904; repr, 1950), II, 365.

9. *Public Advertiser*, 19 Jun. 1769, 2.

10. *Morning Post and Daily Advertiser*, 3 Apr. 1783, 2.

11. Norma Landau, *The Justices of the Peace 1679–1760* (Berkeley and Los Angeles: University of California Press, 1984), 223.

12. *Middlesex Journal or Universal Evening Post*, 24–26 Sept. 1772, 4; 15–17 Oct. 1772, 4; 22–24 Dec. 1772, 4.

13. *London Chronicle*, 20–22 April 1773, 376; *General Evening Post*, 13–15 Jul. 1773, 4; *St James's Chronicle or British Evening Post*, 25–28 Sept. 1773 4; *Middlesex Journal or Universal Evening Post*, 12–14 Oct. 1773, 5; *Gazetteer and New Daily Advertiser*, 2 Jun. 1774, 2; *Morning Chronicle and London Advertiser*, 19 Sept. 1774, 2; *Public Advertiser*, 29 Oct. 1774, 2; *Middlesex Journal and Evening Advertiser*, 22–24 Dec. 1774, 3.

14. *Morning Chronicle and London Advertiser*, 13 Aug. 1776, 2.

15. *Middlesex Journal or Chronicle of Liberty*, 4–7 Jan. 1772, 4; *Morning Post and Daily Advertiser*, 10 Jul. 1777, 6.

16. *London Chronicle*, 2–5 Sept. 1786, 2.

17. *Public Advertiser*, 11 Jun. 1787, 2; *Evening Mail*, 6–8 Jul. 1791, 4.

18. *Public Advertiser*, 3 Jul. 1790, 2.

19. *OBP*, December 1781, trial of John West (t17811205-34).

20. L. D. Schwarz, 'The Standard of Living in the Long Run: London 1700–1860', *Economic History Review*, Second Series, 38, no. 1 (February 1985): 31.

21. Roger Knight, *Britain Against Napoleon: The Organization of Victory 1793–1815* (London: Allen Lane, 2013), 22–3.

22. Lynn MacKay, 'Why They Stole: Women in the Old Bailey, 1779–1789', *Journal of Social History* 32, no. 3 (1999): 623–39. MacKay uses legal year that began in Dec.

23. *OBP*, September 1775, trial of Elizabeth Ives, Eleanor Brown (t17750913-32).
24. *OBP*, July 1776, trial of Mary the Wife of William London, Ann Harvey (t17760710-43).
25. *OBP*, May 1765, trial of Rosa Samuel, Abigal Samuel (t17650522-15).
26. *OBP*, October 1799, trial of Jeremiah Connell, Honora Connell, Mary Waghorne (t17991030-7). Cf. *OBP*, November 1796, trial of Jane Richards (t17961130-14).
27. Lynn MacKay, *Respectability and the London Poor, 1780–1870: The Value of Virtue* (London: Pickering & Chatto), 2013, 38–9.
28. Shepard, Alexandra. 'Minding their Own Business: Married Women and Credit in Early Eighteenth-Century London', *Transactions of the Royal Historical Society* 25 (2015): 53–74, 67.
29. *OBP*, July 1795, trial of Ann Judith Roy, otherwise Ann Judith Taylor (t17950701-10).
30. TNA HO 47/13/39 (23 May 1791).
31. MacKay, 'Why They Stole', 629–30. NB. Mary Griffin was acquitted for receiving because she pointed out that had she been guilty she would never have pawned the goods in her neighbourhood and in her own name: *OBP*, trial of William Davison, Mary Griffin (t17800223-20).
32. 'The Sailor's Widow', *The Lady's Monthly Museum, or Polite Repository of Amusement and Instruction*, 11 (Aug. 1803), 79–84.
33. GHC G ID/12.4, 25 Oct. 1777; LMA P78/NIC/45.
34. Landau, *The Justices of the Peace 1679–1760*, 185.
35. It was replaced by Horsemonger Lane Gaol, built 1792–99.
36. See www.londonlives.org/static/Policing.jsp. London and Middlesex sessions met eight times a year to cope with crime in the metropolis.
37. GHC G ID/12.1, 1 Jun. 1772.
38. Reid, *The Concept of Liberty*, 77; *The Public Advertiser*, 26 Jul. 1768, 2. Cf. *Lloyd's Evening Post*, 27 Jul. 1769, 6.
39. TNA HO 47/29/8 (8 May 1802).
40. Jerry White, *London in the 18th Century: A Great and Monstrous Thing* (London: Bodley Head, 2012), 433 ff.
41. *General Evening Post*, 12–15 Mar. 1785, 1.
42. TNA HO 42/33/125.
43. *The Times*, 28 Mar. 1792, 3.
44. *Public Advertiser*, 29 Sept. 1792, 1; ibid., 11 Oct. 1792, 1.
45. Joseph Cox, *A Faithful Narrative of the Most Wicked and Inhuman Transactions of that Bloody-Minded Gang of Thief-Takers, Alias Thief-Makers, Macdaniel, Berry, Salmon, Eagan, alias Gahagan* (London: printed for Joseph Cox and sold by M. Mechell, 1756).
46. *General Evening Post*, 13–15 Oct. 1785, 1.
47. TNA ACC 1230/006.
48. *London Chronicle*, 20–22 Mar. 1794, 1.
49. *Hoey's Dublin Mercury*, 3–5 Oct. 1771, 1.
50. *General Evening Post*, 12–15 Mar. 1774, 1.
51. Ibid., 11–13 Apr. 1771, 1.
52. *Gazetteer and New Daily Advertiser*, 13 Dec. 1780, 1; *General Evening Post*, 5–7 Mar. 1771, 1.
53. *Public Advertiser*, 10 Jul. 1775, 1.
54. *St James's Chronicle or the British Evening Post*, 20–22 Jul. 1773, 1.
55. *Gazetteer and New Daily Advertiser*, 29 Dec. 1769, 1; *Morning Chronicle and London Advertiser*, 16 Nov. 1775, 2.
56. Francis Place, *The Autobiography of Francis Place*, ed. Mary Thrale (Cambridge: Cambridge University Press, 1972), 81.
57. *Diary or Woodfall's Register*, 31 Dec. 1792, 1; *St. James's Chronicle or the British Evening Post*, 3–5 Jan. 1793, 1.
58. *London Evening Post*, 10–12 Oct. 1771, 1.

59. *General Evening Post*, 16–19 Apr. 1774, 1. *London Courant and Westminster Chronicle*, 18 Sept. 1781, 1.
60. *London Packet or New Lloyd's Evening Post*, 24–26 Dec. 1794, 4.
61. *Public Advertiser*, 29 Jul. 1775, 2.
62. *Middlesex Journal and Evening Advertiser*, 14–17 Jan. 1775, 1. This is the county or 'New Gaol', Southwark.
63. *Public Advertiser*, 24 Aug. 1784, 2; *London Chronicle*, 16–19 Oct. 1784, 2; *Morning Chronicle and London Advertiser*, 3 Dec. 1785, 2.
64. *Public Advertiser*, 15 Nov. 1791, 1.
65. *General Evening Post*, 9–12 Nov. 1776, 1.
66. Hulk Act, 16 Geo. III, cap. 43. Cf. Transportation Act, 19 Geo. III, cap. 74.
67. *Public Advertiser*, 3 Jun. 1777, 2.
68. *Morning Herald and Daily Advertiser*, 8 Oct. 1783, 1; *General Evening Post*, 9–11 Jul. 1778, 1. Ibid., 8–10 Jun. 1780, 1.
69. *London Courant Westminster Chronicle and Daily Advertiser*, 9 Feb. 1782, 1.
70. *St James's Chronicle or the British Evening Post*, 20–22 Aug. 1782, 1; *London Chronicle*, 15–17 Jul. 1783, 2.
71. TNA HO 47/3/56.
72. TNA HO 42/20/52; HO 42/40/196.
73. John Nicol, *The Life and Adventures of John Nicol, Mariner*, ed. John Howell (Edinburgh: William Blackwood; London: T. Cadell, 1822), 119, 112, 110.
74. Roger Knight, 'The First Fleet: its State and Preparation, 1786–1787', in John Hardy and Alan Frost, eds, *Studies from Terra Australis to Australia* (Canberra: Australian Academy of the Humanities, 1989), 121–36, 256–62.
75. Daniel Paine, *The Journal of Daniel Paine, 1794–1797*, ed. R. J. B. Knight and Alan Frost, (Granville, NSW: Ambassador Press, 1983).
76. *Gazetteer and New Daily Advertiser*, 16 Aug. 1769, 2; *Bingley's Journal* 25 Apr.–2 May 1772, 1.
77. TNA HO 47/28/1.
78. TNA ADM 106/1172/159; ADM 354/158/205; ADM 106/1143/53.
79. TNA HO/47/24/36; HO 47/37/6.
80. *London Chronicle or Universal Evening Post*, 30 Apr.–3 May 1774, 6.
81. *London Evening Post*, 18–21 Feb. 1775, 3.
82. Ibid., 13–15 Sept. 1774, 5.

5 Spirited Women

1. State Library of New South Wales, Safe 1/45 (19 Aug. 1789).
2. Michael Lewis, *A Social History of the Navy 1793–1815* (London: Chatham Publishing, 1960; repr. 2004), 48.
3. Margarette Lincoln, *Naval Wives and Mistresses 1750–1815* (London: National Maritime Museum, 2007), 31.
4. Anne Currie, *Henleys of Wapping: A London Shipowning Family, 1770–1830* (London: National Maritime Museum, 1988), 41–2.
5. NMM HNL/77/23:24 (9 Jun. 1797).
6. NMM HNL/77/23:29.
7. NMM HNL/6/28:28.
8. Mary Lacey, *The Female Shipwright* (1773), ed. Margarette Lincoln (London: The National Maritime Museum, 2008), 29, 31; Lincoln, *Naval Wives and Mistresses*, 81.
9. Lincoln, *Naval Wives and Mistresses*, 42; Patricia Y. C. E. Lin, 'Caring for the Nation's Families: British Soldiers' and Sailors' Families and the State, 1793–1815', in *Soldiers, Citizens and Civilians: Experiences and Perceptions of the Revolutionary Wars, 1790–1820*, ed. Alan Forrest, Karen Hagemann and Jane Rendall (Houndmills, Basingstoke: Palgrave Macmillan, 2009), 107.

10. Derek Morris, *Mile End Old Town 1740–1780: A Social History of an Early Modern London Suburb* (London: The East London History Society, 2007), 15–16.
11. J. C. Beaglehole, *The Life of Captain James Cook* (Stanford, CA: Stanfield University Press, 1974), 445.
12. Ibid., 475.
13. BL Egerton MS 2180 f. 28.
14. State Library of New South Wales, R 198.
15. GHC G ID/12.4, 5 Apr. 1777, 5 Dec. 1778; LMA P78/NIC/45.
16. GHC G ID/12.5, 12 Jul. 1783; G 10/12.8, 9 Oct. 1790 and G 12.12, 9 Sept. 1797.
17. GHC G.12.11, 9 Jul. 1796.
18. GHC G ID/12.2, 1 Jun. and 6 Jul. 1771; 28 Mar. 1772.
19. *Read's Weekly Journal or British Gazetteer*, 21 Sept. 1751, 4.
20. See Nicholas Rogers, *Mayhem: Post-War Crime and Violence in Britain, 1748–1753* (New Haven & London: Yale University Press, 2012).
21. GHC G ID/12.7, 25 Mar. and 1 Apr. 1786; G.12.11, 28 Jan. 1797.
22. GHC G ID/12.8, 7 Jun. 1788.
23. TNA ADM 106, 3320, 18 Apr. 1781.
24. J. Stevenson, 'The London "Crimp" Riots of 1794', *International Journal of Social History* 16, no. 1 (1971): 40–58.
25. Codrington to his wife Jane, 27 Dec. 1808, NMM COD 21/1a.
26. Margaret Hunt, *The Middling Sort: Commerce, Gender, and the Family in England 1680–1780* (Berkeley and Los Angeles: University of California Press, 1996), 138–42.
27. LMA E/PNE/I/7/5.
28. Hoh-Cheung Mui and Lora H. Mui, *Shops and Shopkeeping in Eighteenth-Century England* (Kingston, Ontario: McGill-Queen's University Press; London: Routledge, 1989), 60.
29. TNA ADM 106/1231/172.
30. Marcia Pointon, *Brilliant Effects: A Cultural History of Gem Stones and Jewellery* (New Haven & London: Yale University Press, 2009), 26, 21.
31. The painting is now in the Royal Ontario Museum, 959.283.
32. Peter Guillery and Bernard Herman, 'Deptford Houses: 1650 to 1800', *Vernacular Architecture* 30 (1999): 58–84, (p. 63).
33. *The Small House in Eighteenth-Century London: A Social and Architectural History*, Peter Guillery (New Haven & London, 2004), 232.
34. *The Universal Director; or, The Nobleman and Gentleman's True Guide to the Masters and Professors of the Liberal and Polite Arts and Sciences; and of the Mechanic Arts, Manufactures, and Trades, Established in London and Westminster, and their Environs* (London: J. Coote, 1763), 15.
35. Dugaw, Dianne, 'Balladry's Female Warriors: Women, Warfare, and Disguise in the Eighteenth Century', *Eighteenth-Century Life* 9, no. 2 (1985): 1–20; *Gazetteer and New Daily Advertiser*, 2 Apr. 1779, 2; *Morning Post and Daily Advertiser*, 13 Jul. 1779, 2; *London Chronicle*, 23–26 Oct. 1779, 400.
36. Margarette Lincoln, 'Emma Hamilton, War and the Depiction of Femininity in the Late Eighteenth Century', *Journal for Maritime Research* 17, no. 2 (2015): 135–45 (p. 136).
37. *London Chronicle*, 8–10 Dec. 1772, 8.
38. Tim Hitchcock and Michèle Cohen, eds, *English Masculinities 1660–1800* (Harlow, Essex: Longman, 1999), 15.
39. TNA ADM 106/1231/171; ADM 106 2991.
40. TNA HO 47/12/100; cf. HO 47/7/42, HO 47/3/67.
41. Currie, *Henleys of Wapping*, 37.
42. *London Evening Post*, 30 Mar.–1 Apr. 1775, 4; *The London Chronicle*, 27 Feb.–2 Mar. 1790, 208.
43. *Morning Chronicle and London Advertiser*, 13 Oct. 1778, 2.
44. Robert B. Shoemaker, 'The Decline of Public Insult in London 1660–1800', *Past & Present* 169, no. 1 (2000): 97–131.

45. Geoff Quilley, *Empire to Nation: Art, History and the Visualization of Maritime Britain 1768–1829* (New Haven & London: Yale University Press, 2011), 113–18.
46. *The Rambler's Magazine; Or, the Annals of Gallantry, Glee, Pleasure, and the Bon Ton*, vol. 5 (1787), 43–4, 167.
47. Peter Fryer, *Staying Power: The History of Black People in Britain* (London: Pluto Press, 1984), 196–202.
48. Lincoln, *Naval Wives and Mistresses*, 115–18. *The Arguments of Counsel in the Ecclesiastical Court on the Cause of Inglefield . . . on the twenty-second of July. 1786, at giving judgement* (London: J. Murray, 1787), 107.
49. NMM WHW/1/4 (7 May 1812).
50. E. Bligh to J. Bond, 8 Sept. 1784, State Library of New South Wales, MLMSS 1016.
51. BL RP 2802 (iii) (27 Jan. 1800).
52. E. Bligh to J. Bond, 8 Sept. 1784, State Library of New South Wales, MLMSS 1016.
53. Ibid.
54. E. Bligh to J. Bond, 25 Jun. 1788, State Library of New South Wales, MLMSS 1016E.
55. Frances Burney, *The Early Diary of Frances Burney, 1768–1778*, ed. Annie Raine Ellis, 2 vols (London: George Bell and Sons, 1889), 1: 310, Mr Crisp to Miss Burney, 22 Aug. 1774.
56. *GM*, v. 58: pt 2 (1788), 863.
57. Lincoln, *Naval Wives and Mistresses*, 155–8.
58. David Divers and Chris Jarrett, 'Excavations at the Mouth of Deptford Creek, Greenwich Reach', *London Archaeologist*, 9, no. 1 (1999): 6–16; David Divers, 'Excavations on the Site of the East India Company Dockyards and the Trinity House Almshouses, London', *Post-Medieval Archaeology* 38, no. 1 (2004): 17–132.
59. Joseph Cotton, *Memoir on the Origin and Incorporation of Trinity House of Deptford Strond* (London: J. Darling, 1818), 189.

6 Money and Pleasure

1. Eric J. Evans, *The Forging of the Modern State: Early Industrial Britain 1783–1870* (London & New York: Longman, 1983), 33–4.
2. Stephen Inwood, *A History of London* (London: Macmillan, 1998), 332–6.
3. *Morning Chronicle and London Advertiser*, 6 May 1775, 2.
4. Colin Milne, *Sermons* (London: T. Cadell, 1780), 162.
5. Margarette Lincoln, 'Naval Ship Launches as Public Spectacle 1773–1854', *Mariners Mirror* 83, no. 4 (1997): 466–72.
6. *Public Advertiser*, 16 Oct. 1780, 2.
7. Tower Hamlets Local History Library and Archives, P/GOF/1 (23 Jan. 1793).
8. *Lloyd's Evening Post*, 27 Dec. 1776, 628.
9. Pythagoras, *A Vindication of A Right in the Public to a One Shilling Gallery either at the New Theatre Royal in Covent-Garden, Or Somewhere Else* (London: J. Owen, 1792), 35.
10. *A Letter to the Author of the Burletta Called Hero and Leander* (London: G. Kearsley, 1787), 29–30.
11. David Worrall, *Theatric Revolution: Drama, Censorship and Romantic Period Subcultures 1773–1832* (Oxford: Oxford University Press, 2006), 70.
12. David Worrall, *The Politics of Romantic Theatricality, 1787–1832: The Road to the Stage* (London: Palgrave Macmillan, 2007), 67–75.
13. Gillian Russell, *The Theatres of War: Performance, Politics and Society, 1793–1815* (Oxford: Clarendon Press, 1995), p. 139.
14. Worrall, *Theatric Revolution*, 89.
15. Greg Dening, *Mr Bligh's Bad Language: Passion, Power and Theatre on the Bounty* (Cambridge: Cambridge University Press, 1992), 287–99
16. William Upton, *The Words of the Most Favourite Songs, Duets. &c. Sung at the Royal Amphitheatre, Westminster Bridge, and the Royalty Theatre, Well-close Square* (Lambeth: S. Tibson, [1798]), 44.

17. TNA HO 65/1 (22 Jan. 1798).
18. John Bull, 'Palmer, John (1744–1798)', *Oxford Dictionary of National Biography*, Oxford University Press, 2004, http://0-www.oxforddnb.com.catalogue.libraries.london.ac.uk/view/article/21198, accessed 3 Aug 2016.
19. *Morning Chronicle and London Advertiser*, 27 May 1776, 2; *Morning Post and Daily Advertiser*, 13 Sept. 1776, 1.
20. *Morning Chronicle and London Advertiser*, 19 Jun. 1777, 2.
21. Donna T. Andrew, ed., *London Debating Societies, 1776–1799* (London: London Record Society, 1994), 99.
22. *Daily Advertiser*, 22 Apr. 1783, 1.
23. BL Add MS 16947(119).
24. *The Catch Club: a collection of all the songs, catches, glees, duets, &c, as sung by Mr. Bannister, Mr. Arrowsmith [and others] . . . at the Royalty Theatre* (London: J. Griffith, [1787?]), 14.
25. *Morning Chronicle and London Advertiser*, 18 Jan. 1786, 4.
26. Hoh-Cheung Mui and Lora H. Mui, *Shops and Shopkeeping in Eighteenth-Century England* (Kingston, Ontario: McGill-Queen's University Press; London: Routledge, 1989), 120.
27. NMM HNL/6/29 10 [K5:16].
28. *The Town and Country Magazine, or, Universal Repository of Knowledge, Instruction, and Entertainment*, 12 (1780): 182–3; 16 (1784): 64–5.
29. NMM HNL/6/28:22 [K3:90].
30. Henry Morley, *Memoirs of Bartholomew Fair* (London: Chapman and Hall, 1859), 459.
31. Parker's *General Advertiser and Morning Intelligencer*, 9 Sept. 1784, 3.
32. *Public Advertiser*, 13 Oct. 1786, 4.
33. *General Evening Post*, 4–6 Mar. 1777, 1; *Public Advertiser*, 12 May 1777, 4; *London Chronicle*, 21–23 Jul. 1791, 2.
34. *Public Advertiser*, 19 Apr. 1788, 4.
35. *St James's Chronicle or the British Evening Post*, 29–31 Jan. 1788, 4.
36. Dianne Payne, 'London's Charity School Children: The "Scum of the Parish"', *British Journal for Eighteenth-Century Studies* 29 (2006): 383–97.
37. M. G. Jones, *The Charity School Movement* (London: Frank Cass & Co. Ltd, 1938; repr. 1964), 6.
38. *A Hymn to be Sung by the Charity Children, of Deptford, on Sunday, September, the 18th 1791* (Deptford: [n.p.], 1791).
39. *St James's Chronicle or the British Evening Post*, 22–24 Nov. 1768, 1.
40. Daniel O'Quinn, *Entertaining Crisis in the Atlantic Imperium 1770–1790* (Baltimore, Johns Hopkins University Press, 2011), 112–24.
41. *Public Advertiser*, 2 Apr. 1782, 4.
42. *Morning Chronicle and London Advertiser*, 24 Sept. 1781, 4.
43. BL Add MS 16947 f. 17; LMA H05/M/D/01/001 (21 Jun. 1789).
44. John Poland, *Records of the Miller Hospital and Royal Kent Dispensary* (Greenwich: Henry Richardson, 1893), 6–7.
45. *General Advertiser and Morning Intelligencer*, 30 Jan. 1778, 2.
46. *An Account of the Kent Dispensary, in the Broad-way, Deptford* (London: W. Hales, 1785?), 5.
47. LMA H05/M/D/01/001 (24 Sept.1783).
48. Poland, *Records of the Miller Hospital*, 18–22.

7 War with France

1. *The Times*, 25 Jan. 1793, 2.
2. William Wordsworth, 'The Prelude', XI, 108, *Wordsworth Poetical Works*, ed. Thomas Hutchinson, 2nd edn (Oxford: Oxford University Press, 1973), 570.
3. Charlotte Smith, *The Works of Charlotte Smith*, vol. 14, ed. Jacqueline M. Labbe (London: Pickering & Chatto, 2007), 126, 138.

4. *London Chronicle*, 5–8 Jan. 1793, 26.
5. *The Oracle*, 27 Dec. 1792, 4.
6. *St. James's Chronicle or the British Evening Post*, 1–3 Sept. 1791, 1; *Whitehall Evening Post*, 3–6 Sept. 1791, 4; *London Packet or New Lloyd's Evening Post*, 8–10 Jul. 1793, 4.
7. J. Ross Dancy, *The Myth of the Press Gang: Volunteers, Impressment and the Naval Manpower Problem in the Late Eighteenth Century* (Woodbridge: Boydell Press, 2015), 28–9.
8. *World and Fashionable Advertiser*, 8 Jan. 1787, 5.
9. Joseph Farington, *The Farington Diary*, ed. James Greig, 8 vols (London: Hutchinson & Co, [1922]–28), I, 92.
10. *St. James's Chronicle or the British Evening Post*, 14–16 Jan. 1796, 8.
11. Mark Philip, 'Talking about Democracy: Britain in the 1790s', *Reimagining Democracy in the Age of Revolutions: America, France, Britain, Ireland 1750–1850*, ed. Joanna Innes and Mark Philip (Oxford: Oxford University Press, 2013), 107–10; *The Lady's Magazine; or Entertaining Companion for the Fair Sex*, 25 (1794), 701.
12. *Lady's Magazine*, 25 (1794), 380.
13. Dror Wahrman, 'Percy's Prologue: From Gender Play to Gender Panic in Eighteenth Century England', *Past & Present* 159 (1998), 113–60.
14. Francis Place, *The Autobiography of Francis Place* (1771–1854), ed. Mary Thrale (Cambridge: Cambridge University Press, 1972), 57, 73.
15. *Morning Herald*, 30 Mar. 1793, 3.
16. Roger Knight, *Britain Against Napoleon: The Organization of Victory 1793–1815* (London: Allen Lane, 2013), 222.
17. Robert Dozier, *For King, Constitution and Country: The English Loyalists and the French Revolution* (Lexington: University Press of Kentucky, 2015), 85; BL Add MS 16923, p. 10; Add MS 16927, p. 65.
18. *The Star*, 26 Dec. 1792, 3.
19. *GM*, 72 pt 2 (1802), 745.
20. *The Antigallican Songster. Number 1* (London: J. Downes, 1793), 4.
21. *The Anti-Gallican; or Standard of British Loyalty, Religion and Liberty; including A Collection of the Principal Papers, Tracts, Speeches, Poems, and Songs, that have been published on the Threatened Invasion: together with many original pieces on the same subject* (London: Vendor & Hood and J. Asperne, 1804), 228–9.
22. Place, *The Autobiography of Francis Place*, 127–8.
23. *GM*, 65 pt 2 (1795), 1018–23.
24. *Public Advertiser*, 7 Jan. 1793, 3.
25. J. D. Chambers and G. E. Mingay, *The Agricultural Revolution* (London: B. T. Batsford, 1966), 108–9. A quarter equals eight bushels, or approximately one-quarter ton of grain.
26. GHC G.12.11 (27 Jul. 1795).
27. BPP, 1831, VIII, *Select Committee of the House of Lords on Poor Laws and Petitions Praying for the Relief of Pauperism*, 368–71.
28. *Morning Post and Fashionable World*, 13 Jul. 1795, p. 2; 14 Jul. 1795, 3.
29. Adrian Randall, *Riotous Assemblies: Popular Protest in Hanoverian England* (Oxford: Oxford University Press, 2006), 209, 239.
30. *St. James's Chronicle or the British Evening Post*, 11–13 May 1795, 4.
31. London Corresponding Society, *Moral and Political Magazine of the London Corresponding Society* (London: John Ashley, Secretary, 1796), 308.
32. *Gazetteer and New Daily Advertiser*, 10 Jul. 1783, 2; William Richardson, *A Mariner of England: An Account of the Career of William Richardson from Cabin Boy in the Merchant Service to Warrant Officer in the Royal Navy (1780–1819) As Told by Himself* (London: John Murray, 1908), 43.
33. N. A. M. Rodger, *The Command of the Ocean: A Naval History of Britain 1649–1815* (London: Allen Lane, 2004), 360.

34. John Barrell, 'London and the London Corresponding Society', in *Romantic Metropolis: The Urban Scene of British Culture, 1780–1840*, ed. James Chandler and Kevin Gilmartin (Cambridge: Cambridge University Press, 2005), 86, 88; *Selections from the Papers of the London Corresponding Society 1792–1799*, ed. Mary Thale (Cambridge, Cambridge University Press, 1983), 94.

35. William Austin, *Letters from London, Written in the Years 1802 & 1803* (Boston: W. Pelham, 1804), 118, 163.

36. Austin, *Letters from London*, 282.

37. *Morning Chronicle*, 11 Apr. 1794, 4.

38. Matthew McCormack, *Embodying the Militia in Georgian England* (Oxford, Oxford University Press, 2015), 69.

39. *The True Briton*, 25 Dec. 1795, 3; *Moral and Political Magazine of the London Corresponding Society* (1796), 270.

40. Cecil Sebag-Montefiore, *A History of the Volunteer Forces from the Earliest Times to the Year 1860* (London: Archibald Constable & Co. Ltd, 1908), 170–71; TNA HO 42/51/110.

41. *The Parliamentary Register; or, History of the Proceedings and Debates of the House of Commons*, vol. 55 (London: J. Debrett, 1794), 153.

42. *The Times*, 9 Oct. 1797, 3.

43. G. Quilley, *Empire to Nation: Art, History and the Visualization of Maritime Britain 1768–1829* (New Haven: Yale University Press, 2011), 181.

44. TNA HO 42/42/145.

45. *OBP*, January 1799, trial of James Eyres (t17990109-5).

46. TNA HO 47/23/7 ff. 27–30; HO 43/27/9.

47. TNA HO 42/46/130 ff. 286–7.

48. *The New Town and Country Magazine* (1787), 658.

49. NMM WHW/1/7 (6 Jun. 1812).

50. E. Johnson's *British Gazette and Sunday Monitor*, 7 Nov. 1802, p. 3.

51. J. B. Sharpe, *Report . . . For the Better Regulation of Madhouses in England* (London: Baldwin, Cradock & Joy, 1815), 375.

52. NMM LBK/75 (17 Jun. 1800).

53. Jennine Hurl-Eamon, *Marriage and the British Army in the Long Eighteenth Century: 'The Girl I Left Behind Me'* (Oxford, Oxford University Press, 2014), 62–4; Margarette Lincoln, *Naval Wives and Mistresses* (London: National Maritime Museum Publishing, 2007), 15–16.

54. *Gazetteer and New Daily Advertiser*, 27 Feb. 1777, 3.

55. GHC G ID/12.4, 20 Mar. 1779; *St. James's Chronicle or the British Evening Post*, 3–5 Sept. 1782, 4.

56. Helen Doe, *Enterprising Women and Shipping in the Nineteenth Century* (Woodbridge: Boydell Press, 2009).

57. TNA ADM 106/1454 (4 Mar. 1795).

58. ADM 106 1454 (30 Dec. 1795).

59. *General Evening Post*, 24–26 May 1796, 1.

60. John Bohstedt, 'Gender, Household and Community Politics: Women in English Riots 1790–1810', *Past & Present* 120 (1988), 88–122.

61. TNA HO 42/62/104.

62. Roger Knight and Martin Wilcox, *Sustaining the Fleet: War, the British Navy and the Contractor State* (Woodbridge: Boydell Press, 2010), 18.

63. NMM LBK/75 (29 Jun. 1802; 23 Jul. 1802).

64. NMM ADM B/205 (26 Jul. 1802).

65. John Gast, *Calumny Defeated: or, a Compleat Vindication of the Conduct of the Working Shipwrights during the Late Disputes with their Employers* (London: J. Delahoy, 1802), 8.

66. *The Times*, 6 Oct. 1802, 3.

67. C. Northcote Parkinson, *Trade in the Eastern Seas, 1793–1818* (London: Frank Cass & Co. Ltd, 1966), 128–9.
68. P. J. Cain and A. G. Hopkins, *British Imperialism: Innovation and Expansion, 1688–1914* (London: Longman, 1993), 115.
69. *General Evening Post*, 16–18 Sept. 1790, 4.
70. TNA PROB 11/1265/89; PROB 11/1484/66; PROB 11/1501/154.

8 Grand Designs

1. Patrick Colquhoun, *A Treatise on the Commerce and Police of the River Thames: containing an Historical View of the Trade of the Port of London* (London: Joseph Mawman, 1800), table between pp. 24 and 25.
2. [W. Vaughan?], *On Wet Docks, Quays, and Warehouses, for the Port of London; with Hints Respecting Trade* (London: [n.p.], 1793), Preface.
3. *The Sun*, 13 Oct. 1794, 4.
4. *Morning Chronicle*, 8 Jan. 1796, 5.
5. *Morning Post and Daily Advertiser*, 8 Apr. 1779, 2.
6. *Lloyd's Evening Post*, 19–22 Feb. 1796, 208.
7. BPP, 1796, XIV, *Report from the Committee appointed to enquire into the best Mode of providing sufficient Accommodation for the increased Trade and Shipping of the Port of London*, etc., Appendices D, H.
8. *Morning Chronicle*, 25 Apr. 1793, 3.
9. N. Draper, 'The City of London and Slavery: Evidence from the first Dock Companies', *The Economic History Review* 61, no. 2 (2008): 432–66, (p. 460); W. Vaughan, *Reasons in Favour of the London-Docks* (London: [n.p.], 1795), 3.
10. *A Letter to the Right Hon. The Lord Mayor on the Subject of the Intended New Docks to be Established at Wapping* (London: J. Johnson, 1796), 11.
11. Colquhoun, *A Treatise on the Commerce and Police of the River Thames*, xxx–xxxi.
12. *Report from the Committee appointed to enquire into . . . the increased Trade and Shipping of the Port of London*, 164–5.
13. BL Add MS 38231 f. 17.
14. *Whitehall Evening Post*, 16–18 Oct. 1784, 2; 25–27 Nov. 1784, 4.
15. *The Times*, 28 Mar. 1792, 3.
16. John Harriott, *Struggles through Life*, 2 vols (London: C. & W. Galabin, 1807), 1:336.
17. [Vaughan?], *On Wet Docks*, 20.
18. *The True Briton*, 27 Apr. 1795, 1; Walter M. Stern, 'The First London Dock Boom and the Growth of the West India Docks', *Economica* 19, no. 73 (1952): 59–77 (p. 60).
19. *A Letter to the Right Hon. The Lord Mayor*, 42–4.
20. *The Times*, 9 Feb. 1796, p. 2.
21. *Eastward Ho!!! or, Quoz's Letters relative to the Wet Dock Bill, with an Additional Letter*, 3rd edn (London: P. Norman, 1796), 6.
22. Ibid., 18.
23. [Vaughan?], *On Wet Docks*, 4–5.
24. *Observations on a Pamphlet entitled 'A Plan of the London Dock', Shewing the Impracticality of the Proposed Plan* (London: [n.p.], 1794), 4–5.
25. *Wapping Docks Triumphant!!! Or, Quoz Refuted; In an Answer to a Pamphlet entitled Eastward Ho!!!* By an Inhabitant of the East (London: J. Skirven, [n.d.]), 11.
26. BPP, 1799, CXXIII, *Minutes of the Evidence taken at the Committee on the Bill for making Wet Docks, Basons, Cuts, and other Works for the Greater Accommodation and Security of Shipping, Commerce and Revenue within the Port of London*, etc., 43–5.
27. LMA Misc.Ms.79.3.
28. LMA CLC/B/192/F/001/MS11936/361 (20 Jul., 5 Jun., 11 Sept. 1789).
29. *Minutes of the Evidence . . . for making Wet Docks*, 135.

30. Ibid., 229.
31. *Report from the Committee appointed the enquire into . . . the increased Trade and Shipping of the Port of London*, 98–9.
32. Peter D'Sena, 'Perquisites and Casual Labour on the London Wharfside in the Eighteenth Century', *The London Journal* 14, no. 2 (1989): 130–47.
33. *Oracle and Daily Advertiser*, 3 Jan. 1800, 1.
34. LMA ACC/1230/6.
35. Colquhoun, *A Treatise on the Commerce and Police of the River Thames*, xxv.
36. Ibid., 50–76.
37. Ibid., 167–8.
38. Patrick Colquhoun, *A Treatise on the Police of the Metropolis* (London: H. Fry, 1796), 50.
39. Colquhoun, *A Treatise on the Commerce and Police of the River Thames*, 80.
40. Colquhoun, *A Treatise on the Police of the Metropolis*, 78.
41. Colquhoun, *A Treatise on the Commerce and Police of the River Thames*, 190, 198–9.
42. Ibid., 214.
43. Ruth Paley, 'Colquhoun, Patrick (1745–1820)', in *Oxford Dictionary of National Biography*, ed. H. C. G. Matthew and Brian Harrison (Oxford: Oxford University Press, 2004), http://0-www.oxforddnb.com.catalogue.libraries.london.ac.uk/view/article/5992 (accessed 17 Dec. 2016).
44. A Citizen of London, *Observations on a late Publication: intituled, A Treatise on the Police of the Metropolis, by P. Colquhoun, Esq.* (London: H. D. Symonds, [1800]), 21–4, emphasis in original.
45. Ibid., 79.
46. Iatros [David Yates Grant], *A Biographical Sketch of the Life and Writings of Patrick Colquhoun, Esq. LL.D.* (London: G. Smeeton, 1818), 24.
47. Michael E Scorgie, 'Patrick Colquhoun', *Annual Conference Accounting Association of Australia and New Zealand*, 5 vols (1993): 5:6.D.2, 8.
48. *St. James's Chronicle or the British Evening Post*, 26–29 Jul. 1800, 2.
49. LMA ACC/1230, *The Penny Magazine* 1 Jul. 1837, 252–3.
50. J. Ross Dancy, *The Myth of the Press Gang: Volunteers, Impressment and the Naval Manpower Problem in the Late Eighteenth Century* (Woodbridge: Boydell Press, 2015), 59.
51. MLD, PLA/WIDC/1/1/1/1 to PLA/WIDC/1/1/1/4.
52. *GM*, 72 pt 2 (1802), 677.
53. *Lloyd's Evening Post*, 26–29 Dec. 1800, 633.
54. Izumi Watanabe 'The Evolution of Income Accounting in Eighteenth and Nineteenth-Century Britain', *Osaka Keidai Ronshu* 57, no. 5 (2007): 21–34 (pp. 30–31).
55. Royal London Hospital Archives & Museum, RLHLH/A/5/13, 326.
56. MLD PLA/LDC/1/1/1/1, 412.
57. MLD PLA/LDC/1/1/1/1, 347.
58. See www.slavevoyages.org/voyages/S3UVhyfZ.
59. Gary L. Sturgess and Ken Cozens, 'Managing a Global Enterprise in the Eighteenth Century: Antony Calvert of the Crescent, London' (1777–1801), *The Mariner's Mirror* 99, no. 2 (2013): 171–95.
60. Draper, 'The City of London and Slavery', 440.
61. Ottobah Cugoano, *Thoughts and Sentiments on the Evil and Wicked Traffic of the Slavery and Commerce of the Human Species* (London: [n.p.], 1787), 89–91.
62. Ibid., 87, emphasis in original.
63. *The Trial of Edward Marcus Despard, Esquire. For High Treason* (London: M. Gurney, 1803), 174.
64. *Oracle and Daily Advertiser*, 12 Mar. 1799, 3.
65. Patrick Colquhoun, *A Treatise on Indigence; Exhibiting A General View of the National Resources for Productive Labour; with Propositions for Ameliorating the Condition of the Poor . . .* (London: J. Hatchard, 1806), 243.

66. Stern, 'The First London Dock Boom', 71.
67. Ibid., 73.

Conclusion

1. Andrew Knapp and William Baldwin, *The New Newgate Calendar*, 6 vols (London: J. Robins & Co. [1826?]), 5: 372.
2. Joseph Farington, *The Farington Diary*, ed. James Greig, 8 vols (London: Hutchinson & Co. [1922]–28), 7: 72.
3. *The Times*, 22 Dec. 1811, 2.
4. Roger Knight, *Britain Against Napoleon: The Organization of Victory 1793–1815* (London: Allen Lane, 2013), 94, 260.
5. *Public Ledger*, 22 Feb. 1796, 3.
6. *The Morning Chronicle*, 29 Sept. 1807, 3.
7. Roger Morriss, 'Government and Community: the Changing Context of Labour Relations, 1770–1830', in *History of Work and Labour Relations in the Royal Dockyards*, ed. Kenneth Lunn and Ann Day (London: Mansell, 1999), 31–2.
8. *OBP*, September 1800, trial of George Thomas (t18000917-147).
9. See Knight, *Britain Against Napoleon*, 38.
10. TNA ADM 6/403, 22 Jan. 1805.
11. Cobbett's *Weekly Political Register*, 27 Jul. 1805, 7.
12. Edward Ward, *A Collection of the Writings of Mr. Edward Ward*, 2 vols (London: A. Bettesworth, 1717), 2: 216.
13. Peter Linebaugh, *The London Hanged: Crime and Civil Society in the Eighteenth Century* (Harmondsworth: Penguin, 1991), chapters 9, 11, 12.
14. 'Commercial Credit', *The Belfast Monthly Magazine* 6, no. 32 (1811), 238–42, p. 241.
15. David Hughson [Edward Pugh], *London; being an Accurate History and Description of the British Metropolis and its Neighbourhood, to Thirty Miles Extent from an Actual Perambulation*, vol. 6 (London: J. Stratford, 1809), 322.
16. BPP 1813–14, VIII, Minutes of the Evidence taken before the Select Committee of the House of Commons on Petitions Relating to East-India-built Shipping, 78, 353, 399.
17. Helen Doe, 'The Thames Merchant Yards in the Napoleonic Wars', in *Shipbuilding and Ships on the Thames*, ed. Roger Owen (London: Greenwich Industrial History Society, 2006), 10–19.
18. John E. Barnard, *Building Britain's Wooden Walls: The Barnard Dynasty c. 1697–1851* (Oswestry: Antony Nelson, 1997), 93.
19. Iowerth Prothero, *Artisans and Politics in Early Nineteenth-Century London. John Gast and his Times* (London: Methuen, 1979; repr. 1981), 62.
20. *Don Juan*, X, 82 in Byron, George Gordon, Lord, *Lord Byron – The Major Works*, ed. Jerome J. McGann (Oxford: Oxford University Press, 1986), 719.

BIBLIOGRAPHY

Manuscript Sources

British Library (BL)

004977492, An Outline Plan of His Majesty's Dock at Deptford, 1774
Add MS 16919–16928, Original letters . . . relating to the Association for Preserving Liberty
Add MS 16947, Autograph letters of inhabitants of Greenwich and Deptford
Add MS 38231, Letters to the 1st Earl of Liverpool
Egerton MS 2180, Original Letters addressed to John Douglas D. D.
RP 2802, Various copy manuscripts

Greenwich Heritage Centre (GHC)

G ID/12.1 to G ID/12.8, Greenwich Workhouse Minute Books, 1764–91
G.12.9 to G.12.11, Greenwich Workhouse Minute Books, 1790–98

London Metropolitan Archives (LMA)

ACC/1230, Records of Patrick Colquhoun
CLC/B/192/F/001/MS11936/361, Sun Insurance Office Ltd: policies
E/PNE, Records of the Paine family
H05/M/D/01/001, Ledger of the Governors of the Kent Dispensary, 1783–1837
Misc.Ms.79.3, Evidence in support of petitions against . . . wet docks at Wapping
P78/NIC, Records of the parish of Saint Nicholas, Deptford

Museum of London Docklands (MLD)

PLA/LDC/1/1/1/1 to PLA/LDC/1/1/2/1, London Dock Company records
PLA/WIDC/1/1/1/1 to PLA/WIDC/1/1/1/4, West India Dock Company Records

BIBLIOGRAPHY

The National Archives (TNA), Kew, London

ACC 1230, Correspondence and autobiographical notes of Patrick Colquhoun
ADM 106, Navy Board Records
ADM 106/1143/53, Samuel Seddon, Piccadilly . . . instructions to his agent
ADM 106/1172/159, Samuel Seddon, Piccadilly . . . gaoled at Maidstone
ADM 106/1193/89, Letter from Dudman, Adams and Barnard
ADM 106/1193/148, Benjamin Slade, account of anchors
ADM 106/1193/175, Benjamin Slade, account of purchases
ADM 106/1204/72, Letter from Deptford and Woolwich Shipwrights
ADM 106/1204/116, Petition of sailmakers at Deptford
ADM 106 1205/118, Benjamin Slade on composition for seasoning ships timber
ADM 106/1205/9, Benjamin Slade on price of bark
ADM 106/1231/171, Petition of Mary Slade on behalf of her husband, Josias
ADM 106/1231/172, Benjamin Slade, list of stores purchased
ADM 106/1454, Letter from William Barnard
ADM 354/158/205, John Clevland . . . accused of embezzling junk
HO 42/, Home Office: Domestic Correspondence
HO 42/15/81, Letter from Charles Marsham, MP for Kent
HO 42/20/52, Memorandum from Col. John Rolle, MP for Devon
HO 42/33/125, Report of the case of George Webster
HO 42/40/196, Memorandum from the Commissioners of the Transport Service
HO 42/42/145, Secret information about the London Corresponding Society
HO 42/46/130 ff. 286–287, Letter from Edward Thompson about the coal heavers' riot
HO 42/51/110, Letter from magistrate of Shadwell on use of volunteers to quell mob
HO 42/62/104, Memorandum about radical groups in Wapping and Ratcliff, 1801
HO 47/, Home Office: Judges' reports on criminals
HO 47/3/56, Joseph Mawbey on receipt of petition
HO 47/3/67, Report on petition . . . in the name of Rebecca Harley
HO 47/7/42, Report on petition from D. Carter, prisoner's wife
HO 47/7/96, Report of Joseph Mawbey on a collective petition
HO 47/12/100, Report on petition from Mary Randall, prisoner's wife
HO 47/13/39, Report on petition on behalf of Mary Martin
HO/47/24/36, Report on petitions on behalf of William Ford
HO 47/28/1, Report on petitions on behalf of John Hopwood
HO 47/29/8, Report on petitions on behalf of Charles and William Gill
HO 47/37/6, Report on petitions on behalf of Mary Connell
HO 65/1, Home Office Letter Book (General), 1795–1811
PROB 11/, Prerogative Court of Canterbury: will registers

National Maritime Museum (NMM), Greenwich, London

ADM B/205, Board of Admiralty In-Letters
COD 21/, Admiral Sir Edward Codrington, letters to father and wife
HNL/, Michael Henley & Son
LBK/75, Letterbooks of Henry Fletcher & Son, Shadwell Dock
WHW/1, James Whitworth, letters to his wife

Royal London Hospital Archives & Museum

RLHLH/A/5/13 and RLHLH/A/5/14, House Committee minutes, 1794 to 1808

BIBLIOGRAPHY

State Library of New South Wales

MLMSS 1016, Elizabeth Bligh letters, 1781–1807
R 198, Waistcoat of Tahiti Cloth
Safe 1/45, Letter from William Bligh to his wife Elizabeth describing the *Bounty* mutiny

Tower Hamlets Local History Library and Archives

P/GOF/1, Diary of Elijah Goff, 1788–1796

Unpublished Theses

Knight, R. J. B. 'The Royal Dockyards in England at the Time of the American War of Independence', PhD thesis, University of London, 1972
J. G. Moher, 'The London Millwrights and Engineers 1775–1825', PhD thesis, University of London, 1989

Newspapers and Journals

The Belfast Monthly Magazine
Bingley's Journal
The Craftsman; or Say's Weekly Journal
Daily Advertiser
Diary or Woodfall's Register
E. Johnson's *British Gazette and Sunday Monitor*
Evening Mail
Gardeners' Chronicle & New Horticulturist
Gazetteer and New Daily Advertiser
General Advertiser and Morning Intelligencer
General Evening Post
Gentleman's Magazine (*GM*)
Hoey's Dublin Mercury
Independent Chronicle
The Lady's Magazine; or Entertaining Companion for the Fair Sex
The Lady's Monthly Museum, or Polite Repository of Amusement and Instruction
Lloyd's Evening Post
London Chronicle
London Chronicle or Universal Evening Post
London Courant and Westminster Chronicle
London Courant Westminster Chronicle and Daily Advertiser
London Evening Post
London Packet or New Lloyd's Evening Post
Middlesex Journal and Evening Advertiser
Middlesex Journal or Chronicle of Liberty
Middlesex Journal or Universal Evening Post
The Monthly Register and Encyclopedian Magazine
Moral and Political Magazine of the London Corresponding Society
Morning Chronicle and London Advertiser
Morning Herald
Morning Herald and Daily Advertiser
Morning Post and Daily Advertiser
Morning Post and Fashionable World
The New Town and Country Magazine

The Oracle
The Oracle and Daily Advertiser
Parker's General Advertiser and Morning Intelligencer
The Penny Magazine
Public Advertiser
Public Ledger
The Rambler's Magazine; Or, the Annals of Gallantry, Glee, Pleasure, and the Bon Ton
Read's Weekly Journal or British Gazetteer
St. James's Chronicle or the British Evening Post
The Star
The Sun
The Times
The Town and Country Magazine, or, Universal Repository of Knowledge, Instruction, and Entertainment
The True Briton
Whitehall Evening Post
World and Fashionable Advertiser

Internet Sources

History of Parliament Online, www.historyofparliamentonline.org
Legacies of British Slave Ownership, www.ucl.ac.uk/lbs
Locating London's Past, www.locatinglondon.org
London Lives 1690–1800, www.londonlives.org
Old Bailey Proceedings Online (*OBP*), www.oldbaileyonline.org
Oxford Dictionary of National Bibliography (*ODNB*), www.oxforddnb.com
The Trans-Atlantic Slave Trade Database, www.slavevoyages.org

British Parliamentary Papers (BPP)

1795–96, XIV. *Report from the Committee appointed to enquire into the best Mode of providing sufficient Accommodation for the increased Trade and Shipping of the Port of London*, etc.
1798–99, CXXIII. *Minutes of the Evidence taken at the Committee on the Bill for making Wet Docks, Basons, Cuts, and other Works for the Greater Accommodation and Security of Shipping, Commerce and Revenue within the Port of London*, etc.
1813–14, VIII. *Minutes of the Evidence taken before the Select Committee of the House of Commons on Petitions Relating to East-India-built Shipping*
1831, VIII (227). *Select Committee of the House of Lords on Poor Laws and Petitions Praying for the Relief of Pauperism*

Books, Pamphlets, Articles

An Account of the Kent Dispensary, in the Broad-way, Deptford. London: W. Hales, [1785?]
The Anti-Gallican; or Standard of British Loyalty, Religion and Liberty; including A Collection of the Principal Papers, Tracts, Speeches, Poems, and Songs, that have been published on the Threatened Invasion: together with many original pieces on the same subject. London: Vendor & Hood and J. Asperne, 1804
The Antigallican Songster. Number 1. London: J. Downes, 1793
The Arguments of Counsel in the Ecclesiastical Court on the Cause of Inglefield . . . on the twenty-second of July. 1786, at giving judgement. London: J. Murray, 1787
The Catch Club: a collection of all the songs, catches, glees, duets, &c, as sung by Mr. Bannister, Mr. Arrowsmith [and others] . . . at the Royalty Theatre. London: J. Griffith, [1787?]

Declaration of those Rights of the Commonalty of Great-Britain without which they cannot be Free. London: [n.p.], *c.* 1775

Eastward Ho!!! or, Quoz's Letters relative to the Wet Dock Bill, with an Additional Letter, 3rd edn. London: P. Norman, 1796

Elements of Geography for the Use of Mr Alexander's Academy, Hampstead. London: printed for the author, 1785

A Hymn to be Sung by the Charity Children, of Deptford, on Sunday, September, the 18th 1791. Deptford: [n.p.], 1791

A Letter to the Author of the Burletta Called Hero and Leander. London: G. Kearsley, 1787

A Letter to the Right Hon. The Lord Mayor on the Subject of the Intended New Docks to be Established at Wapping. London: J. Johnson, 1796

Observations on a Pamphlet entitled 'A Plan of the London Dock', Shewing the Impracticality of the Proposed Plan. London: [n.p.], 1794

Proceedings Relative to Ships Tendered for the Service of the United East-India Company, from the First of January, 1780, to the Thirty-First of March, 1791; with an Appendix. Vol. 530. London: E. Cox, 1802

The Trial of Edward Marcus Despard, Esquire. For High Treason. London: M. Gurney, 1803

The Universal Director; or, The Nobleman and Gentleman's True Guide to the Masters and Professors of the Liberal and Polite Arts and Sciences; and of the Mechanic Arts, Manufactures, and Trades, Established in London and Westminster, and their Environs. London: J. Coote, 1763

Wapping Docks Triumphant!!! Or, Quoz Refuted; In an Answer to a Pamphlet entitled Eastward Ho!!! By an Inhabitant of the East. London: J. Skirven, [n.d.]

* * *

Andrew, Donna T., ed. *London Debating Societies, 1776–1799.* London: London Record Society, 1994

Austin, William. *Letters from London, Written in the Years 1802 & 1803.* Boston: W. Pelham, 1804

Barnard, John E. *Building Britain's Wooden Walls: The Barnard Dynasty c. 1697–1851.* Oswestry: Antony Nelson, 1997

Barrell, John. 'London and the London Corresponding Society', in *Romantic Metropolis: The Urban Scene of British Culture, 1780–1840.* Edited by James Chandler and Kevin Gilmartin. Cambridge: Cambridge University Press, 2005

Barrow, John, bart. *Travels in China: containing descriptions, observations and comparisons made and collected in the course of a short residence at the Imperial Palace of Yuen-min-yuen, and on a subsequent journey from Pekin to Canton.* London: T. Cadell & W. Davies, 1804

Beaglehole, J. C. *The Life of Captain James Cook.* Stanford, CA: Stanfield University Press, 1974

Bohstedt, John. 'Gender, Household and Community Politics: Women in English Riots 1790–1810', *Past & Present* 120 (1988): 88–122

Bull, John. 'Palmer, John (1744–1798)', *Oxford Dictionary of National Biography.* Oxford University Press, 2004

Burney, Frances. *The Early Diary of Frances Burney, 1768–1778.* Edited by Annie Raine Ellis, 2 vols. London: George Bell and Sons, 1889

Byron, George Gordon, Lord. *Lord Byron – The Major Works.* Edited by Jerome J. McGann. Oxford: Oxford University Press, 1986

Cain, P. J. and A. G. Hopkins. *British Imperialism: Innovation and Expansion, 1688–1914.* London: Longman, 1993

Chambers, J. D. and G. E. Mingay. *The Agricultural Revolution.* London: B. T. Batsford, 1966

A Citizen of London. *Observations on a late Publication: intituled, A Treatise on the Police of the Metropolis, by P. Colquhoun, Esq.* London: H. D. Symonds, [1800]

Cobbett, W. *Parliamentary History of England, from the Earliest Period to the Year 1803.* Vol. 36. 1801–3. London: T. C. Hansard, 1820

Cock, Randolph. '"The Finest Invention in the World": The Royal Navy's Early Trials of Copper Sheathing, 1708–1770'. *Mariner's Mirror* 87, no. 4 (2001): 446–59

Colquhoun, Patrick. *A Treatise on Indigence; Exhibiting A General View of the National Resources for Productive Labour; with Propositions for Ameliorating the Condition of the Poor . . .* London: J. Hatchard, 1806

—— *A Treatise on the Commerce and Police of the River Thames: containing an Historical View of the Trade of the Port of London.* London: Joseph Mawman, 1800

—— *A Treatise on the Police of the Metropolis.* London: H. Fry, 1796

Cotton, Joseph. *Memoir on the Origin and Incorporation of Trinity House of Deptford Strond.* London: J. Darling, 1818

Cox, Joseph. *A Faithful Narrative of the Most Wicked and Inhuman Transactions of that Bloody-Minded Gang of Thief-Takers, Alias Thief-Makers, Macdaniel, Berry, Salmon, Eagan, alias Gahagan.* London: printed for Joseph Cox and sold by M. Mechell, 1756

Cugoano, Ottobah. *Thoughts and Sentiments on the Evil and Wicked Traffic of the Slavery and Commerce of the Human Species.* London: [n.p.], 1787

Currie, Anne. *Henleys of Wapping: A London Shipowning Family, 1770–1830.* London: National Maritime Museum, 1988

Dancy, J. Ross. *The Myth of the Press Gang. Volunteers, Impressment and the Naval Manpower Problem in the Eighteenth Century.* Woodbridge: Boydell Press, 2015

Defoe, Daniel. *A Tour Thro' the Whole Island of Great Britain.* London: Penguin, 1971; first published 1724–6

Dening, Greg. *Mr Bligh's Bad Language: Passion, Power and Theatre on the Bounty.* Cambridge: Cambridge University Press, 1992

Divers, David. 'Excavations on the Site of the East India Company Dockyards and the Trinity House Almshouses, London'. *Post-Medieval Archaeology* 38, no. 1 (2004): 17–132

—— and Chris Jarrett. 'Excavations at the Mouth of Deptford Creek, Greenwich Reach'. *London Archaeologist* 9, no. 1 (1999): 6–16

Doe, Helen. *Enterprising Women and Shipping in the Nineteenth Century.* Woodbridge: Boydell Press, 2009

—— 'The Thames Merchant Yards in the Napoleonic Wars', in *Shipbuilding and Ships on the Thames.* Edited by Roger Owen, 10–19. London: Greenwich Industrial History Society, 2006

Dozier, Robert. *For King, Constitution and Country: The English Loyalists and the French Revolution.* Lexington: University Press of Kentucky, 2015

Draper, N. 'The City of London and Slavery: Evidence from the first Dock Companies'. *The Economic History Review* 61, no. 2 (2008): 432–66

D'Sena, Peter. 'Perquisites and Casual Labour on the London Wharfside in the Eighteenth Century'. *The London Journal* 14, no. 2 (1989): 130–47

Dugaw, Dianne. 'Balladry's Female Warriors: Women, Warfare, and Disguise in the Eighteenth Century'. *Eighteenth-Century Life* 9, no. 2 (1985): 1–20

Evans, Eric J. *The Forging of the Modern State: Early Industrial Britain 1783–1870.* London & New York: Longman, 1983

Farington, Joseph. *The Farington Diary.* Edited by James Greig. 8 vols. London: Hutchinson & Co. [1922]–28

Fryer, Peter. *Staying Power: The History of Black People in Britain.* London: Pluto Press, 1984

Gast, John. *Calumny Defeated: or, a Compleat Vindication of the Conduct of the Working Shipwrights during the Late Disputes with their Employers.* London: J. Delahoy, 1802

Grant, David Yates [Iatros]. *A Biographical Sketch of the Life and Writings of Patrick Colquhoun, Esq. LL.D.* London: G. Smeeton, 1818

Guillery, Peter. *The Small House in Eighteenth-Century London: A Social and Architectural History.* New Haven & London: Yale University Press, 2004

—— and Bernard Herman. 'Deptford Houses: 1650 to 1800'. *Vernacular Architecture* 30, no. 1 (1999): 58–84

Harriott, John. *Struggles Through Life*. 2 vols. London: C. & W. Galabin, 1807

Hasted, Edward. *The History and Topographical Survey of the County of Kent*, 2nd edn. 12 vols. Canterbury: W. Bristow, 1797–1801

Hitchcock, Tim and Michèle Cohen, eds. *English Masculinities 1660–1800*. Harlow, Essex: Longman, 1999

Hughson, David [Edward Pugh]. *London; being an Accurate History and Description of the British Metropolis and its Neighbourhood, to Thirty Miles Extent from an Actual Perambulation*. Vol. 6. London: J. Stratford, 1809

Hume, Robert D. 'The Value of Money in Eighteenth-Century England: Incomes, Prices, Buying Power – and some Problems in Cultural Economics'. *Huntington Library Quarterly* 77, no. 4 (2015): 373–416

Hunt, Margaret. *The Middling Sort: Commerce, Gender, and the Family in England 1680–1780*. Berkeley and Los Angeles: University of California Press, 1996

Hurl-Eamon, Jennine. *Marriage and the British Army in the Long Eighteenth Century: 'The Girl I Left Behind Me'*. Oxford: Oxford University Press, 2014

Inwood, Stephen. *A History of London*. London: Macmillan, 1998

Jones, M. G. *The Charity School Movement*. London: Frank Cass & Co. Ltd, 1938; repr. 1964

Knapp, Andrew and William Baldwin. *The New Newgate Calendar*, 6 vols. London: J. Robins & Co. [1826?]

Knight, Roger. *Britain Against Napoleon: The Organization of Victory 1793–1815*. London: Allen Lane, 2013

—— 'The First Fleet: its State and Preparation, 1786–1787', in *Studies from Terra Australis to Australia*. Edited by John Hardy and Alan Frost. Canberra: Australian Academy of the Humanities, 1989

—— 'Pilfering and Theft from the Dockyards at the Time of the American War of Independence'. *Mariner's Mirror* 61, no. 3 (1975): 215–25

—— and Martin Wilcox. *Sustaining the Fleet 1793–1815: War, the British Navy and the Contractor State*. Woodbridge: Boydell Press, 2010

Knights, Mark. 'The 1780 Protestant petitions and the culture of petitioning', in *The Gordon Riots: Politics, Culture and Insurrection in Late Eighteenth-Century Britain*. Edited by Ian Haywood and John Seed. Cambridge: Cambridge University Press, 2012

Lacey, Mary. *The Female Shipwright*. Edited by Margarette Lincoln. London: The National Maritime Museum, 2008; first published 1773

Landau, Norma. *The Justices of the Peace 1679–1760*. Berkeley and Los Angeles: University of California Press, 1984

Lewis, Michael. *A Social History of the Navy 1793–1815*. London: Chatham Publishing, 1960; repr. 2004

Lin, Patricia Y. C. E. 'Caring for the Nation's Families: British Soldiers' and Sailors' Families and the State, 1793–1815', in *Soldiers, Citizens and Civilians: Experiences and Perceptions of the Revolutionary Wars, 1790–1820*. Edited by Alan Forrest, Karen Hagemann and Jane Rendall. Houndmills, Basingstoke: Palgrave Macmillan, 2009

Lincoln, Margarette. 'Naval Ship Launches as Public Spectacle 1773–1854'. *Mariners Mirror* 83, no. 4 (1997): 466–72

—— *Naval Wives and Mistresses 1750–1815*. London: National Maritime Museum, 2007

—— 'Emma Hamilton, War and the Depiction of Femininity in the Late Eighteenth Century'. *Journal for Maritime Research* 17, no. 2 (2015): 135–45

Linebaugh, Peter. *The London Hanged: Crime and Civil Society in the Eighteenth Century*. Harmondsworth: Penguin, 1991

London Corresponding Society. *Moral and Political Magazine of the London Corresponding Society*. London: John Ashley, Secretary, 1796

McCormack, Matthew. *Embodying the Militia in Georgian England*. Oxford: Oxford University Press, 2015

Macdonald, Janet. *The British Navy's Victualling Board, 1793–1815: Management Competence and Incompetence*. Woodbridge: Boydell Press, 2010

MacKay, Lynn. *Respectability and the London Poor, 1780–1870: The Value of Virtue*. London: Pickering & Chatto, 2013

—— 'Why They Stole: Women in the Old Bailey, 1779–1789'. *Journal of Social History* 32, no. 3 (1999): 623–39

McLeod, A. B. and A. M. G. 'John Cleveley the Elder's "The Floating Out of the Cambridge": Problems and Patrons'. *The Mariner's Mirror* 100, no. 4 (2014): 449–54

Mainwaring, William. *An Address to the Grand Jury of the County of Middlesex*. London: H. Reynell, 1785

Milne, Colin. *Sermons*. London: T. Cadell, 1780

Morley, Henry. *Memoirs of Bartholomew Fair*. London: Chapman and Hall, 1859

Morris, Derek. *Mile End Old Town, 1740–1780: A Social History of an Early Modern London Suburb*. London: The East London History Society, 2002

—— and Ken Cozens. *London's Sailortown 1600–1800*. London: The East London History Society, 2014

—— and Ken Cozens. 'The Shadwell Waterfront in the Eighteenth Century'. *The Mariner's Mirror* 99, no. 1 (2013): 86–91

—— and Ken Cozens. *Wapping 1600–1800*. London: The East London History Society, 2009

Morriss, Roger. 'Government and Community: the Changing Context of Labour Relations, 1770–1830', in *History of Work and Labour Relations in the Royal Dockyards*. Edited by Kenneth Lunn and Ann Day. London: Mansell, 1999

Mui, Hoh-Cheung and Lora H. Mui. *Shops and Shopkeeping in Eighteenth-Century England*. Kingston, Ontario: McGill-Queen's University Press; London: Routledge, 1989

Namier, Sir Lewis and John Brooke. *The History of Parliament: The House of Commons 1754–1790*. London: HMSO, 1964

Nicol, John. *The Life and Adventures of John Nicol, Mariner*. Edited by John Howell. Edinburgh: William Blackwood; London: T. Cadell, 1822

O'Quinn, Daniel. *Entertaining Crisis in the Atlantic Imperium 1770–1790*. Baltimore: Johns Hopkins University Press, 2011

Paine, Daniel. *The Journal of Daniel Paine, 1794–1797*. Edited by R. J. B. Knight and Alan Frost. Granville, NSW: Ambassador Press, 1983

Paley, Ruth. 'Colquhoun, Patrick (1745–1820)', *Oxford Dictionary of National Biography*. Edited by H. C. G. Matthew and Brian Harrison. Oxford: Oxford University Press, 2004

Parkinson, C. Northcote. *Trade in the Eastern Seas, 1793–1818*. London: Frank Cass & Co. Ltd., 1966

The Parliamentary Register; or, History of the Proceedings and Debates of the House of Commons. Vol. 55. London: J. Debrett, 1794

Payne, Dianne. 'London's Charity School Children: The "Scum of the Parish"'. *British Journal for Eighteenth-Century Studies* 29 (2006): 383–97

Philip, Mark. 'Talking about Democracy: Britain in the 1790s'. *Reimagining Democracy in the Age of Revolutions: America, France, Britain, Ireland 1750–1850*. Edited by Joanna Innes and Mark Philip, 101–14. Oxford: Oxford University Press, 2013

Phillips, Watts. *The Wild Tribes of London*. London: Ward and Lock, 1855

Pietsch, Roland. *The Real Jim Hawkins: Ships' Boys in the Georgian Navy*. Barnsley: Seaforth Publishing, 2010

Place, Francis. *The Autobiography of Francis Place*. Edited by Mary Thrale. Cambridge: Cambridge University Press, 1972

Ploeg, Sophie. *Staged Experiences: Architecture and Rhetoric in the Work of Sir Henry Wotton, Nicholas Hawksmoor and Sir John Vanbrugh*. Groningen, Netherlands: Rijksuniversiteit Groningen, 2006

Pointon, Marcia. *Brilliant Effects: A Cultural History of Gem Stones and Jewellery*. New Haven & London: Yale University Press, 2009

Poland, John. *Records of the Miller Hospital and Royal Kent Dispensary*. Greenwich: Henry Richardson, 1893

Powell, Dulcie. 'The Voyage of the Plant Nursery H.M.S. Providence, 1791–1793'. *Economic Botany* 31, no. 4 (1977): 387–431

Prothero, Iowerth. *Artisans & Politics in Early Nineteenth-Century London. John Gast and his Times*. London: Methuen, 1979; repr. 1981

Pythagoras. *A Vindication of A Right in the Public to a One Shilling Gallery either at the New Theatre Royal in Covent-Garden, Or Somewhere Else*. London: J. Owen, 1792

Quilley, Geoff. *Empire to Nation: Art, History and the Visualization of Maritime Britain 1768–1829*. New Haven & London: Yale University Press, 2011

Randall, Adrian. *Riotous Assemblies: Popular Protest in Hanoverian England*. Oxford: Oxford University Press, 2007

Reid, John Phillip. *The Concept of Liberty in the Age of the American Revolution*. Chicago and London: University of Chicago Press, 1988

Richardson, William. *A Mariner of England: An Account of the Career of William Richardson from Cabin Boy in the Merchant Service to Warrant Officer in the Royal Navy (1780–1819) As Told by Himself*. London: John Murray, 1908

Rodger, N. A. M. *The Command of the Ocean. A Naval History of Britain, 1649–1815*. London: Allen Lane, 2004

Rogers, Nicholas. *Mayhem: Post-War Crime and Violence in Britain, 1748–1753*. New Haven and London: Yale University Press, 2012

—— *The Press Gang: Naval Impressment and its Opponents in Georgian Britain*. London: Continuum, 2007

Rudé, George F. D. *Hanoverian London, 1714–1808*. Berkeley and Los Angeles: University of California Press, 1971

Russell, Gillian. *The Theatres of War: Performance, Politics and Society, 1793–1815*. Oxford: Clarendon Press, 1995

Schaffer, Simon. '"The Charter'd Thames": naval architecture and experimental spaces in Georgian Britain', in *The Mindful Hand: Inquiry and Invention from the Late Renaissance to Early Industrialisation*. Edited by Lissa Roberts, Simon Schaffer and Peter Dear, 279–307. Amsterdam: Edita – the Publishing House of the Royal Netherlands Academy of Arts and Sciences and University of Chicago Press, 2007

Schwarz, L. D. *London in the Age of Industrialization: Entrepreneurs, Labour Force and Living Conditions, 1700–1850*. Cambridge: Cambridge University Press, 1992

—— 'The Standard of Living in the Long Run: London 1700–1860'. *Economic History Review*, Second Series, 38, no. 1 (1985): 24–41

Scorgie, Michael E. 'Patrick Colquhoun'. *Annual Conference Accounting Association of Australia and New Zealand*. 5 vols ([n.p.]1993): 5:6.D.2

Sebag-Montefiore, Cecil. *A History of the Volunteer Forces from the Earliest Times to the Year 1860*. London: Archibald Constable & Co. Ltd, 1908

Sharpe, J. B. *Report . . . For the Better Regulation of Madhouses in England*. London: Baldwin, Cradock & Joy, 1815

Shepard, Alexandra. 'Minding their Own Business: Married Women and Credit in Early Eighteenth-Century London'. *Transactions of the Royal Historical Society* 25 (2015): 53–74

Shoemaker, Robert B. 'The Decline of Public Insult in London 1660–1800'. *Past & Present* 169 (2000): 97–131

Smith, Adam. *An Inquiry into the Nature and Causes of The Wealth of Nations*. Edited by Edwin Cannan, 2 vols. London: Methuen, 1904; repr. 1950

Smith, Charlotte. *The Works of Charlotte Smith*. Vol. 14. Edited by Jacqueline M. Labbe. London: Pickering & Chatto, 2007

Stern, Walter M. 'The First London Dock Boom and the Growth of the West India Docks'. *Economica* 19, no. 73 (1952): 59–77

Stevenson, J. 'The London "Crimp" Riots of 1794'. *International Journal of Social History* 16, no. 1 (1971): 40–58

Stow, John. *A Survey of London*. London: John Wolfe, 1598

Sturgess, Gary L. and Ken Cozens. 'Managing a Global Enterprise in the Eighteenth Century: Antony Calvert of the Crescent, London (1777–1801)'. *The Mariner's Mirror* 99, no. 2 (2013): 171–95

Sumner, James. *Brewing Science, Technology and Print, 1700–1880*. London: Pickering & Chatto, 2013

Sutherland, Lucy S. *A London Merchant, 1675–1774*. London: Frank Cass, 1962

Syrett, David. *Shipping and the American War, 1775–83: A Study of British Transport Organization*. London: Athlone Press, 1970

Thale, Mary, ed. *Selections from the Papers of the London Corresponding Society 1792–1799*. Cambridge, Cambridge University Press, 1983

Thomas, James. *The Poll for the Knights of the Shire for the County of Surrey. Taken at Guildford in the said County, the 20th and 21st days of October, 1774*. Guildford: J. Russell, 1774

Upton, William. *The Words of the Most Favourite Songs, Duets. &c. Sung at the Royal Amphitheatre, Westminster Bridge, and the Royalty theatre, Well-close Square*. Lambeth: S. Tibson, [1798]

[Vaughan, W.?], *On Wet Docks, Quays, and Warehouses, for the Port of London; with Hints Respecting Trade*. London: [n.p.], 1793

Vaughan, W. *Reasons in Favour of the London-Docks*. London: [n.p.], 1795

Wahrman, Dror. 'Percy's Prologue: From Gender Play to Gender Panic in Eighteenth Century England'. *Past & Present* 159 (1998): 113–60

Ward, Edward. *A Collection of the Writings of Mr. Edward Ward*. 2 vols. London: A. Bettesworth, 1717

Watanabe, Izumi. 'The Evolution of Income Accounting in Eighteenth and Nineteenth-Century Britain'. *Osaka Keidai Ronshu* 57, no. 5 (2007): 21–34

White, Jerry. *London in the 18th Century: A Great and Monstrous Thing*. London: Bodley Head, 2012

Worrall, David. *Theatric Revolution: Drama, Censorship and Romantic Period Subcultures 1773–1832*. Oxford: Oxford University Press, 2006

—— *The Politics of Romantic Theatricality, 1787–1832: The Road to the Stage*. London: Palgrave Macmillan, 2007

INDEX